The European Financial Crisis: Debt, Growth, and Economic Policy

Thank you for all your support
— without you we couldn't do
what we do.
  — Rob

The European Financial Crisis: Debt, Growth, and Economic Policy

Robert Godby
University of Wyoming
Department of Economics and Finance

The European Financial Crisis: Debt, Growth, and Economic Policy
Copyright © Business Expert Press, LLC, 2014.

First published in 2014 by
Business Expert Press, LLC
222 East 46th Street, New York, NY 10017
www.businessexpertpress.com

ISBN-13: 978-1-60649-706-7 (paperback)
ISBN-13: 978-1-60649-707-4 (e-book)

Business Expert Press Economics Collection

Collection ISSN: 2163-761X (print)
Collection ISSN: 2163-7628 (electronic)

Cover and interior design by Exeter Premedia Services Private Ltd., Chennai, India

First edition: 2014

10 9 8 7 6 5 4 3 2 1

Printed in the United States of America.

For Sascha and Jochen. Thank you for everything during my year in Germany, and I apologize for the many beers that were ruined by discussion of the Euro Crisis. No good deed ever goes unpunished.

Abstract

The European debt crisis has posed a challenge for many people to understand, both non-Europeans and Europeans alike. Even economists, finance specialists, and market commentators are often uncertain of its causes or in the interpretation of events ongoing, or of past events that have taken place that then shaped the current situation. Typically, this lack of comprehension results from a lack of understanding of how European institutions work, the structure of European politics and the Eurozone, the economics of the financial system, or the relationship of debt markets to current government policies in the European Union (EU). The purpose of this book is to describe the causes and outcomes of the European debt crisis (to the date of publication) within the context of three questions most often asked about the debt crisis: (i) what happened, (ii) why did it happen, and (iii) why has the crisis been so difficult for policy makers to address? The book attempts to answer these questions in a straightforward, scholarly, and thoughtful fashion, thereby developing a wider understanding of the crisis in its entirety for the reader. The book is by no means meant to be an exhaustive treatment on any of the issues it discusses. There are now, and will continue to be, many new and very detailed academic papers and monographs on each of the topics described, and some are referred to along with contemporary news reports should the reader wish to explore further. With this approach the book should be useful for those people who wish to better understand the events of the European financial crisis over the past four years, but who do not need to acquire an exhaustive background in EU institutions, debt markets, recent European history, and economic policy making. For that reason this book will have appeal to undergraduate students in business, economics, politics, or interdisciplinary studies looking for an approachable yet detailed overview of the crisis, for graduate classes seeking similar goals and laypeople or professionals interested generally in the topic or with a need to acquire a basic understanding of the topic. Furthermore, the book can also serve as an introduction in courses or settings that lead to deeper discussion of the economic, political, and financial issues it presents.

Keywords

European debt crisis, European politics, European Union, EU, European integration, sovereign debt, currency union, monetary policy, fiscal policy, EU institutions, debt crisis timeline, the Euro, Greek debt crisis, macroeconomics, recession, banking union, Eurozone, bailouts, currency risk, bond risk, financial uncertainty, central bank policy, central bank independence, Germany, ECB, European Central Bank, IMF, International Monetary Fund, the troika, European unemployment.

Contents

Acknowledgements

The problem with trying to thank everyone by name that helped make this book possible is that I will be bound to inadvertently forget someone. With that in mind let me first offer a heartfelt thanks to everyone who helped me in the thinking, writing, rewriting, and publishing of this book. You know who you are and I really appreciate all the help and support you gave me during that entire process.

There are also a few acknowledgements I would be negligent not to recognize explicitly and they follow. Thank you first to Pforzheim University for hosting me during my stay in Germany when preparations for this book began, especially Karl-Heinz, and Rudi who were instrumental in making my stay possible. Thank you also to those at the European Central Bank, European Commission, and at the Bundesbank who patiently answered my questions and shared their viewpoints during the research for this book.

I also cannot thank Stephanie Anderson enough for her help. She was also on sabbatical from Wyoming when I was and in Germany during 2011 and 2012. It was her email conversations with me in that time that were the catalyst that drove the writing of this book. Once that began, Stephanie likely regretted having ever mentioned the topic but gamely read my tedious drafts and helped immensely to improve them.

Of course, any errors left remain mine alone.

Finally, thanks to Sascha and Jochen, who went out of their way to make me feel welcome in Germany. Both often found themselves being forced to be sounding boards for my ideas when they probably would've preferred to have just been allowed to enjoy their beer in peace. I will always consider your friendship the most important benefit of my stay in Deutschland.

PART I

Introduction: Understanding the Problem—Why Is This So Hard?

CHAPTER 1

Introduction: Where There's Smoke, There's Fire

August 2009

Smoke hung heavily over Athens. Unforgiving winds blowing out of central Europe spread searing flames toward Greece's ancient capital. As residents fled the scorching embers and deadly heat, leaving homes and livelihoods behind, to escape late August wildfires, none could have known that the conflagration pursuing them would cause the beginning of an ordeal that would dash the dreams of millions, ruin personal fortunes, topple governments, and threaten to destroy the aspirations of an entire continent long after the blaze engulfing the forests north of democracy's birthplace was extinguished. The ashes of the pine trees, olive groves, and burned foundations left after the Greek wildfires of 2009 would eventually cultivate the seeds of an economic and political crisis with repercussions affecting financial markets across the globe. This would also not be the last time Athens would be aflame, although future fires would be fueled by economic desperation and political frustration instead of tinder-dry woods.

In September 2009, perceived failures in the Greek government's response to the wildfires, coupled with years of apparent neglect of the firefighting service and suspicions that the forest fires were the arson of unscrupulous land developers, ignited new calls for the ouster of Greece's sitting center-right New Democracy party. The government was not in a strong position, having already been stung by a string of earlier corruption scandals. Holding only a one-seat majority in the Greek Parliament, Prime Minister Kostas Karamanlis called a snap election in hopes of consolidating his party's power over the main opposition Pan Hellenic Movement (PASOK) and several smaller parties. That early-September decision proved a disaster. New Democracy was punished by voters, receiving its lowest vote share in party history (up to that time), and the returns of the

Greek Legislative election of October 2009 set in motion the events of the what has since become known as the Euro crisis.

To many, it is hard to believe, but the seemingly never-ending Euro crisis has been an ongoing headline for 4 years. Germany's chancellor Angela Merkel once warned it would be a marathon.[1] It began in late 2009 in the shadow of the financial crisis of 2008. After the October election, the new center-left Greek government of George Papandreou assumed office and began to sort through the ledger of the previous government. In doing so, it was shocked to find a deficit much larger than expected. The required restatement of the government's fiscal position revealed that, for years, previous Greek governments had hidden massive debts from the rest of the European Union (EU) and had obscured the fact that Greece had not met debt and deficit commitments that all countries in the "Eurozone," the 17 EU member states using the euro as their common currency, are required to meet.[2]

Missing the targets was not surprising. Other countries in the past, including the largest economies in the bloc, France and Germany, had also failed to meet these targets, especially the deficit target set at 3% of gross domestic product (GDP). The recent global financial crisis and subsequent government actions taken across the continent to stabilize markets had left several other Eurozone governments outside of the EU-mandated fiscal guidelines. Deficits were not new. What shocked markets was the scale of the revelation; Greece's estimated government deficit for 2009 was more than tripled, revised from a previous 3.7% of GDP to 12.5% shortly after the new government took office. By April 2010, new EU figures suggested the deficit was even larger—nearer to 14%.[3] The implications of this admission forced investors worldwide to reconsider their faith in the safety of sovereign debt, a faith that had been used to rescue the world financial system in the aftermath of the 2008 global market crash. Questioning the solvency of sovereign debt threatened to undermine the greatest source of strength and until now seemingly the only source of certainty in a still fledgling world financial recovery.

Such revisions in official statistics are typically very rare. In Greece, however, such revisions were part of a repeated pattern that in hindsight make the revelations of 2009 seem less surprising. Since 2005 the EU had expressed reservations no less than five times regarding the biannual reporting of Greek debt and deficit figures. The EU's own statistical agency Eurostat had first suggested Greece was guilty of misreporting its numbers in 2004. World circumstances had changed since the early part of the decade, and concerns that had once been ignored now became deadly serious, threatening still fragile international markets. On November 10, 2009, the European Economic and Financial Affairs Council (ECOFIN) issued a statement demanding the Greek government rectify its reporting issues and calling for an investigation of the ongoing reporting problems.[4] In its August 2010 follow-up report, the European Commission identified two primary problems that had caused the repeated pattern of upward revisions including the most serious one the previous October: poor accounting procedures and poor governance influencing fiscal reporting. The latter problem was far more troubling than the former as it implied the reported state of Greek finances could be more dependent on electoral and political cycles than on the true state of affairs. While stated more diplomatically, Greece was charged with allowing official agencies to "cook the books" when politically expedient. This had been a quiet suspicion all along, but the new deficit revisions in 2009 created a tipping point in financial markets. Such problems would no longer be ignored. What else had been overlooked or misreported in other states? Was sovereign debt really as safe as credit agencies had rated it? This was all too eerily similar to the mistakes made in the U.S. housing crisis that led to the failure of the investment bank Lehman Brothers and the world financial crisis just ended. The Euro crisis was now well underway.

The newest Greek revisions and their scale forced many observers to question whether Greece could remain solvent for long, or if, in fact, the country was solvent at all given all official figures were now in question. While very serious concerns, these questions also had important implications for the fledgling financial recovery still underway after the world financial crisis that had followed the Lehman collapse. What might have seemed in the past like only an arcane statistical adjustment to the general public had shocked the financial world, whose attention had previously been occupied mostly by the fallout of the U.S. financial crisis and subsequent global recession. Markets had become risk averse following that crisis, a dramatic change from market sentiments prior to 2008 when problems of accounting or debt were often overlooked by many market participants. As markets in the United States and elsewhere collapsed after the investment bank Lehman Brothers failed in September of that previous year, the ensuing credit crisis and market deleveraging was only staunched by the combined efforts of the world's major economies, using their own sovereign credit to fill the void left when private institutions stopped lending. Panicked by the insolvency of major international institutions, private credit markets had dried up as creditors questioned the solvency of all private debtors and stopped lending altogether. Without access to credit, the world financial economy had come to a sudden stop. Only credit extended by sovereign governments broke the freeze, with the credit backed by what the world saw as the only remaining safe asset—sovereign debt. Backed by these efforts and despite a global recession, the worst since the Great Depression, the financial crisis of 2008 began to turn in early 2009 when world markets began a tentative recovery, finding their feet again only with the aid and reassurance that countries would backstop their economies and financial systems using their own good credit.

In this context, one can understand why Greece's revelations had been such a shock. The lifeline that had been credited with saving the world economy suddenly seemed much less secure, or at least potentially so. After the Greek debt and deficit disclosures, the assumption of sovereign debt's perceived safety was now clearly questionable. Sovereign debt crises are never pretty and have a tendency to spread. Admissions that the books had been cooked and that Greek debt was not the safe asset once imagined gave rise to what had been previously unimaginable or at least unspoken—the safety of sovereign debt was potentially uncertain, and with it the nascent financial recovery underway worldwide. Although the troubles of Greece in and of themselves were serious, the implication that the assets used to backstop recent global financial rescues could be questioned implied that those efforts could all become undone. Greek debt, which had been considered investor-grade by ratings agencies and comparable to the major economies' in the EU as late as 2009, was soon downgraded to junk in the months following. In many ways, this new sovereign debt crisis appeared to be a replay of what had only just recently happened 2 years earlier to cause the U.S. financial crisis when another unquestioned asset, mortgages, had been revealed to be far less safe than assumed. Markets worldwide feared another "Lehman moment" could be just around the corner, with predictable financial fallout. They reacted accordingly. In the first summer of this new crisis, the euro's exchange rate plunged by 20% and major market declines were seen from New York to Tokyo.

As the crisis unfolded in late 2009 and early 2010, the costs of refinancing Greek debt soared, doubling from a year earlier and reaching yields of almost 10% on 10-year bonds and triple that of Germany, the union's strongest economy. After a series of denials from both the EU and the Greek government regarding the need for a bailout, the Greek government in Spring 2010 was forced to admit defeat and approach the EU and the International Monetary Fund (IMF) for €110 billion in aid. The country could no longer afford to finance their national debt or raise liquidity in private markets. The group that would later be referred to as "the Troika"—the European Central Bank (ECB), the EU and the IMF, administered the first of what would eventually be six bailouts by fmid-2013. What had been unimaginable only a year before was now a shocking reality. A member of the EU was on the verge of national default. The threat of such a default, it was feared, endangered the entire global economy. After the Lehman Brothers' failure of 2008 the danger was clear. The collapse of a country that was integral to the EU and completely integrated into the world financial system could have cascading effects far beyond what a single bank failure like Lehman's had caused. The financial systems of Europe and even the world could come unraveled. It could even lead to the demise of the euro itself.

For many though, such fears are hard to understand. Why would the near failure of a small economy that makes up only 2.5% of Eurozone economy threaten to unravel the whole currency union? It is a good question, and the effects Greece's disclosures have had on the euro and Portugal, Italy, Ireland, Spain, and the rest of the currency union are not easily or simply explained. The answer and the questionable stability of Europe's common currency revealed by those Greek revelations reflect real problems in the concept and construction of the Eurozone. Although blame for the Euro crisis has most often been on the countries derisively referred to by the acronym "PIIGS" or "GIPSI" both inside and outside Europe, culpability for the crisis can be apportioned much more widely.[5] Beginning with flaws in the design and governance of the Eurozone, understanding how the Euro crisis arose and therefore what can be done to solve it requires much more than simply pointing the finger at those countries now at its center. The concept of the euro as a common currency came from high ideals and lofty ambitions for Europe and its citizens. From an economic perspective though, its implementation was always a compromised project, one in which policies and practices for economic governance were created as much for political expediency as for economic and financial prudence. To understand how the problems of a small nation often credited as the cradle of democracy could threaten an entire global financial system requires careful examination and the answers are not simple.

Four years after the crisis began, five additional bailouts in Europe have been required—for Ireland in 2010; for Portugal in early 2011; for Greece again in spring of 2012; for Spain's banking system in summer of 2012; and then for Cyprus in spring of 2013. As the crisis has marched on, focus has turned from national debt levels of member states to banking and liquidity problems caused by the Euro system's structure, to structural imbalances in the Eurozone and the need for political reforms in the common currency area's fiscal governance. When conditions finally began to improve in Europe's sovereign debt markets in late 2012, they did so only after the ECB was forced to take an action that would never have been possible politically 3 years earlier. The ECB accomplished what four previous bailouts had failed to by unveiling its "big bazooka" and announcing it would provide potentially unlimited liquidity to support the euro and the debt of Eurozone members if necessary.

To those unfamiliar with the Eurozone but familiar with financial crises, such a solution to a financial crisis seems obvious, but it requires an understanding of how the EU and the Eurozone works to understand why this action was only taken 3 years after the crisis began. The policy also addressed only the liquidity shortage in the Eurozone that had been present since the first Greek revelations, lifting crisis conditions in most sovereign debt markets. It came far too late though to avoid the damage 3.5 years of crisis had wrought on European economies. By the end of 2012, the entire region was collectively in recession and unemployment rates in some states had topped 25%. The past 4 years have seen riots in the cities of Portugal, Ireland, Spain, and Greece. Governments have fallen as severe recessions have bred political instability. Only time and additional action will determine whether solvency risk in Europe has also been addressed, but crisis conditions there have spread well beyond financial markets. Despite billions of euros in bailout aid, and years of political wrangling over financial firewalls, fiscal reform, and new banking unions, and the continued suffering of millions of newly unemployed people, lost fortunes, and dashed dreams, the question still remains whether default will be limited to losses already incurred in the crisis or whether defaults will continue and become more disorderly, increasing the threat to European and world markets as time goes on. Although the euro seems safer than it has at some points during the crisis, it still remains to be seen whether the currency union will survive, and whether the grand project begun 50 years ago toward European political and economic integration will continue.

The following attempts to describe the events of the Euro crisis and to interpret why the crisis has unfolded as it has. It further attempts to describe the background of the crisis. Fundamentally, the crisis arose, as with the financial crisis in 2008, due to a worldwide misperception of financial risk, but its roots begin long before 2008. To understand the crisis one has to understand the EU and have a sense of history to understand what it was meant to accomplish. Furthermore, understanding the crisis requires understanding why the EU and the Eurozone operate as they do. One has to understand the design of its common currency, and have an understanding of the economic concerns that might affect a common currency's stability. Finally, in the context of these constraints, one needs to understand the economic circumstances that brought the crisis about.

Unlike the world financial crisis of 2008, whose causes may be traced to imperfect and lax regulation, new and exotic financial instruments, myopic and even reckless decision making by market participants and institutions, and the scale and complexity of international financial markets, the Euro crisis is even more complex. It has never been merely an economic or financial crisis, one that could be solved by engineering a clever economic, financial, or regulatory response. It has, at its heart, been an economic and political crisis, and its solution requires both appropriate and complex economic responses, but more importantly, difficult political reforms. European reaction and policy making since the crisis began has been constrained by the principles and design of its political and institutional framework, a framework that did not imagine such a crisis would occur.

The following attempts to describe the complexity of that framework, the implications for policy making throughout the crisis it has imposed and potential reforms that could help circumstances moving forward. The book also attempts to describe the conditions that led to the crisis, and how the structural flaws in the implementation of the common currency affected those conditions. Finally, the book attempts to briefly outline problems that lie ahead for the Eurozone and in doing so attempts to assess where its future might lie.

Throughout, the book will refer to specific countries as necessary but will also refer to collections of countries in an effort to generalize the effects of the crisis. It will also focus mainly on the original 12-member countries of the Eurozone in describing outcomes that preceded the crisis and in describing outcomes since. This is for two reasons. First, the five countries that have joined the Eurozone since 2007 (in order—Slovenia, Malta, Cyprus, Slovakia, and Estonia) have acceded relatively recently, between 2008 and 2011. Secondly, the newest five member states are very small, with a combined output accounting for only 1.5% of the total value of 2009 Eurozone output.[6] Although the effects of the crisis have been severe not only in the original 12-member states but also in these new countries, notably Cyprus, only Cyprus will be discussed as crisis fallout in that country has been a direct result of decisions made to aid Greece. With respect to the original 12 states to use the Euro, the five most problematic will be referred to as the "GIPSI" states to denote the order in which Greece, Ireland, Portugal, and Spain received bailouts or aid, and Italy which remains the largest and most threatening country in the crisis, but which has not yet (as of this writing) received any official-aid package. To differentiate and define groups of countries further, "southern" countries will refer to those troubled economies on the southern Eurozone periphery (Portugal, Spain, Italy, and Greece), and northern countries to the Netherlands, Germany, Austria, and Finland, which have been the strongest economies throughout the crisis.

As the Euro crisis nears a half decade, it is possible we may be approaching a new stage in the drama, one that might allow the crisis to slowly come to a conclusion. Alternatively, the crisis may only have evolved from a financial and economic one to a political crisis that threatens to undermine a grander dream of forming a greater Europe. The outcome remains unclear. Conditions in troubled countries threaten a political backlash of populism, one that could have unpredictable consequences. Similarly, stronger countries at the core of the Eurozone are now also experiencing economic pain—both from the reduced demand caused by the deep recessions and near-depression-like conditions in the originally troubled countries, and due to austerity actions elsewhere. How the Eurozone responds to these challenges is unclear. It is possible that political leadership could emerge to change course and deliver effective actions, which may or may not lead to fundamental changes in the structure of the Eurozone and possibly even its membership, but which allow the Eurozone and the larger project of European integration to move forward. It is, however, also possible that the crisis is only entering another troubled chapter that takes it even further from a resolution that leaves the union intact. The smoke over Athens and the Eurozone has not yet cleared enough to determine the direction the future will take.

PART II

The Imperfect Architecture of the Eurozone

Introduction

Much like a house with a shaky foundation becomes unstable over time, much of the Euro crisis can be blamed on the faulty architecture of the European monetary union, or "Eurozone"—the group of countries that collectively share the euro as their common currency. While early in the crisis European leaders often blamed their misfortune on the world financial crisis of 2008 that began in the United States, much of the cause of the crisis can be traced to how the euro and EU were designed. In particular, one can identify three sources of problems that contributed to the crisis occurring and that now makes it much worse: a governmental architecture that undermines effective crisis response, a flawed economic architecture that created an unstable monetary union, and a socio-political architecture that causes national policies in the face of the crisis to alienate the European people that European member governments are eventually accountable to. Combined, these three flaws interact in a way that reinforced the destabilizing effects of each, and has led to a crisis that has only worsened over time despite efforts to reverse it. These flaws also undermine the potential for an effective resolution, and may threaten to derail efforts to economically integrate Europe that lay behind the creation of euro in the first place.

The Euro crisis has in large part been shaped by the institutions and governmental structure of the EU as much as it has by economics. To understand the Euro crisis one has to have an appreciation of how the EU works, how it has been shaped by the history of European integration efforts, and the political dynamics this shared history has created among the member states. Policy making in the crisis has not been successful in developing swift and comprehensive solutions because of the institutional structure governing decision making, resulting in a response often characterized as "too little too late" or "kicking the can down the road." This has led to uncertainty in markets and the effect that often policy responses to the crisis seem to have worsened instead of improved it. To discern how the EU's framework may have constrained policy, it can be useful to compare the framework that governs the Eurozone to that of the United States. Both the United States and European economies have faced recent financial crises but efforts to confront both were vastly different. The time it has taken to arrest the Euro crisis cannot be blamed on a lack of knowledge regarding possible policy responses in the face of financial crisis—a long body of policy options has been developed over the experiences of the past century. Using such approaches proved effective and swift in the United States in late 2008 or early 2009 yet Europeans were slow to adopt what seemed like obvious solutions. The result has been a much slower resolution and a worsening of the situation. This can be traced in part to differing political preferences in Europe, to the construction of the decision-making institutions that govern the EU, and to the political incentives these structures have created. These structures have also alienated electorates in many countries who feel that decisions have been made without accountability to the people.

Events and outcomes preceding the crisis were also instrumental in creating it. While the trigger of the Euro crisis may be traced to Greece's debt revelations in October 2009, or even further back to the worldwide financial crisis that unfolded in 2008 after the failure of the investment bank Lehman Brothers in the United States, symptoms of impending problems began to emerge long before either of these events. These include most obviously problems in the sovereign debt bookkeeping of Greece, which first became an issue for European regulators as early as 2004.[1] They also included less obvious symptoms that began to manifest themselves almost as soon as the euro was adopted as the single common currency among Eurozone states in 2002. Just as with the U.S. housing crisis that turned into the worldwide financial crisis of 2008, signs of impending problems in Europe were readily apparent in hindsight, but not perceived as obvious beforehand. Economic activity and financial flows that contributed to the crisis were visible well before the Euro crisis began in 2009, but they were most often dismissed as transitional, temporary, or misinterpreted altogether. For example, trade patterns and the credit flows to finance them emerged after the adoption of the euro that left southern country's financial systems in the Eurozone very vulnerable. These financial flows were misinterpreted by many as signs of economic convergence that proponents of a single currency had predicted would occur, but in hindsight they reflected dangerous credit imbalances. The causes of the trade patterns and financial flows are fundamental—they reflected differences in productivity that existed long before the creation of the euro, and that have persisted and in some cases worsened, since.

Not everyone has been surprised by the Euro crisis, many economists had suggested such a crisis was inevitable as soon as the monetary union announced plans to form. These economists, mostly in the United States but also in Europe appealed to the theory of "optimal currency areas" to suggest that Europe's monetary union did not meet the criteria necessary to ensure its stability.[2] Specifically, the economies adopting the euro as their single currency, first 12 countries and now 17, are much too different.[3] To satisfy the conditions necessary to allow a single currency to function well, theory requires several conditions to be present. Politically, however, ensuring the necessary conditions existed to maintain a single stable currency has not proven possible since the euro was adopted. Member states have neither demonstrated the internal political will necessary to ensure such conditions were created, nor have they ensured externally that supranational institutions exist with the power to ensure these conditions are implemented. Doing so would require ceding significant national sovereignty to Europe, something that has proven too politically unpalatable for countries to accomplish. While designers of the single currency knew reforms were likely necessary, leaders found that dealing with these issues was too easily deferred in the early years of the currency when it appeared the monetary union was functioning smoothly. Unfortunately, such changes have proven very difficult to adopt after the Euro crisis had begun and when they are most needed.

The following three chapters briefly review the historical context leading to the formation of the political institutions of the EU, the economic forces that have contributed to the crisis occurring, and the institutional framework that has hampered policy making once the crisis had begun. Understanding all of these ideas is necessary if one is to be able to understand the present or to forecast how the crisis might yet evolve. The causes of the Euro crisis can be traced to a flawed architecture in the economic design of the monetary union and a flawed implementation of the institutions meant to achieve monetary stability. This flawed implementation can be traced to a problem of governance—specifically a lack of a strong federal system developed over 60 years of European integration efforts. The governmental system adopted to organize the supranational institution the EU has become also inherently creates a distance from electorates. This has led to a populist backlash during the crisis, especially in many of the worst-hit countries, in reaction to policies adopted to save the euro, the monetary union, and even the entire effort to create the EU. The Euro crisis may be the final act in a tragic irony—the monetary union meant to be the final stage of European integration may instead cause the effort to unite Europe to fail altogether. Only time will tell whether the crisis will serve as the catalyst to finish the European integration project or lead to its delay or abandonment altogether.

CHAPTER 2

The Flawed Governmental Architecture of the Eurozone

The European Monetary Union was developed within the context of a greater European integration project. Within that context and given the inertia of over 40 years of progress, the union could not be reconfigured to suit a currency union. Instead, the currency union had to be configured within the context of the EU. This has proven problematic from an economist's point of view as Europe's governance does not include a body with the incentives to make Europe-wide decisions in the interest of the union, regardless of the interests of individual member states. The supranational institution that is the EU does not have a strong federal decision-making authority over the nations it includes. This has led to three serious problems: (i) it has undermined the EU's ability to respond to the crisis effectively by adopting policies across the monetary union that might normally be expected to be used in such a crisis; (ii) it has undermined the creation of new political and economic institutions necessary to rectify problems in the economic architecture of the union; and (iii) because the crisis has required economic transfers between states, it has allowed the wealthiest and economically strongest country's interests to become the most important ones—the idea of a union of equals has not been achieved. How a lack of a strong federal supranational system has led to these faults is best described in the context of the EU's history.

A Brief History of the EU and the Euro

Europe will not be made all at once, or according to a single plan. It will be built through concrete achievements which first create a de facto solidarity.

Robert Schuman, Schuman Declaration, May 9, 1950

The fusion (of economic functions) would compel nations to fuse their sovereignty into that of a single European State.

Jean Monnet, founder of the European
Movement, April 3, 1952[4]

The road to a common European currency began in the aftermath of World War II with the drive to politically integrate the continent. Excessive nationalism in Europe was seen as the primary reason the 20th century's first four decades had been marred by two world wars, leaving the continent in ruins. Ensuring the creation of a united Europe able to overcome the experience of the recent past and avoid similar national conflicts in the future became the political goal of many postwar European politicians and statesmen. Likely, the best known of them with respect to what was to become the EU was Jean Monnet. The drive for such pan-European integration after World War II was most famously and influentially given impetus by Winston Churchill's address of September 19, 1946 at the University of Zurich where he called for the creation of a United States of Europe:

We must build a kind of United States of Europe. In this way only will hundreds of millions of toilers be able to regain the simple joys and hopes which make life worth living. The process is simple. All that is needed is the resolve of hundreds of millions of men and women to do right instead of wrong and to gain as their reward blessing instead of cursing ...

The structure of the United States of Europe, if well and truly built, will be such as to make the material strength of a single state less important. Small nations will count as much as large ones and gain their honor by their contribution to the common cause.[5]

The speech ended with a call for the formation of a Council of Europe to begin the process of forming the United States of Europe. The idea of a Untied States of Europe as Churchill envisioned was not welcomed by all—some nationalist interests in Europe feared such an effort could one day usurp the sovereignty of individual states, but these fears were overcome and a Council was formed in 1949 and continues to exist, with

47 member states comprising most of the northern hemisphere and administrating the European Court of Human Rights among other organizations. While this organization is entirely separate from what would become the EU, its organization would later create the template for the ensuing governance structures of the EU. The tension between nationalist interests with reticence to cede sovereignty to a continental-wide power, and federalists who argued for supranational European institutions led to the adoption of a governance structure in the Council of Europe that attempted to satisfy both motives. The result was a form of dual governance—a Council of Ministers representing the national interests of each member country, and a Parliamentary Assembly functioning as a supranational body representing the greater interests of Europe. This type of federal structure, while diplomatically sidestepping nationalist/federalist differences and since duplicated later in the EU and its predecessor efforts has left Europe without strong federal governance.

Postwar efforts to reconstruct Europe and the Berlin Blockade of 1949 resulted in the recognition of the need for stronger economic and security ties among nations than the Council of Europe provided. To create this and to avoid the conflicts of the past it was understood a binding French–German reconciliation was necessary. On May 9, 1950, such efforts were given voice in a speech by Robert Schuman, France's foreign minister and influential former prime minister. This speech, since referred to as the *Schuman Declaration*, is considered the founding idea of what has since become the current EU, as it appealed to leaders "to make war not merely unthinkable, but materially impossible."[6] The means of ensuring European peace would be developed through economic as well as political integration. The resulting Treaty of Paris, signed on April 18, 1951 created the European Coal and Steel Community (ECSC) among France, Germany, Italy, and the Benelux countries (Belgium, the Netherlands, and Luxembourg). Its purpose was to coordinate and consolidate the economic interests of member states to more quickly achieve war-time reconstruction, raise living standards, and to ensure European peace by pooling the coal and steel production capability of all six nations, which had historically been central to national munitions production. It was also the first supranational European governmental institution and its governance structure would influence those institutions that were to follow.

Governance of the ECSC was directed by several institutions, each of which was the forerunner of similar institutions used today in the EU. The executive body governing the ECSC was the High Authority, which would eventually evolve into the European Commission of the EU. Its charge was to work in the interest of the community of nations and not national interests. The ECSC also had a Common Assembly with consultative power to the High Authority, but no direct legislative authority, and made up of 78 members appointed or elected by their constituent states. This body was the forerunner of the modern European Parliament in the EU. The Special Council of Ministers comprised a third governance body, and was made up of representatives from the member states' national governments. This group has evolved into the modern Council of Ministers in the EU. The High Authority required the consent of the Special Council in all areas of executive action except coal and steel where the Council of Ministers were only advisory to the High Authority.[7] In this way, national interests were represented in non-coal and steel decisions as Council rules requiring unanimity in decision making allowed members to veto actions not in their country's interest.

Formation of the ECSC was only the first of what was envisaged to be three supranational communities that would bind a federal Europe, the other two being the European Defence Community and European Political Community. Nationalist interests, however, particularly those in France where the Defence Community was rejected by the French Parliament, led to the curtailment of additional political integration efforts and resulted instead in a focus on European economic integration in the following decade. The Treaties of Rome, signed on March 25, 1957 created the European Atomic Energy Community (Euratom) and the European Economic Community (EEC), with both beginning operation in 1958. These new communities focused on coordinating and consolidating economic interests in Europe, with the former coordinating atomic energy activities and the latter charged with managing the creation of a customs union allowing for the eventual adoption of a free and common market for goods and services, labor, and capital among member states. The EECs early activities focused on common transport and agricultural policies and it rapidly became the most important of the three communities.

Governance of all three communities was similar and some institutions such as the Parliamentary Assembly (the Common Assembly until 1962) and Court of Justice were shared. The Brussels Treaty of 1965 merged the three communities into the European Communities (EC) beginning in July 1967, integrating their governance into a single set of institutions. The Special Council of Ministers had now evolved into the Council of European Communities, while the Commission of the European Communities was defined to serve as the overall ECs' executive body. Organizationally, with these changes Europe moved closer to a single governance structure managing its economic and political integration.

Nationalist sentiments in the EC began to grow and resist the process of supranational integration efforts, particularly in France after the election of Charles De Gaulle as the new French president in late 1958. This was most apparent in debates regarding the enlargement of the EC. Pressures to allow enlargement of membership in the EC beyond the original "inner six" countries resulted in Denmark, Norway, Ireland, and the United Kingdom submitting membership applications in 1960. France, fearing its foreign-policy interests could be undermined by this wider expansion, particularly the addition of the United Kingdom, vetoed British admission to the EC. This resulted in the suspension of the remaining countries' membership processes and a victory for France's nationalist interests.

The conflict between nationalist and federalist efforts came to a head in 1965, when French concerns regarding their sovereignty over agricultural policy resulted in "the empty chair" crisis the withdrawal of French representation from the Council of European Communities over its use of majority voting, which had undermined the principle of national vetoes. The result was the Luxembourg Compromise of 1966, which reinstituted the practice of vetoes in matters of national interest, and this practice continues to this day. While nationalist/federalist tensions had been present since the creation of the EC, this was a fundamental decision, protecting national interests over European ones. The result would constrain the future formation of strong federal European governance in the eventual formation of the EU. De Gaulle's opposition to the supranational authority of EC institutions also resulted in the first informal European leader's summits in 1961 as an attempt to offset the growing power of the EC's supranational authority. While these early meetings did not initially create a permanent nationalist counterweight to federal EC power, they eventually resulted in the creation of a new European institution in 1975, the European Council. This body, now the pre-eminent decision-making body in the executive branch of the EU is made up of member heads of state, and in matters of national interest, decision making allows vetoes to be exercised.[8]

This concession to nationalist interests though, far from undermining further integration actually revitalized it, allowing political integration to begin again and a strong central Council kick-started economic integration efforts, which had stalled in the 1970s without the creation of the promised customs union and free-trade zone the original EEC was supposed to create.[9] It also allowed enlargement of the European Communities. In 1973, the United Kingdom, Denmark, and Ireland were all formally admitted. In 1976 the European Parliament formalized the process of member elections, resulting in the first elections in all member states in 1979.[10] Further enlargement occurred in the 1980s, with Greece joining in 1981 and Spain and Portugal in 1986.[11] In 1986 the Single European Act was signed, modifying the original Treaties of Rome to begin the process of deeper political and economic integration that was to become the current European Union. Forty years after Churchill's speech in Zurich, the political and economic integration of Europe was well underway, but the balancing of nationalist and supranational interests would continue to define the union's governance.

The final framework to achieve the goals of an economically integrated Europe emerged in the Delors Report (1989), which framed the stages and process by which the monetary union should occur.[12] In 1992, the Maastricht Treaty outlined the new rules under which the European Union would function. With respect to governance, the structure of the EU would be based on "three pillars": the European Community pillar, the Common Foreign and Security Policy pillar, and the Justice and Home Affairs pillar. Each pillar was largely an extension of existing institutional structures, with the latter two pillars specifying intergovernmental structures within the Union necessary to define foreign policy and the operation of a borderless Europe. The European Community was again in practice the most influential, defining now the supranational institutions of the EU by largely preserving the governance structures previously put in place.

Decision making in the EU would be governed by an executive branch, the European Commission. The Commission's guidance and accountability flowed directly from the European Council composed of member heads of state. The Legislative branch would be composed of the Council of the EU (sometimes referred to as the Council of Ministers) composed of member-state cabinet ministers or appointed representatives, and the European Parliament. To protect nationalist concerns, both councils would suspend special majority voting rules in favor of member-state vetoes in treaty matters regarding governance of the EU, or matters of national interest. EU-wide interests would be reflected in the appointed European Commission and the European Parliament, the latter continuing as a directly elected body with seats elected by member-country electorates proportional to member-state populations. This structure continues today. Legislative direction is defined by the European Council through agreement of national leaders. The Commission then proposes legislative action, which the EU Parliament and Council of Ministers act upon. The Judicial branch is administered by the European Court of Justice, arbitrating matters regarding EU-wide law. The Court includes a member from each nation in the EU. This EU governance structure is shown in Figure 1.

Overall, the path chosen to achieve European integration has led to an EU-wide governance structure that is a hybrid of almost all democratic political institutions that have preceded it. It is not a single federal system, nor is it a confederation of nations. It is a structure that in some areas is closely coordinated and even supranational, but in others remains strictly intergovernmental. It is this latter characteristic of the relationship that has proven most relevant in the crisis, as intergovernmental decision making has defined the response of the Eurozone and by extension the EU due to the need to respect national interests on the European Council. Because some governments have been unwilling to consider EU policies that might undermine their strength back home, this has constrained policy making in the crisis by weakening or avoiding altogether strong EU-wide responses to the crisis. Specifically, any policy that might imply an intergovernmental transfer of wealth to other nations has been especially hard to agree upon, and this in particular has undermined aid to the most troubled countries in the Euro crisis, or in creating new institutions that could strengthen the union. Simply put, the structure of the EU system implies that domestic

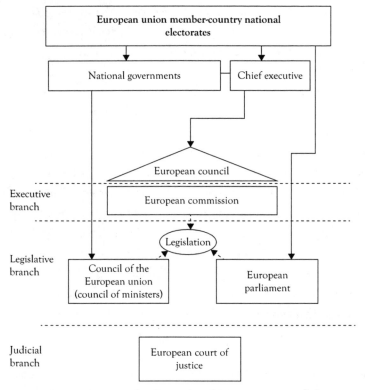

Figure 1. Governance in the European Union consists of three branches. The executive branch, headed by the European Commission is directed by the European Council, which defines the direction of the EU through its membership of elected heads of state. The legislative branch is composed of the Council of the EU (Council of Ministers) and the EU Parliament, while the judicial branch is composed of the court shown. Legislative action (broken arrows) is proposed by the executive, but then requires approval from the two arms of the legislative branch. Solid arrows in the diagram identify responsibility for appointment of the members in each body of government. National electorates elect their own governments and heads of state, along with a European Parliament. Heads of the member states or their delegates compose the memberships of the European Council and Council of Ministers, respectively. Matters of foreign policy or national interest require unanimity in both councils' decisions, thus national interests are safeguarded. Federal or Europe-wide interests, represented by the European Commission in the executive branch and the European Parliament in the legislative branch will always be constrained by this structure as EU-wide decision making, directed by the European Council requires unanimous national consent to proceed, and the Council of Ministers' approval to be successfully enacted into EU law.

politics in individual states can have important implications on EU-wide decision making.

If one were to compare the EU to a similarly sized economic and monetary union, the United States would be a natural comparison. In the United States, 50 states share the same currency, and have almost completely free trade between them. Upon casual inspection, the economic fundamentals are broadly similar across the EU and the United States. Each has an approximately comparable population and GDP.[13] Both include only developed economies. Socially, European ancestry in the United States is still obvious in the laws, institutions, and cultures that make up the country. There are, however, important differences. Fundamentally, a united Europe is still an unfinished project. In economic matters affecting the entire Eurozone or the whole EU, it is still a confederation, one that makes difficult decisions slowly based on consensus of the member nations.[14] The emergence of Angela Merkel, Chancellor of Germany, and Nicholas Sarkozy, the President of France as the primary decision makers during the Euro crisis from 2009 until 2012 (when Sarkozy was defeated in the French presidential election), is in itself indicative of the vast difference in the constructions of governance of the two unions. Europe's governance, dominated by these two leaders presiding over Eurozone's largest two economies, would be comparable to imagining in a time of national economic crisis, not the president of the United States but the governors of New York and California dominating the political debate. In the United States, strong federal governance has ensured this does not occur. In Europe, however, ensuring federal interests rise above regional ones has not been possible.[15] Instead, a kind of economic government has been created in which healthier and wealthier economies have the greatest power in dictating policy if their resources are necessary to accomplish a given policy. This has been the case during the Euro crisis as policies regarding bailouts and collective action have required significant outlays of financial resources.

Formation of the Euro

The formation of the European Monetary Union can be regarded as the final stage in the economic integration of Europe. Efforts to achieve closer economic integration began to occur in the late 1960s. At the Hague

Summit of 1969 the European Council delegated Pierre Werner, then Prime Minister of Luxembourg the task of reporting on how the EC might avoid exchange rate volatility among its member states. The result was the Werner Plan published in 1970, which recommended a common currency or irrevocably fixed exchange rates among member currencies to occur over a period of 10 years in three stages. The first stage was seen as the most important as it would set the stage for the transference of economic policy across the EC from national governments to a single centralized, community-wide body. In effect, the report called for a greater political integration to achieve economic goals and not surprisingly given the previous discussion regarding the conflict between nationalist and supranational visions, the plan was not adopted.

In 1972 after the breakdown of the Bretton Woods fixed exchange rate system, concerns mounted in the EC regarding exchange rate volatility and the negative impacts such risk implied for closer economic integration and trade in the EC. The first EC attempt to overcome this problem was to adopt an idea from the Werner Plan to establish a cooperative semi pegged exchange rate system in which currencies would be allowed to fluctuate by only ±2.25% between countries. This arrangement was referred to as the "the snake in the tunnel" due to the fact that exchange rates could move within an upper and lower limit. By the late 1970s it was clear this arrangement had failed to reduce the exchange fluctuations it was meant to address and in 1979 the European Monetary System (EMS) was created. Exchange rates were based on a new reference currency referred to as the European Currency Unit (ECU), which in turn was based on the values of the participating countries' currencies. Again exchange rates of individual countries were pegged within a range of ±2.25% of the ECU value, with a wider band of ±6% allowed for the Italian lira. The EMS also proved to be a volatile system. Over time because of the German Bundesbank's (the German central bank's) strict anti-inflation policies, the Deutsche Mark became the central currency within this system and other currencies had to follow the Bundesbank's lead to maintain their exchange rates.

By the late 1980s member countries were primarily using national interest rates to maintain their EMS exchange rate targets. Differences in economic conditions and policy priorities across member states led to a crisis in the system in September 1992 as speculators recognized several countries would not be able to maintain their exchange rates given domestic economic conditions. What is referred to as a "time inconsistency" problem occurred, that is, countries that had committed to a fixed exchange rate regime earlier now found it optimal to renege on that commitment.[16] On "Black Wednesday," September 16, 1992, under intense pressure from currency speculators in international exchange markets, Britain was forced to withdraw from the EMS. The conflict between very weak domestic economic conditions and the high interest rates (over 10%) necessary to maintain exchange rate targets proved unworkable. The following day Italy also withdrew from the EMS as it was also unable to maintain exchange rate targets. When the French franc also came under speculative pressure the following year, EMS target ranges were widened to 15% to accommodate it. While in principle the EMS was still functioning, in practice the system had completely broken down and was no longer providing the exchange rate stability it was meant to create.

Given the fact that in order to maintain their exchange rates countries had been forced to follow German economic monetary policy, effectively German economic policy had become European policy, much to the dissatisfaction of many other EC member states. To avoid this outcome and control what was perceived in some countries as Germany's excessive influence, it became clear to many that the close economic integration Europe desired could only be accommodated with a single currency across states. Adopting such a system would commit countries to exchange rate parity and allow Europe-wide monetary policy to be determined for all of Europe, avoiding the problems the EMS experienced. Following the outline recommended in the 1989 Delors Report, the Maastricht Treaty of 1992 defined the new EU and conditions under which a new single currency would be adopted: the euro.

The euro first came into existence in 1999 as a virtual currency, used only as a unit of account among the original 11 participating EU countries. In 2001 Greece was also approved to become part of the euro at the start of the following year, joining France, Germany, Luxembourg, Spain, Italy, Portugal, Belgium, the Netherlands, Finland, Ireland, and Austria now often referred to collectively as the Eurozone or "Euro-Group." At the beginning of 2002, the euro replaced national currencies in participating countries to great fanfare. The euro's introduction as the single currency of the monetary union fueled optimism it would replace the U.S. dollar as the world reserve currency. The following decade never lived up to such hopes but the euro has emerged as the only major alternative to the dollar in international finance.

Because countries of the Eurozone must coordinate economic policies more closely, the Euro Group of finance ministers meet on a regular basis, typically a day before EU-wide meetings of the ECOFIN.[17] Since the Euro crisis began, it has also been common for Euro Group heads of state to convene "Euro-summits" to decide crisis policy in a manner similar to how the EU Council of Ministers becomes the European Council when heads of state represent their nations. Again, these meetings have been unofficial, but have served to ensure policy coordination across Eurozone countries.

The implementation of the euro as a common currency was also seen by many as a critical political achievement, one that since World War II had been decades in the making, as shown in Figure 2. It was anticipated that the creation of the Eurozone would ensure significant economic benefits for those countries participating. In some quarters, specifically

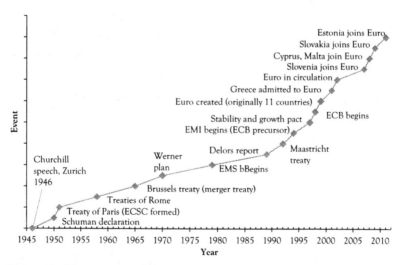

Figure 2. The process of European economic integration over time. Major treaties occurred through the 1950s and 1960s. Efforts to stabilize currency exchange rates among member countries in the European Community began in the 1970s and led directly to the creation of the Euro in 1999. Eurozone enlargement has occurred since 2001 and it now includes 17 countries as of 2013.

Germany and northern Europe, it was thought the euro would end the threat of inflation across the continent through the enshrinement of sound continent-wide monetary policy. Other countries saw the creation of the euro as a spur to growth, easing trade and creating better access to credit markets, particularly those countries in the south. In general, the euro was expected to create the conditions for "economic convergence," the condition in which all member economies' standards of living converge to a common outcome, bringing greater prosperity to the entire union. This promise has since led to additional countries joining the currency, including Slovenia in 2007, Cyprus and Malta in 2008, Slovakia in 2009, and Estonia in 2011. Latvia will join in 2014 and Lithuania also hopes to be included by 2015.

Ironically, the political accomplishment the Eurozone represents was accomplished in large part by avoiding the political compromises necessary to create a supranational political union. The monetary union was accomplished without ceding national sovereignty formally from areas that would need to be if the currency union were to remain stable.[18] Despite the hopes of the original visionaries, a "United States of Europe" was never created. Instead the EU and the Eurozone in particular represent a hybrid governmental institution that is far more economically than politically integrated. The Eurozone is a supranational economic government, however, politically the institution could be considered to behave more often like confederation, with intergovernmental relationships defining its political direction. The difficulties in achieving a consensus in which a stronger federal union might have emerged were sidestepped throughout the evolution of the current Eurozone; from the original ECSC, through the creation of the EC and finally to the current EU and Eurozone, the latter intended to one day cover almost all of the EU.

As a social creation, the current EU and Eurozone embody the social and political realities that have been present in Europe as they evolved. Social conditions, political, cultural, and historical, defined the boundaries of the political and economic integration achieved. While the Eurozone and EU may yet evolve into a more supranational or federal entity, one that considers first the greater welfare of the continent, the current system prioritizes the interests of the individual states within it. Relations between states reflect wealth, power, and more local interests first. Lacking a strong central decision-making mechanism, policy throughout the Euro crisis has been implemented piecemeal, reacting to conditions instead of anticipating them, and has not been able to define the type of integrated response necessary to deal with the challenges the Euro crisis presents. It remains to be seen whether greater political integration will be forced to emerge out of necessity in order to preserve the accomplishments so far achieved, or whether incremental development will continue, and with it the continued risk and uncertainty the Euro crisis represents.

CHAPTER 3

The Flawed Economic Architecture of the Eurozone

A European currency will lead to member nations transferring their sovereignty over financial and wage policy as well as monetary affairs. It is an illusion to think that states can hold on to their autonomy over taxation policies.

Hans Tietmeyer, President of the Deutsche Bundesbank (1993–99), 1991.[1]

As noted in the previous chapter, the implementation of the euro created an economic union that was designed to fit the political constraints of the EU. These constraints caused the currency union to lack important characteristics that have proven important and even essential to the stability of common currency areas. Successful monetary unions have historically required three characteristics that require states to cede sovereignty over monetary and fiscal policy for the good of the currency: economic integration and the ability to manage and react to external and internal shocks; a common fiscal framework allowing collective transfers and if necessary, collective debt; and strong central bank able to act as a lender of last resort in the common currency. The European monetary union, however, was critically lacking in several of these features when it was launched. The first two conditions are consistent with the conditions necessary to form an "optimal currency area." The third characteristic, the presence of a strong central bank that can act as a union-wide lender of the last resort has proven invaluable in financial crises for over a century and Europe's central banking arrangement has proven problematic during the Euro crisis. The design of the European monetary union's economic architecture, has contributed to the Euro crisis becoming as serious as it has, and has also hindered its recovery. Much of the effort to address the Euro crisis has focused on trying to establish these missing elements.

Optimal Currency Areas

The theory of an optimal currency area was first developed in 1961 by the Canadian economist Robert Mundell and was part of the work that won him the Nobel Memorial Prize in Economics in 1999. Since a monetary union permanently fixes exchange rates between a set of countries at parity, to be credible the commitment must be binding. As was demonstrated by Europe's previous experiences with setting a fixed exchange rate system, such commitment is necessary to ensure that fixed exchange rates can be maintained. Otherwise, countries will leave the system when it becomes advantageous to do so. Currency speculation will also hasten the breakdown of fixed exchange rates when it becomes likely such defections are about to happen. To ensure a currency union is stable the benefits of joining must outweigh the costs of continuing membership and the circumstances necessary to ensure this is likely to occur is what the theory of optimal currency areas describes.

The benefits of adopting a common currency arise from three effects a monetary union provides: reduced transaction costs in trade between countries; greater price transparency between goods from different countries; and less economic uncertainty caused by the reduction of exchange rate volatility. The first benefit occurs through the elimination of the costs of currency exchange, the second fosters greater trade and price competition to the benefit of consumers, while the third improves trade and investment decisions. When these benefits increase, the greater is the trade and economic integration between the countries in a currency union, and the creation of a common currency is generally assumed to also increase trade among the participating countries.

The primary cost of a currency union is the loss of a country's ability to use independent monetary policy to manage its economy or to adjust to a country-specific economic shock. If a recessionary shock were to occur to a country, in the absence of a currency union a country's exchange rate can be sacrificed to allow expansionary monetary policy to be used to increase employment. Monetary policy may be used to stimulate growth through lower interest rates causing greater investment, while simultaneously causing depreciation in the country's exchange rate, stimulating trade with the rest of the world. When a country is part of a currency union, however, this monetary policy option is lost as the country no longer controls its currency. Policy responses to aid adjustment to macroeconomic shocks then must occur either through fiscal policy (expansion of government expenditures, lower taxes to stimulate growth, or both), labor migration, or through a reduction in the price of goods within the affected country relative to others, allowing it an expansion of exports within the currency union. For countries in a currency union, the use of fiscal policy to react to a recessionary shock may be limited if a country cannot borrow at reasonable rates from international finance markets. Such rates require a country does not have an unsustainable debt load.

Labor mobility—allowing people move to other countries with better economic conditions, allows citizens to adapt to a shock by moving within the currency union. Labor mobility, however, may be limited because of cultural and linguistic factors or immigration restrictions. Such restrictions may include outright laws against such movement or, as in the case of Europe, differences in social or pension programs that make such relocation difficult. The last choice, and the most injurious to a country's people, is referred to as an *internal devaluation,* and occurs as costs in a country are reduced by recessionary conditions and a lack of employment and demand, primarily through a reduction in wages, which improves a country's trade competitiveness. Clearly, labor migration and internal devaluation impose the costs of adjustment to a macroeconomic shock on the people within the country, and if adjustment requires either to occur, political pressure may build to rethink currency membership.

The willingness of a country to accept the loss of its ability to affect its terms of trade through monetary policy may in part depend on a country's policy preferences. These often differ, for example, German society tends to have a much higher preference for low inflation relative to unemployment than say, Italy, due in part to the experiences of Germany prior to World War II. Foregoing the ability to independently set monetary policy, eliminating its potentially inflationary use as a means of macroeconomic adjustment to shocks may be preferred in some countries (e.g., Germany) over the use of monetary policy to stabilize employment or output at the cost of inflation. Such inflationary preferences might also increase the benefit of a monetary union since commitment to a common currency effectively ties the hands of policy makers with respect to inflation rates. For countries with the opposite preference, however, the loss of independent monetary policy can be seen as a loss of economic sovereignty. A currency union also eliminates the ability of a country to use inflation to ease the real costs of its debt burden—in other words by "printing money" to pay a portion of the debt. Again policy preferences within a country determine whether a country is willing to give up such sovereignty to joining a currency union.

Overall, a successful monetary union will require that the conditions of an optimal currency union are present. If they are, deeper economic integration occurs after the common currency is implemented. Despite the fact that a currency union eliminates the use of monetary policy, the ability to react to internal or country-specific economic shocks is preserved if countries maintain the fiscal space to do so—that is, if they have the ability to borrow using sovereign debt, or if they can rely on support from the other members of the union through transfers or a form of shared debt. Preserving the ability to react to shocks in this way can then ensure the benefits of remaining in a currency union outweigh the costs of adjustment if members face the risk country-specific economic shocks.

Since the costs of joining a monetary union may fall predominantly on labor through internal devaluation, accepting a monetary union requires the people within participating countries to be willing to allow the collective interests of the union to transcend their own national interests. Such solidarity, possibly caused by cultural or economic ties across countries may not only lend political support for a common currency but may also create the political willingness to share resources to aid other countries through transfers when needed. Allowing collective transfers or collective debt to help support another country's fiscal position could provide the means for affected countries to stabilize their economies through the use of other member's resources. The ability of a monetary union as a whole to use fiscal transfers and joint debt liability to react to internal country-specific shocks or external shocks that affect the entire union would also be greatly facilitated by strong union-wide federal governance.

A Flawed Optimal Currency Area?
The Implementation of the Euro

Given the economic theory regarding the sources of costs and benefits of a monetary union, Europe's implementation of the euro can be compared with the criteria known to be important to create a sustainable union to determine whether the currency had the potential for instability problems. The economic conditions that would enhance the benefits of a currency union and reduce its costs are shown in Table 1, along with an evaluation of how countries of the Eurozone score collectively with respect to these characteristics. Additionally, the social characteristics that would enhance a country's willingness to accept the tradeoffs implied by a monetary union are also shown. The chart shows the areas most problematic have included differential debt levels among states, labor market mobility, wage flexibility, and limited cohesion among states. Each of these characteristics has played a part in the evolution of the Euro crisis. These flaws were also foreseen before the euro was implemented.

From the first efforts to begin the process of implementing a single currency in Europe, critics have questioned the euro's prospects. In 1992, sixty-two German economists signed a document warning against the implementation of the common currency. The adoption of the euro and Maastricht Treaty were challenged in the country's constitutional

Table 1. *Optimal Currency Area Characteristics of the Eurozone*

Optimal Currency Area Criteria	Eurozone Area Conditions
Economic criteria	
Degree of trade openness and integration	High
Product diversification	High
Labor mobility	Low
Wage flexibility	Low
Level of debt	Varies from low to high
Fiscal transfers possible	Officially limited
Social criteria	
Homogeneous policy preferences	Regional/limited
High degree of solidarity with other nations	Regional/limited

Sources: OECD, Gáková and Dijkstra (2008), and Baldwin and Wyplosz (2004).

courts in 1997.[2] Criticism of the project was also common in the United States, where American economists in both the Federal Reserve and academia voiced skepticism over plans for the euro's success.[3] Europe's justification for implementation of the euro relied on the high degree of trade openness already present on the continent and the idea that reducing the costs of this trade would greatly expand it among the members of the union. Since the euro's adoption many authors have suggested this trade effect has indeed occurred but estimates of the degree trade might have increased vary. Some early authors writing before the euro had been implemented estimated the currency union could increase trade flows among member countries by 40% or more in the long run. More recent studies have indicated far less of an impact (between 5% and 20%). Some have even suggested that the euro has not meaningfully increased trade among countries at all.[4] Overall, the more recent results suggest the benefits of adopting the common currency may have been small and hard to establish, potentially undermining the benefits perceived in the Eurozone for its adoption. If the costs the monetary union imposes were to mount in affected countries, as they potentially have during the Euro crisis, this could undermine the willingness of countries to remain committed to it.

Justification of the European currency union also relied on the likelihood that country-specific shocks would affect members of the Eurozone. Such internal shocks should be less likely to occur when member economies are well diversified since sector-specific shocks affecting only single countries or regions would be less likely. With respect to product diversification, Europe, at least among most of its original members, was and remains highly diversified and therefore less apt to be affected regionally by sector-specific shocks, at least in product markets.[5]

Skepticism regarding the EU's ability to avoid defections from the currency focused on the inability of specific countries to reduce the cost of country-specific shocks, and the ensuing political pressure this would create to abandon the euro. Labor market adjustment would be very difficult as labor markets are relatively rigid in most European countries, with high union presence and strict labor laws regarding worker protections. According to the Organization for Economic Cooperation and Development's (OECD) labor market protection index, Eurozone countries' average rank exceeds the OECD average and is eight times that of the United States (see Figure 1), making labor market and wage adjustment very difficult in the event of an economic downturn.

Furthermore, while ensuring labor mobility across countries was a core goal when the process of European economic integration began, language and cultural differences across countries limit this goal in practice. In comparison to American labor mobility, the levels found in the Eurozone have been estimated to be two and a half times lower.[6] Wage inflexibility, coupled with limited labor mobility implies adjustment to a country-specific shock would be slow without other policy interventions. Given the above conditions, to maintain popular support of the currency union, the ability to remain able to effectively employ fiscal policy in response to a shock would seem especially important in the Eurozone.

The ability to use fiscal policy to stabilize an economy requires the ability to borrow. This, in turn, depends on a country's perceived ability to service their pre-existing debt load. When this debt load is higher, higher interest rates are usually necessary to compensate lenders for the additional risk of default such a debt burden creates, reducing a country's ability to borrow. International financial markets are also volatile and

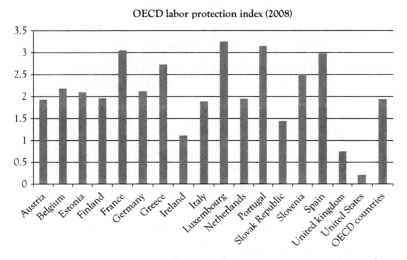

Figure 1. OECD strictness of national employment protection index. The high index scores of EU countries relative to the United States indicate how difficult it is to use labor market adjustment to adapt to economic conditions. In a currency area this makes internal devaluation very difficult for countries to achieve.
Source: OECD.

prone to sudden swings in market sentiment, potentially causing interest rates to increase, drying up credit. While such swings can occur quickly, adjustment of a country's debt burden is a slow process thus restoring confidence can be a very slow process, made slower by the effect limited credit can have on economic growth. To avoid such an outcome, countries need to maintain "fiscal space," ensuring that debt loads are small enough that should additional fiscal action be needed, the additional debt necessary to finance it is perceived to be sustainable.

With the implementation of the euro in 1999, while control of monetary policy in each participating country was relinquished in favor of the use of the common currency across states, fiscal policies governing government expenditures and taxation by country were left effectively independent. This did not mean, however, that fiscal policy was not also limited. The Maastricht Treaty did specify critical fiscal requirements, the "Maastricht Convergence Criteria" limiting annual government deficit levels to no more than 3% of GDP, and ratios of national debt to GDP to no more than 60%.[7] These debt and deficit policies were meant to ensure debt brakes existed within the currency union to ensure access to markets, thereby maintaining monetary union stability. The criteria were to be enforced by rules described in the European Stability and Growth Pact (SGP) adopted at the original urging of Germany, which reasoned that there was a need for such a pact to ensure countries adhered to the Maastricht Criteria. To accomplish this, the SGP specified sanctions for the failure to meet these terms, including fines and even the suspension of EU expenditures within the country. The SGP was eventually signed into law in 1997.

Almost immediately after the euro replaced national currencies, however, the Maastricht and SGP rules were violated by some countries. As Figure 2 illustrates, debt–GDP levels across the original 12 Eurozone countries have varied significantly but in general have grown over time. This growth was occurring even before the world financial crisis of 2008 and the Euro crisis began in 2009, and since then these levels have increased substantially. With respect to violations of Treaty requirements, first Portugal was found to be in violation in 2002, and then Greece in 2005, but sanctions were not imposed. In 2002 and 2003, France and Germany, the two largest countries in the Eurozone accounting for 50%

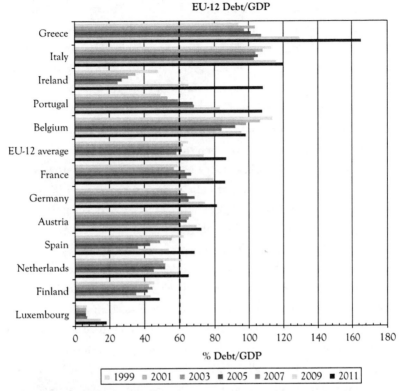

Figure 2. Debt–GDP levels for the original 12 Eurozone countries. Since the inception of the euro, some countries have had relatively higher debt–GDP ratios, indicating that access to financial markets could potentially be problematic. Several also saw debt loads rise as a proportion of national income after the euro was implemented, despite Maastricht Criteria meant to limit such debt growth. By 2009 and the beginning of the Euro crisis a majority of countries had debt–GDP ratios greater than the 60% specified in the Maastricht Treaty (dashed line). Source: Eurostat.

of Eurozone output both exceeded the 3% deficit rule. In 2003 France and Germany also exceeded the 60% debt–GDP rule, which they have broken every year since. Germany's failure to achieve Maastricht targets was primarily due to the costs of reunification with the former East Germany. France had missed the targets after a severe economic slowdown in the early 2000s. In each case the EU commission began sanction proceedings as directed under SGP, but both countries successfully lobbied against any punitive action being taken against them. More importantly, they also lobbied for a reinterpretation of the SGP rules.[8] This was to have significant influence on the future course of events in the Eurozone.

At the European Council Meeting on March 22 and 23, 2005, member states agreed to German–French proposals that would change rules defined in the SGP regarding violations of the SGP accord. Their proposals allowed the inclusion of special circumstances under which the Maastricht convergence requirements need not be strictly met. Specifically, if debt–GDP requirements were met, deficit rules could be loosened. The structural deficit (deficit adjusted for the business cycle) could now be considered to allow for loosening of deficit limits when economies slowed, allowing counter-cyclical fiscal expenditures to expand when necessary. Furthermore, deficit limits would also be waived if deemed necessary by the severity of an economic downturn, or if expenditures were undertaken to enhance future productivity, and "all other relevant factors." These ideas had merit from an economic perspective. The measures allowed for large-scale public infrastructure investment, like that occurring in the former East Germany. Relaxing the Maastricht limits also ensured increased austerity would not be necessary to meet them exactly when the opposite type of fiscal policy might be called for in the event of an economic slowdown. Ironically, the strict rules Germany had successfully ensured were adopted to protect the Eurozone were undermined by the later efforts of Germany with the help of France to relax them.

Unfortunately, the loosening of Maastricht and SGP requirements made nearly impossible any type of fiscal controls, should a government wish to avoid them for economic or political reasons, and it allowed countries to pursue wider variations in fiscal stance than beforehand. As shown by the rise in debt–GDP across countries in Figure 2, the French–German effort to avoid sanctions set a standard and practice that was to continue—deficits and debt limits began to be missed repeatedly by several countries in the Eurozone—each time, justified on the wider grounds now available to governments to waive Maastricht limits.[9] The net result of the rising debt–GDP levels was to reduce the potential fiscal space, the ability countries had to borrow on international financial markets. This was also potentially destabilizing to the currency union, as it increased the possibility countries could face a debt crisis if borrowing as a means of servicing debt obligations became difficult.

One means of easing such instability would be to allow transfers between countries, or joint liability among countries, effectively allowing one country to borrow using another's credit-worthiness. The idea of transfers though and the principle of joint liability was explicitly rejected in the Maastricht Treaty.[10] The reason this was prohibited came primarily from concerns voiced by countries when the treaty was written. Some countries were concerned that allowing such transfers would only create moral hazard. In the presence of such an arrangement it was felt that members of the currency union would have no incentive to reduce deficits or debt, as should they find access to credit markets cut, they could instead receive transfer support from other states.[11]

Given the lack of a "European identity" and the lack of a cultural solidarity among the populations of member countries, this caveat to the treaty was not surprising. The lack of such sentiments would naturally cause the public within each member nation to prefer protecting their own fiscal burdens to aiding other countries with "bailouts" or "transfers." Without such unity, transfers would be politically unpopular and difficult to employ should they be needed to stop the Eurozone from unraveling if countries faced crises that threatened their exit otherwise. This has been clearly demonstrated in the current crisis as bailouts to southern periphery countries have been widely unpopular in the other countries that have financed them. Furthermore, the idea of Euro bonds, that is, bonds that allow the joint liability for debt to support countries cut off from credit markets has also been soundly rejected, particularly by northern countries, most vocally Germany.

Overall, from an economic perspective the implementation of the euro as a single currency was potentially flawed and prone to instability. While trade integration and diversification suggested that the benefits of a currency union could be significant and that country-specific shocks should not occur often, much of the Eurozone lacked the ability to deal with such shocks and therefore, if they were to occur the economic and political costs could be large. Since the treaty structure of the Eurozone intentionally limits transfers among union members, countercyclical aid to offset the costs of such events would not be available from the rest of the Eurozone. In these circumstances, country-specific shocks would inflict greater costs on affected countries, potentially resulting in countries reconsidering currency membership. Domestic politics in a downturn would be prone to discount the benefits of the currency union and instead focus on the costs of such shocks. To avoid the possibility of defections from the euro, the European currency union intentionally did not include an exit procedure should a country choose or be forced to leave the euro.

Not including an exit process was meant to signal commitment to a common currency, avoiding the time inconsistency problem that had caused Europe's previous fixed exchange rate efforts to fail. This did not ensure, however, that such an event was impossible. The lack of exit rules, deemed necessary to solve the time inconsistency problem, also created a different and potentially destabilizing problem. Should a country choose or be forced to leave the union, the consequences of such an action would be unclear as no procedure existed to define how this would occur. Any such exit would therefore be "chaotic," greatly increasing the uncertainty of such a situation.

In general, the structure of the European monetary union was not necessarily optimal and could be potentially destabilized by regional or country-specific shocks, both due to the original design and the evolution of the rules following the euro's adoption. While the diversification of European economies may have suggested that regional shocks were less likely on the production side of the economy, the implementation of the euro also may not have considered seriously enough how the central banking architecture of the monetary union could cause the financial sectors of each country to be more prone to destabilizing shocks.

The EU's Monetary System: The Eurosystem

To administer the euro as the single currency in the Eurozone, the central banking structure among participating countries had to be reformed to create a single central bank responsible for monetary policy. Since the currency-union members are sovereign states, it was not deemed politically possible to merge their central banks into one large institution. Instead, a new central bank was brought into existence. This was accomplished in a two-stage process, first by the creation of the European Monetary Institute (EMI) in 1994, which took over the administration of the European Exchange Rate Mechanism (ERM) and oversaw the coordination and convergence of member state monetary policies in preparation for the adoption of the euro. In May 1998 the original 11 members of the euro met the convergence conditions necessary to form the currency union and in June 1998 the second stage of the process began with the adoption of the ECB and the European System of Central Banks (ESCB), which consists of the central banks of all EU members and the ECB, replacing the EMI.[12]

The "Eurosystem" forms the central banking architecture of the Eurozone and refers to a subset of the ESCB banks consisting of the ECB and the national central banks of the countries participating in the euro as shown in Figure 3. The ECB is presided over by a president, vice-president, and four directors who make up the Executive Board, with appointments staggered and lasting 8 years. Appointments to the ECB's Executive Board are recommended by the EU Council of Ministers and approved by heads of state or EU member governments. During the Euro crisis two presidents have governed the ECB, Jean-Claude Trichet of France until October 31, 2011, and Mario Draghi of Italy from November 1, 2011 to the present. The Executive Board and the governors of each of the 17 Eurozone national central banks form the Governing Council, responsible for all monetary policy decisions including interest rate policy in the currency area. Policy decisions of the Governing Council are determined by majority vote every 2 weeks and, by the treaty articles of the EU, must remain independent with no member of the ECB or national bank allowed to be influenced by any member state government, EU institution, or other body. Monetary policy, once determined by the Governing Council, is implemented by the ECB, which issues instructions to the national central banks of the Eurozone who carry it out.

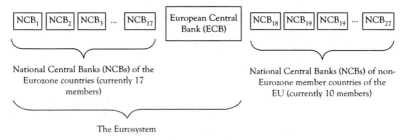

Figure 3. Structure of the ESCB.

A central bank most often has three inter-related functions. It is usually responsible for ensuring the stability of the financial system; it can act as a lender of last resort to ensure that banks and nations have access to credit when necessary; and it controls monetary policy, the availability of money in the economic system for transactions and private lending. To maintain stability in a currency, the conduct of such functions should occur outside political influence to avoid the conflict of political and economic goals, thus the bank must also be politically independent.

For example, in the United States, the Federal Reserve or "Fed" serves as the politically independent entity performing all three of these tasks. It determines U.S. monetary policy to achieve two, sometimes conflicting, mandates it is required by law to fulfill: to maintain employment by maintaining conditions for growth, and to maintain price stability. By controlling monetary policy and indirectly the levels of interest and underlying credit conditions across all 50 states the Fed attempts to achieve both of these goals, but often it can face tradeoffs. The Fed can loosen policy and create better conditions for growth in some areas, even though this may cause inflation in others. As part of monetary policy, it can also intervene in bond markets and take other actions that soothe conditions if they become turbulent. The Fed can act as a lender of last resort by lending directly to banks if they are cut from credit. The Fed can also use this lender of last resort function to provide credit to government through bond market purchases. The ability of the Federal Reserve to use each of these actions proved very important during the financial crisis of 2008 and its aftermath. While controversial, most economists and other observers credit the swift and effective use of these instruments with helping to quell the U.S. crisis by early 2009.

By comparison, the sole purpose of the Eurosystem is to ensure price stability through the ECB as defined in the treaty articles of the EU. As a result the Eurosystem's greatest concern with respect to monetary policy has been inflation. In practice, price stability has been interpreted to imply that the inflation rate across the Eurozone should be kept below 2%. Unlike the Federal Reserve, the ECB is mandated only to maintain price stability; therefore, its ability to use monetary policy to stimulate growth is very limited. If one country or region faces recession, it likely will not see monetary policy relief if this threatens inflationary conditions in other countries. During the Euro crisis, credit relief to southern states could have reduced the damage their recessions have inflicted on state finances by providing additional support to employment and output conditions as the debt crisis unfolded in 2009 and 2010. Monetary policy, however, did not loosen during this period but in fact tightened in mid-2011 as concern rose regarding potential inflationary conditions in stronger northern states.

Like the German banking system where strong bank independence is preferred and upon which much of the Eurosystem design was based, separation of regulatory authority from the actual central bank is assumed to enhance the central bank's political independence. Bank regulations are therefore not under ECB supervision, but instead remain the responsibility of the individual member nations. The European Banking Authority (EBA), a separate agency from the ECB coordinates the EU banking system.[13] The Council of European Banking Supervisors was formed to coordinate banking regulation within the EU in 2004. It was superseded by the EBA in 2011. National authorities are also responsible for the stability of banks within their jurisdictions including for deposit insurance which, across the EU must insure the first 100,000 euro in bank deposits from loss in the event of bank failure. If a national banking crisis were to arise, the national treasury and by extension the taxpayers of that country only are responsible for any costs incurred to support the banking system.

Within the EU framework the ECB cannot act as a lender of last resort. Specifically, common interpretation of treaty rules prohibits the ECB from acting directly as a lender of last resort to sovereign states as such actions would violate the EU's "no-bailout" policy.[14] Furthermore, by being unable to directly purchase national debt, the ECB largely refrained from entering into global financial markets to maintain lower sovereign debt rates of member countries at the start of the Euro crisis and since has done so under very specific conditions. The intent of the policy was to eliminate moral hazard and to create a debt brake for states as otherwise states might not perceive that they face the discipline of private markets to control their fiscal decisions. Within countries, national central banks may engage in emergency lending as a lender of last resort only to institutions within their jurisdiction should such actions prove necessary, but such actions must be coordinated with the ECB and other central banks to ensure such actions do not undermine overall monetary policy.[15]

One concern that has arisen with allowing national central banks to police their own banking systems has been the fact that there are a variety of rules and practices by country with respect to bank supervision and, in the event of a banking failure, each has different practices and procedures governing bank resolution or shut down. During the Euro crisis, there have been remarkably few banks closed. Instead, bank rescues have occurred, and this has typically protected bank creditors at taxpayers' expense. The lack of a common set of procedures has created the risk that in some countries regulators may be unwilling to impose losses on creditors and "resolve" illiquid institutions. Such reticence could occur if a regulator feared a credit market backlash at other institutions in their country, potentially worsening a banking crisis in their country. They could also avoid such decisions for political reasons.

Differences in practices can also have competitive effects. Creditors, fearing severe potential losses in one jurisdiction over another in the event of a bank insolvency could avoid those countries they perceive to present the greater risk, putting banks in the more severely regulated country at a competitive disadvantage with respect to raising capital or attracting deposits. A lack of well-defined rules also adds to the uncertainty in a banking crisis. Such concerns, and the possibility that closing banks could have political repercussions, can create a moral hazard problem that undermines the independence of the central banking system with respect to bank regulation. Such concerns could be avoided with a common set of regulatory rules and procedures common across countries—a so-called banking union.

Banking Instability and Sovereign Risk in the Eurosystem

Monetary unions are most successful when they are least likely to experience country-specific shocks. Such shocks expose countries to the greatest drawback of a currency union—the inability to use monetary policy to adjust, which transfers the costs of adjustment to the shock onto the public. The costs of the shock are then made worse if a country has limited wage flexibility or labor mobility as many countries in Europe have, as a lack of wage and price flexibility causes market adjustment to take much longer. When the euro was being implemented, economic diversification across countries in the Eurozone suggested regional or country-specific shocks as opposed to a union-wide shocks were less likely to occur. While labor and wage mobility were limited, since country-specific shocks were presumed to be unlikely the potential costs these flaws could create were potentially discounted. Such reasoning, however, focused on the idea that country-specific shocks would arise in the production economy, not the financial sector. After the Greek revelations regarding their public debt in 2009, however, markets quickly came to the realization that financial markets in the Eurozone were in fact quite susceptible to financial crisis, in large part because of the common currency union's structure. While Eurozone members adopted a common currency, the evolution of rules governing fiscal discipline had not created a convergence in fiscal discipline. This and the structure of the Eurosystem and its distribution of responsibilities created the Achilles heel of the monetary system—the problem posed by the national banking systems.

For various reasons depending on the country, the Euro crisis has manifested itself first as a financial crisis, and national banking systems have created the country-specific risks that have destabilized the currency union. In Greece, Ireland, Italy, Spain, and Cyprus real estate bubbles led to highly leveraged banks, much as it did in the United States in the mid-2000s. Furthermore, across Europe, exposure to now-questionable Greek debt, in addition to the price decline in world securities after the 2008 U.S. Financial Crisis and ensuing global recession, created more bank weakness. The Eurosystem's structure, with responsibility for national financial systems falling alone on the individual countries, has caused banking crises arising in these conditions to create country-specific liabilities that have then helped create sovereign debt crises. Ireland, for example, was forced to take a national bailout in 2010 after the costs of a banking system rescue were so high that international finance markets effectively cut credit to the nation. The sudden increase in sovereign debt caused by the combined effects of a recession and bank rescues increased public debt from 24.8% in 2007 to over 108% by 2011 as shown in Figure 2. World financial markets reacted to the sudden risk in Ireland's apparent ability to service its debt sustainably, more than doubling sovereign interest rates to levels approaching 9% in 2010. The result was an unsustainable debt level, leaving Ireland with what appeared only two inevitable choices. It could leave the euro and default on its sovereign debt, or request outside aid—a "bailout." Ireland chose the latter, requesting a bailout in November 2010.

The relationship of bank failures to sovereign debt has sometimes been referred to as the "Doom Loop." Within the EU framework the Eurosystem can act as a lender of last resort, though only to banks. If a financial institution finds credit is unavailable as might occur in a financial crisis, the national central bank whose jurisdiction the institution is located in can provide temporary Emergency Liquidity Assistance (ELA) in return for collateral as a stopgap measure until private credit is reestablished. The collateral eligible to be used for such actions includes that country's sovereign bonds. In the event such a bailout is deemed necessary, the costs of the bailout are assumed by the treasury of the country involved and financed through sovereign debt. The doom loop occurs as a consequence of the following chain of events:

1. Bank asset values fall as a consequence of a financial shock, for example, the effect the financial crisis of 2008 had on real-estate market loans.
2. Banks then experience illiquidity as markets become concerned of their solvency and cut-off credit.
3. National governments step in to stabilize their financial systems by providing liquidity to banks. If the bank system requires a large bailout, countries must increase their debt, often substantially.
4. Concerns about the country's sovereign debt sustainability and solvency in reaction to bailout costs drive sovereign rates up.
5. Banks, as large holders of domestic bonds, see their asset values fall further as bond prices are inversely related to interest rates.
6. The result is worse liquidity at the banks returning the loop to Step 1 and self-fulfilling bank illiquidity and sovereign debt crises emerge.

This process allows a state in the Eurozone to potentially be forced into crisis by the weakness of its banking system. This is unlike in other jurisdictions like the United States where larger banking unions across states ensure that such a crisis would not result in potential insolvency of the individual state where the bank is located. For example, New York state cannot be bankrupted by its own banks. As part of a larger banking union in 2008, failing banks in New York and across the United States were bailed out by the federal system, and the banking crisis did not trigger a series of state debt crises.[16] Access to a larger federal system allows the doom loop to be broken as large (relative to the GDP) troubled banking systems no longer require the state in which the banks are located to be solely responsible for the financing necessary to stabilize the banking system. In effect, joint debt liability of the federal system across all states ensures banking crises do not trigger state debt crises. The design of the Eurosystem and the prohibition of joint debt liability, however, create just the opposite outcome in the Eurozone, creating exactly such instability.

To summarize, the choice to avoid creating a banking union, coupled with the lack of a federal fiscal union that would allow direct transfers of resources across the currency union, along with the prohibition of joint debt liability, have had fundamental consequences in the Euro crisis. Conditions in the Eurozone cause the potential effects of a country-specific shock to be severe because of the limited labor market flexibility. The design of the central banking system creates the situation that should a country experience a financial crisis it will be much more likely to experience a fiscal or sovereign debt crisis. The lack of a system allowing federal transfers or debt issuance backed by the entire Eurozone then causes a sovereign debt crisis to rapidly escalate into a crisis in which default and a withdrawal from the Eurozone are potential outcomes.

To avoid chaotic exits of countries in the Eurozone under these circumstances during the Euro crisis, a series of bailouts financed by the rest of the Eurozone, the EU, and the IMF, something never intended in the original design of the European monetary union have been used. The terms of these bailouts have been very protective of the financing countries' contributions as creditors and required recipient countries to institute very painful, dramatic, and politically unpopular reforms. The result of the bailouts has been to suspend the economic sovereignty the original design of currency union attempted to protect in these countries, resulting in a severe populist backlash against bailout terms that appear to favor creditors over the people in the affected nations. This in turn has highlighted the final architectural flaw in the Eurozone. Efforts to more deeply integrate the Eurozone entail a necessary tradeoff between democracy, national sovereignty, and economic integration in the Eurozone as discussed in the next chapter.

CHAPTER 4

The Flawed Sociopolitical Architecture of the Eurozone

The introduction of the common currency was in no way just an economic decision. Monetary Union is demanding that we Europeans press ahead resolutely with political integration.

Gerhard Schröder, August 30, 1999

As a monetary union represents a lasting commitment to integration which encroaches on the core area of national sovereignty, the EMU participants must also be prepared to take further steps toward a more comprehensive political union.

Annual Report of the Deutsche Bundesbank, 1995

Rodrik's Trilemma

Efforts to create a more deeply integrated Europe, at least economically, have been detailed in the previous two sections. The implementation of the European monetary union created a common currency zone and central banking architecture without the necessary incentives to create a complementary convergence in fiscal policies or "fiscal union" that would protect the currency union from instability. Also missing in the implementation of the currency union was a "banking union," changes in financial and banking regulation that would have prevented country-specific financial crises in the Eurozone from escalating into destabilizing fiscal and sovereign debt crises. Implementing the missing elements of the currency union would have required greater acceptance of supranational governance and ceding of national sovereignty than could be achieved politically in Europe at the time the euro was adopted. As noted in the above quotes, while the EU lacked a deep political integration, the euro's designers and those involved with its implementation knew such changes were necessary. The problem, however, was not that the designers of the European monetary union were insufficiently far-sighted to design institutions capable of creating deeper economic and political integration. The problem was that given the political constraints of the time, economic integration that maintained national sovereignty was seen as a stepping stone to future political integration. To design a system that can achieve deep economic integration while simultaneously protecting national sovereignty in economic policy and maintaining direct political democracy over the supranational governance of Europe invokes a sociopolitical impossibility. Attempting to achieve these three goals requires suspension of a problem recognized for over a decade and referred to as the "international trilemma of globalization." Given what designers knew must occur, the implementation of the euro combined with a set of national sovereign governments was an intermediate step toward a larger political integration of Europe.

Dani Rodrik (2000) penned the political trilemma to describe the political and economic challenge of globalization. His insight recognized that deeper global integration cannot be achieved while preserving national sovereignty in policy making and maintaining democratic politics that allow domestic preferences to determine governmental policy. Diagrammatically, the trilemma is shown in Figure 1.

Rodrik noted that deeper international economic integration, allowing free flow of trade and capital would require a tradeoff. Countries that wish to be open and to compete for international trade and capital cannot

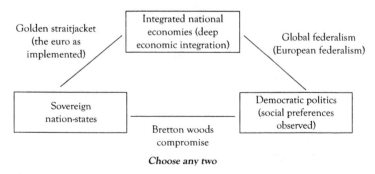

Choose any two

Figure 1. Rodrik's international trilemma applied to Europe.
Source: Rodrik 2000.

interfere with economic transactions. For this reason if countries wished to remain in control of international economic policies within their jurisdictions, the political space from which policies can be drawn would be greatly reduced, decreasing the role of democracy in the formation of economic policy. Competition among nations would require that policies become harmonized to international norms regardless of domestic preferences if deep economic integration were to be achieved. Rodrik termed this outcome the Golden Straitjacket. He noted that within the world, the space of political policy has grown narrower and narrower for this reason.

With respect to Europe's monetary union, the adoption and design of the common currency was consistent with this set of choices, and resulted in an even more limited set of possible government policies given the conditions necessary to maintain a stable common currency. Adopting the euro necessitated giving up national monetary policy and limiting fiscal policy to the convergence criteria defined in the Maastricht Treaty. Government roles move toward becoming technocratic entities in these areas, administering economic and social policies consistent with maintenance of the common currency regardless of the national electorates' preferences. Monetary policy is determined entirely by technocratic Euro system and ECB, while fiscal policy is supposed to be limited to policies consistent with the Maastricht Criteria, regardless of public preferences otherwise. Achieving deeper economic integration and the adoption of the common currency implied adjustment costs to economic shocks would have to be imposed on the nations' citizens, again, consistent with the Golden Straitjacket outcome. Those costs, however, remain high because governments have been unable to find the political will to reduce labor market and wage rigidities in the union. In Rodrik's trilemma, the need to balance the requirements of deep integration implied by the euro, combined with the governance structure adopted for the EU leaves no room for social preferences expressed in democratic politics if they are contrary to the policies required for deep integration. Elected member state governments are locked to those policies necessary to maintain the currency regardless of electoral preferences.

Alternatively, Rodrik suggested deep global economic integration and democratic politics could occur simultaneously, evolving into a kind of "global federalism," but this would necessitate the eclipse of the nation state as the primary economic policy maker. In Europe, this outcome might be referred to European Federalism, a situation in which deeper economic and political integration simultaneously take place. This could be achieved by the creation of supranational European governance, elected or electorally accountable directly to the people of Europe. Deep economic integration that is accountable to the people would require that deep political integration occur—the implementation of a European federal system. Nation states would then only administer their territories within this framework, with some differences in taxation and regulation possible among jurisdictions as long as they did not interfere with economic activity. This outcome might be closest to Churchill's 1946 suggestion of a United States of Europe, in which small states would be as important as larger ones and people's focus would be on a common cause. As noted in the previous chapters, however, movement toward such political integration has been difficult throughout the history of European integration efforts. Since the 1950s there has been a conflict between the objectives of greater political integration and national sovereignty at the governmental level as negotiations over European governance have occurred, and even at the public level there has been skepticism to such efforts. Such public skepticism was apparent when efforts to adopt a European Constitution were thwarted by unsuccessful referenda in the Netherlands and France in June 2005 despite ratification in 18 other states. Still, policy efforts continue to attempt to eliminate the "democratic deficit" in central EU institutions, with an objective of making European governance more democratic. Rodrik's insight was that eventually the combination of the deep economic integration implied by the common currency and deep political integration that is accountable to the people will result in the elimination of sovereign nation states, at least in most matters of economic policy making.

The third alternative Rodrik noted was that the outcome that occurred before the movement toward greater globalization, which he termed the Bretton Woods compromise. In general, nation states remained in control of economic policy consistent with the preferences of their electorates and routinely used capital controls and trade restrictions in the postwar period through the early 1990s. Rodrik noted that until the 1970s and 1980s, two agreements, the international Bretton Woods agreement, which allowed capital flow limits to maintain a system of fixed exchange rates, and the

General Agreement on Tariffs and Trade (GATT), both allowed limits to trade flows consistent with national democratic preferences. The existence of these limits, however, ensured deep economic integration across countries did not occur. Deeper integration occurring internationally across countries has resulted in both agreements no longer being relevant. The GATT was superseded by the World Trade Organization, which has worked to limit trade and capital controls, and the collapse of the Bretton Woods Agreement in the 1970s was consistent with greater capital mobility that has occurred worldwide in the past four decades since. The result of both outcomes has been a movement internationally toward trade liberalization and a narrowing of political options as defined by the Golden Straitjacket. This reflects Rodrik's observation that maintaining nation states with fully independent policies determined by domestic political preferences cannot occur if deep economic integration allowing the free flow of capital and goods is desired.

In Europe, this third alternative could describe economic integration until mid-1970s, with greater efforts toward economic integration moving Europe slowly toward the straitjacket outcome with a narrowing of the potential set of national economic policy choices. The breakdown of the ERM and fixed exchange rate regimes exemplified the political tradeoff nations faced when they imposed conditions on their economies necessary to support their fixed exchange rate. Britain's withdrawal from the ERM in the early 1990s was caused by this conflict—faced with an electorate that demanded policies that were not consistent with those necessary to support its fixed exchange rate, the government withdrew from the ERM. The implementation of the euro, with its lack of an exit method does not offer states this option thus a divergence between the policy preferences of a national electorate and the policies necessary to maintain currency union membership can potentially create a political instability as social frustration grows when governments appear to ignore the preferences of the societies they govern.

Europe's adoption of the euro was undertaken with the apparent assumption that greater political integration would occur in the years after its adoption. As described in previous chapters, such integration did not occur before the Euro crisis began, and since then skepticism of European integration has been growing across the Eurozone, particularly in countries most impacted by the crisis. According to polls, in most countries in Europe support for greater political and economic integration and the EU in general have fallen as unemployment rates have risen across the Eurozone. In countries that have required bailouts, or for which access to international credit markets has been reduced or cut off, the austerity policies necessary to satisfy international creditors and bureaucratic mandates from the European Commission have become deeply unpopular. A populist backlash has resulted in unstable political environments across the Eurozone, especially in Greece and Italy, where anti-European parties whose platforms include leaving the euro have often received the most votes in recent national elections. This political backlash has been in part fed and made worse by the perception among citizens in these countries that their votes have no impact on the policies their countries have taken, and is an on the ground example of the type of alienation Rodrik described could occur in his straitjacket outcome.

If opinion polling and election outcomes are any indicator, the adoption of the euro created a technocratic role for national governments in implementing economic policy that has now undermined people's trust in Europe-wide institutions and their willingness to move toward the political integration necessary to politically stabilize the currency union.[1] Reliance on technocratic solutions imposed by recent bailouts during the Euro crisis (described in more detail in later chapters), and the imposition of technocratic governments in Italy and Spain, and EU-mandated austerity plans across the Eurozone during the Euro crisis have only worsened people's perceived alienation from the European political process. Such alienation threatens to only compound the political instability currently present in the Eurozone and ironically threatens to undermine support for greater economic and political integration across Europe at exactly the time when it appears to be most necessary.

Overview: The Effects of Europe's Governmental, Economic, and Sociopolitical Flaws

The effects of the three general architectural design flaws present in the Eurozone, the governmental, economic, and sociopolitical, undermine the three characteristics successful monetary unions usually have: the ability to manage and react to external and internal shocks; a common fiscal frame-work allowing collective transfers and if necessary, collective debt; and strong central bank able to act as a lender of last resort in the common currency. The inability of Europe to achieve a greater political union resulted in a currency union that has become technocratic in nature and seemingly removed from the people, especially since the Euro crisis has begun.

Together the economic design of the monetary union and the Eurosystem, combined with the lack of a federal system to coordinate broad, effective, and timely continent-wide economic policies have contributed to conditions in the union that have precipitated and wors-ened the crisis, and crippled European policy response. By adopting the euro and giving up their sovereign currencies, Eurozone members adopted a common currency without a sovereign. The European mon-etary union's ability to solve the current crisis was hamstrung by its economic and monetary architecture and lack of a federal system. With-out the waiving of long-standing policy stances regarding joint fiscal actions role of the ECB, finding policy solutions that reduced pressures in markets proved very difficult. In the longer term the union will not only have to address the shortcomings in its system regarding national debt brakes as envisioned by the Maastricht Criteria, but also by adopt-ing a wider federal system that creates a system of mutual support in the common interest.

In the end to save the euro, "more Europe" appears necessary. In a very important speech in July 2012, one in which the ECB pledged to "do whatever it took" to preserve the euro, Mario Draghi, the president of the ECB compared the European monetary union to a bumblebee.[2] He remarked that, like the bee, the monetary union should not have been able to fly, yet it did for almost a decade before the shortcomings in its design caught up with it. To continue flying these will have to be addressed. In addition to the economic and financial union already created, Europe will have to ensure it has a stronger fiscal and banking union than in the euro's original design. This will require more supranational governance, not less and this will require states to cede additional sovereignty to support the constraints maintaining the European monetary implies. In adopting a more supranational approach with common fiscal and banking policies, the Eurozone will also have to become more democratic and less techno-cratic, allowing European governance to be more responsive to the will of the people it governs. As is often the case with unstable structures, unex-pected tremors can lead to their imminent collapse without immediate remedial work to repair them. The financial crisis of 2008 provided not only a tremor but also an earthquake, and the damage resulting was the Euro crisis. Since then, the Eurozone has struggled to repair the founda-tions of an edifice now already occupied.

PART III

Evolution of the Euro Crisis

CHAPTER 5

Flight of the Bumblebee: Precrisis Structural Imbalances and Their Influence in the Eurozone

Introduction

Although like a bumblebee the Eurozone was not supposed to be able to fly, initially it did not seem to matter. For over half a decade general growth and greater prosperity seemed to be the common outcome across most of the monetary union. In the first years of the euro from 2001 to 2007, the original 12 countries of the Eurozone (EU-12) experienced average annual real GDP growth rates of over 2.7%, even despite a recession and weak recovery in the United States, which impacted Eurozone exports. While not all countries experienced uniform growth as shown in Figures 1 and 2, rates of growth were high across most of Europe. Furthermore, the EU-12 countries outperformed the United States' economy during the majority of years over this period. Only the world financial crisis of 2008 and 2009 caused this record of growth to falter as the bursting of the U.S. housing bubble also signaled the bursting of similar bubbles across much of Europe.

While the world financial crisis was severe, the U.S. economy returned to growth by 2010. In Europe, however, the onset of the Euro crisis has proven to be a significant challenge and resulted in wide disparities in economic outcomes across nations. What had appeared to be a successful integration of Eurozone economies had actually masked structural imbalances that now challenged the Eurozone's recovery. Northern countries, particularly Germany, Austria, Finland, and the Netherlands, which had lagged southern and Eurozone economies as a whole in the first 5 years after the euro went into circulation now accounted for the majority of Eurozone

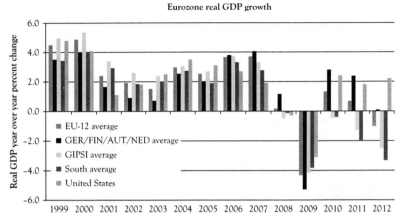

Eurozone real GDP growth

Figure 1. **Real GDP growth rates in the Eurozone were relatively high over the first 9 years of the euro's introduction (1999–2007) with the original 12 Eurozone countries (EU-12 countries averaging better growth than the United States. Performance, however, varied by region with northern economies (Germany, Finland, Austria, and The Netherlands) lagging the rest of the Eurozone until 2006 when Germany began to overcome the malaise caused by reunification. In 2008 GIPSI (Greece, Ireland, Portugal, Spain, and Italy) and southern (Greece, Italy, Spain, and Portugal) countries experienced contraction similar to the United States, whereas northern countries still experienced some growth, causing the EU-12 overall to average a positive though near-zero growth rate. In 2009, most European countries experienced recessions, but following that year northern countries, the EU-12 as a whole, and the United States returned to positive growth rates. In contrast, GIPSI and southern countries (Greece, Spain, Portugal, and Italy) continued to experience contraction for 5 years after the U.S. financial crisis began in 2008.** Source: Eurostat.

growth following 2009. In contrast, southern periphery and GIPSI countries (Greece, Ireland, Portugal, Spain, and Italy—the "south" plus Ireland) experienced a coordinated downturn that now might be called a depression. As of 2013, levels of unemployment in these nations now range from near 15% to over 25%, with unemployment rates for youth under 25 years of age ranging from 35% to over 50%. Adjustment in these countries to the shock of the world financial crisis, and then the sovereign debt concerns that define the Euro crisis, has been particularly difficult, in large part due to the flaws of the currency union outlined in the last few chapters. They were also worsened by a series of serious structural imbalances that were allowed to build during the precrisis years of the currency union.

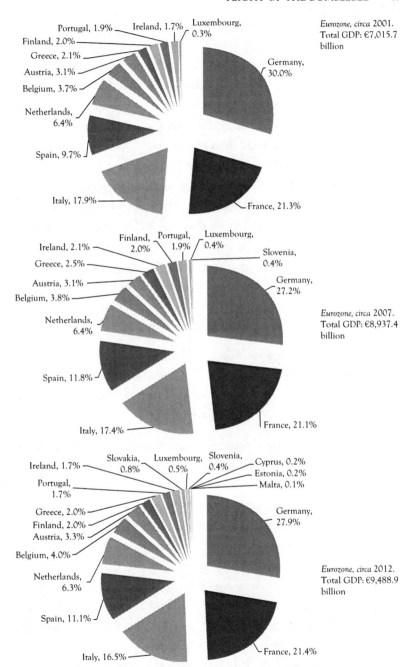

Eurozone, circa 2001.
Total GDP: €7,015.7
billion

Eurozone, circa 2007.
Total GDP: €8,937.4
billion

Eurozone, circa 2012.
Total GDP: €9,488.9
billion

Figure 2. Eurozone country composition and shares of total output.
Percentages indicate share of total Eurozone GDP at market prices in
that year.
Source: Eurostat.

Correction of these imbalances will require structural adjustments within the most affected economies—productivity enhancing actions such as labor market liberalization and social reinvestment in both human capital and infrastructure will have to occur. In the interim, increased competitiveness under a common currency will require internal devaluation (wage–cost reduction) in the most affected countries, imposing the greatest costs of adjustment on the public. This will create political challenges that may further undermine acceptance and dedication to the project of European integration and the euro. The following section attempts to describe the structural imbalances present in the Eurozone prior to the Euro crisis, how they contributed to the onset of the crisis, and how they have changed while the crisis has been underway. Addressing such imbalances will require difficult and painful adjustments, and like a ship in trouble far from shore, the repairs will have to be made while the ship sails on. The alternative may be that some countries could leave the Eurozone if such organizational and structural adjustments cannot be made.

Structural Imbalances: Trade Imbalances, Productivity Levels, and Their Influence on the Credit Crisis

In addition to the sudden changes in international debt markets or market tolerance to risk seen in 2008 and 2009, the Euro crisis has also been caused in part by a set of structural imbalances that have been present since the start of the currency union. The common currency has created a very difficult environment for some countries to economically compete within, due to long-standing differences in productivity and competitiveness. There was always a disparity in competitiveness across the countries that entered the currency union in 1999 through 2001. The problem of competitiveness, however, was ignored when the currency union was established, in part because it was generally assumed that the creation of a currency union and common trade area would create equilibrating flows that would allow competitive convergence to occur. Such assumptions may have been politically expedient; however, differences in competitiveness among nations under a common currency also posed risks to both the weaker countries and the stability of the union as a whole.

Basic trade theory suggests that countries that do not enjoy similar productivities or capacities for the production of goods and services could eventually begin to experience rising debt and deficit if fundamental changes do not occur with respect to the competitiveness among these nations. Since a trade deficit implies that a country spends more than it earns, persistent trade deficits must be financed by increasing inflows of credit or net foreign investment.[1] In normal circumstances, when a country finds itself uncompetitive with others in a trade environment, floating exchange rates could adjust to rebalance trade. United under a single currency, however, such adjustment between member countries cannot occur in the Eurozone. Alternatively, in a complete fiscal and monetary union such as the United States, a federal governance system can dictate fiscal and transfer policies to alleviate problems across disparate regions in the country. Again, the Eurozone has no significant and similar transfer facilities. While the EU created a monetary union, it failed to complete what some architects also might have originally envisioned for in a fully integrated Europe—a single federal system that would coordinate EU economic and social outcomes within a truly federal system. This has led to a situation where trade imbalances caused by relative productivity shifts can neither be addressed by currency devaluation due to the adoption of a common currency, nor internally through transfers.

Consider the original 12 members of the Eurozone. Structural imbalances in productivity and competitiveness between countries were present when the euro was adopted as evidenced by Figures 3 and 4. As Figures 3a and 3b show, labor productivity was always much lower in southern than northern periphery countries, particularly in Germany, Austria, The Netherlands, and Finland (collectively referred to as "northern" countries). These productivity differences originated for many reasons, typically due to structural factors including the education levels of labor and the types of specialized industry in each country, and also due to policy factors that create more rigid labor markets in southern states. While labor productivity as a measure of national productivity grew across the union following the euro's adoption, productivity increased more in northern countries. This is shown in Figure 3b, which shows how the ratio of northern countries' collective average productivity levels evolved relative to that of southern countries. Combined with the fact that wages grew faster in the south relative to northern countries in the period before 2008 as shown by the inflation outcomes in Table 1, the north's cost advantage with respect to labor grew over time, leaving southern countries with an increasing cost disadvantage relative to northern economies.

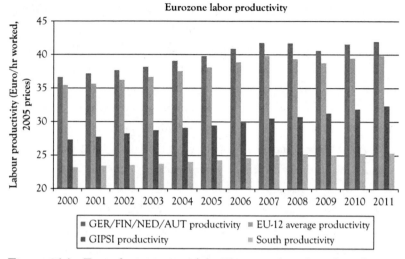

Figure 3(a). From the initiation of the Eurozone there have been large differences between labor productivities in northern and southern periphery states. Although productivity growth occurred throughout the decade in all regions, the gap between southern countries and the rest of the Eurozone has only widened over the period. This has resulted in cost advantages affecting trade patterns in the Eurozone, particularly between northern and southern countries as the north's cost advantages increase. Comparison of GIPSI and southern countries' outcomes indicate the differences between labor productivities in Ireland and other troubled countries. Source: OECD.

Simultaneously, as cost advantages grew in northern countries relative to the south, trade deficits widened southern countries, while in northern countries, greater trade surpluses emerged (Figure 4). Across the EU-12 countries, external trade balances did not change significantly thus the data suggest that the change in regional deficits and surpluses between north and south was in large part created by internal trade flows within the currency union. This is also indicated by the change in flows that occurred after 2008. While northern economies and other economies worldwide recovered in 2009 after the world financial crisis, persistent recessions continued in southern and GIPSI countries. The resulting reductions in trade deficits in the south as import consumption fell were mirrored by reductions in northern trade surpluses, while the overall EU-12 balance was relatively unaffected. This suggests that the increased trade surpluses in northern countries before 2008 were supported by southern countries' trade deficits.[2]

It is important to note that while Ireland has often been grouped with southern countries throughout the Euro crisis, it is structurally quite

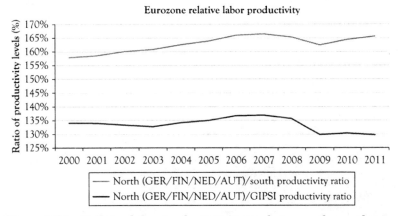

Eurozone relative labor productivity

Figure 3(b). Relative labor productivity ratios between the northern periphery and southern Eurozone countries. Since 2000 the ratio of northern productivities (Germany, Austria, the Netherlands, and Finland averaged annually) to southern productivities (Greece, Portugal, Spain, and Italy averaged annually) has increased over time, indicating southern labor has fallen behind in productivity relative to northern economies. As inflation has been higher over the same period in southern countries, wages grew faster in southern economies and therefore these countries fell behind their northern trade partners in terms of overall cost competitiveness.
Source: OECD.

different. Since the euro was created, Ireland has enjoyed the second highest trade surplus as a percentage of GDP in the Eurozone, exceeded only by Luxembourg, and persistently higher than any northern country. As shown in Figure 9a, Irish levels of productivity were greater than the rest of the southern countries as indicated by the difference between average southern countries' productivity levels and that of the south combined with Ireland (GIPSI productivity levels). In the Eurozone, in fact, Irish productivity has only been exceeded by Luxembourg's since the euro was created, and exceeds all northern periphery countries. Further, when Irish annual productivity levels are averaged with southern countries, the ratio of north to GIPSI countries' average productivity falls over time, indicating that growth in labor productivity in Ireland was greater than in the southern periphery or northern states. While inflation rates prior to 2008 were higher in Ireland than in northern Eurozone countries, this was offset by productivity gains allowing the country to remain very competitive.

Structural differences between north and south in competitiveness and trade flows were both worsened by differences in policy and by policy

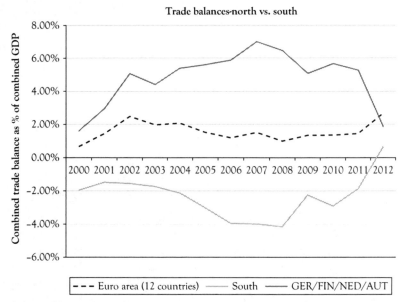

Figure 4. Trade balances (exports less imports as a percentage of GDP) were persistently negative for southern countries (Portugal, Italy, Greece, and Spain) during the 2000s and deficits increased as credit conditions became easier after 2004. Similarly, northern states experienced growing trade surpluses throughout the period leading up to the crisis. Growth in surpluses mirrored deficits in southern states both in the periods leading up to 2008 and afterward during the Euro crisis. Aggregate trade balance across the EU-12 countries remained stable and slightly positive through the period, suggesting that the change in trade balances was the result of internal trade flows.
Source: Eurostat.

incentives that were created with the construction of the Eurozone. The creation of the single currency greatly increased the access to credit markets enjoyed by some countries. Southern states saw interest rates fall to levels nearly equal to those enjoyed by the traditionally low-interest economies like Germany (Figure 5). These countries then took advantage of the newly opened capital markets the creation of the euro allowed, increasing borrowing in both the private and public sectors. This activity fueled growth in government and private-sector consumption and created bubbles in real estate and property prices that, while increasing GDP growth, masked the weaker economies underlying them and the worsening structural imbalances occurring.

With rapidly growing economies, southern countries faced no pressure to make the politically difficult decisions required to reign in public spending or restructure their economies to maintain or improve their internal

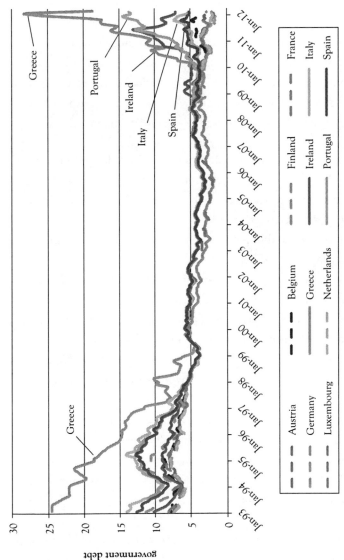

Figure 5. Prior to the formation of a common currency, interest rates for sovereign debt of the EU-12 countries were quite divergent. With the creation of the euro, interest rates for these countries converged to nearly equal rates. Divergence only occurred again during the financial crisis of 2008 and after Greek debt revelations in 2009. This figure does not include the improvement in interest rates seen in the fall of 2012 and 2013.

Source: Eurostat.

competitiveness. As a consequence, productivity relative to northern European trade partners continued to fall and costs rose in these nations relative to their northern neighbors. Northern economies faced the opposite conditions. The creation of the euro did not greatly affect their credit conditions. With trade barriers and exchange costs eliminated, and having historically had higher wages, internal competitiveness within the Eurozone demanded a focus in these countries on productivity gains. Policies that had previously been priorities in these countries after the 1990s' financial crisis in the case of Finland, the challenges of reunification in Germany, and adjustment to "Dutch disease" in the Netherlands, became even more important, leading to increases in their relative productivity within the union.[3]

As relative productivities diverged through the decade, the primary beneficiaries of the trade patterns that developed were Germany and to a lesser extent other northern European states. Sustained purchasing under these conditions for southern economies remained possible only through expanded credit markets and in part these were financed by the mounting trade surpluses accruing to northern countries in the form of foreign investment. Northern economies improved and grew due to the internal trade advantages productivity growth provided. This was reinforced by the lack of an exchange rate appreciation that such emerging trade patterns would have created in the absence of a monetary union. Southern economies, though weakened by eroding trade competitiveness caused by the same forces, did not experience slowing growth as shown in Figure 1, due to favorable cyclical conditions caused by real-estate and consumption bubbles. Their economies remained buoyed by the credit flowing in from northern trading partners and the international "savings glut" that in part drove property bubbles in North America and the rest of the world through the mid-2000s. Differences in property prices relative to the rest of the Eurozone and northern countries in particular are apparent from the inception of the euro until 2007 (Figure 6).

In hindsight, it is clear that consumption and real-estate bubbles were mistaken for economic convergence across Eurozone countries, at least politically, and structural reforms, particularly in southern countries, that would have sped productivity improvements while enhancing the stability of the currency union, were not implemented. Economic expansion continued in GIPSI countries, primarily fueled by the real-estate and

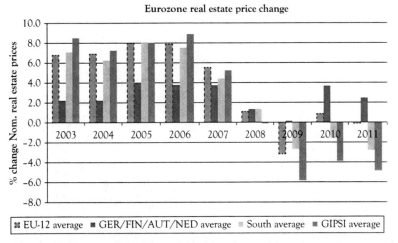

Figure 6. Real-estate price appreciation throughout the Eurozone and in GIPSI countries exceeded that of northern trade-surplus countries (Germany, Finland, Austria, and the Netherlands) by two to three times from 2003 to 2007. These trends reflected Europe-wide conditions.

Source: OECD, Eurostat and GlobalPropertyGuide.com and author's computations.

public-service sectors, despite the widening trade deficits emerging in European trade. What was not clearly understood and partially hidden by the apparent growth in economic activity in the southern economies was the importance of leverage and debt on the economic statistics observed.

The adoption of the euro was in part justified by the potential to create greater economic convergence among the participating countries. Growth rates in the south after the adoption of the euro did appear to suggest economic convergence; competitive differences across states in the Eurozone were being overcome by greater growth in the south but these figures were illusory. Persistent trade deficits between relatively less wealthy southern countries and wealthier northern partners should have been viewed as an unhealthy divergent force—weaker countries' trade sectors were falling victim to the more competitive north. In fact, the opposite view emerged. Convergence and trade deficits were not viewed as mutually exclusive. It was presumed resulting net foreign-investment flows from trade surplus countries to their southern neighbors caused by persistent trade deficits would result in increased productivity-enhancing investment in southern countries. Investment returns could be expected to be higher in southern "catch-up" countries as new investment could be expected to yield greater returns in those countries than in countries with higher productivity. In theory, the accumulating debt faced by southern countries in the presence of trade deficits then need not have detracted from debt sustainability if returns to such investments were higher than the cost of debt service. The evidence, however, does not support this optimistic viewpoint. While investment, in part driven by credit, increased in southern and GIPSI countries relative to northern ones (Figure 7), the data suggests productivity improvements were not forthcoming to cause such convergence to occur. High investment growth in southern countries, while higher relative to northern economies was not to have been allocated to productivity-enhancing activities, but instead to debt-financed real-estate bubbles where investment occurred in the form of new construction. This investment differential and trade deficits that appear to have financed a portion of the

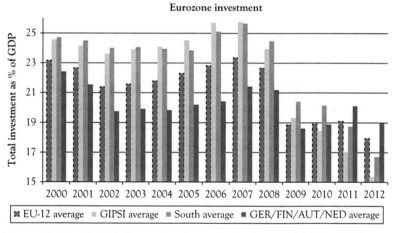

Eurozone investment

EU-12 average   GIPSI average   South average   GER/FIN/AUT/NED average

Figure 7. Trade imbalances in the period prior to 2008 should have financed net foreign investment flows in southern and GIPSI countries. It appears this did occur as investment slowed in Germany, Finland, Austria, and The Netherlands relative to southern states during this period. Given the productivity data, which showed productivity improved for northern states relative to southern ones during the same time, the data is consistent with investment flows financing nonproductivity increasing activities such as real-estate construction. Such flows would be consistent with the emergence of a real-estate bubble in southern countries indicated by the price data shown in Figure 6.
Source: IMF, World Economic Outlook Database.

investment flow collapsed in 2008 in the wake of the world financial crisis and ensuing Euro crisis. The result has been a collapse in southern and GIPSI economies that has yet to be recovered from.

Trade imbalances appear not only to have financed real-estate investment, but they also fueled both government and private debt. Reductions in gross national saving as shown in Figure 8 indicate how both private and public savings declined in southern and GIPSI countries, especially during the real-estate boom that occurred between 2004 and 2008. As shown in Figure 8, savings were always lower in southern and GIPSI countries relative to the rest of the union. In part, this was driven by the larger public sectors and larger deficits in southern countries. This debt pattern and the presence of larger public sectors are shown by the higher debt–GDP ratios in these countries shown in Figure 9. Government debt expanded in the south but stronger growth in the middle part of the decade allowed southern countries to expand the public sector without greatly impacting their debt–GDP ratio for much of the decade.

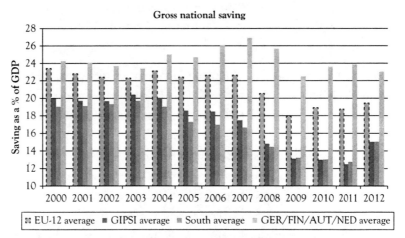

Figure 8. Credit inflows between 2000 and 2007 in southern and GIPSI countries also reduced gross domestic savings as both households and government took on additional debt, particularly in the period 2003–2007. This is consistent with increased home prices in the GIPSI and southern economies, and the period of a rising trade deficit. The impact of the recessions following the financial crisis in 2008 and Euro crisis from 2009 onward is apparent across all countries shown, but especially for southern and GIPSI nations.
Source: OECD Economic Outlook Database.

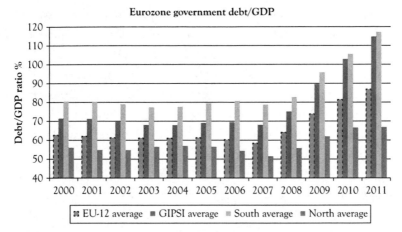

Figure 9. Government debt relative to GDP remained higher in southern and GIPSI countries relative to their northern neighbors. Given that growth was also higher in these countries relative to the Eurozone through part of the decade, it indicates that public-sector debt grew more quickly as well. Debt–GDP growth greatly accelerated across Europe but especially for southern and GIPSI countries after the financial crisis of 2007 and then the Euro crisis in late 2009 and 2010. Toward the end of the period only northern countries' debt–GDP ratios have stabilized, reflecting their stronger economic growth.
Source: Eurostat.

Once the financial crisis of 2008 occurred, property bubbles collapsed. Rapid and severe recessions followed, causing the unsustainability of debt levels in the private and public sectors in southern countries and Ireland to become apparent. These private and public debt levels are shown as they evolved from 2001 to 2011 for the EU-12 countries and Cyprus in Figure 10. From 2001 to 2007, real estate and consumption booms were financed by additional private debt accumulation. By 2011, serious recessions and banking crises caused public debt to balloon as debt–GDP ratios grew much more quickly than in the rest of Eurozone. Simultaneously, the overhang of accumulated private debt created significant uncertainty in the Eurozone as the same economic conditions made private debt much riskier and contributed to the banking crises that emerged. In Ireland and Spain in particular, failing real-estate loans caused severe stresses to the banking systems. Countries throughout Europe that saw private debt levels climb were now far more susceptible to banking crises as the quality of loans underlying those private debts rapidly diminished by the sudden crash in real-estate prices after 2007.

Private and public debt-GDP levels.

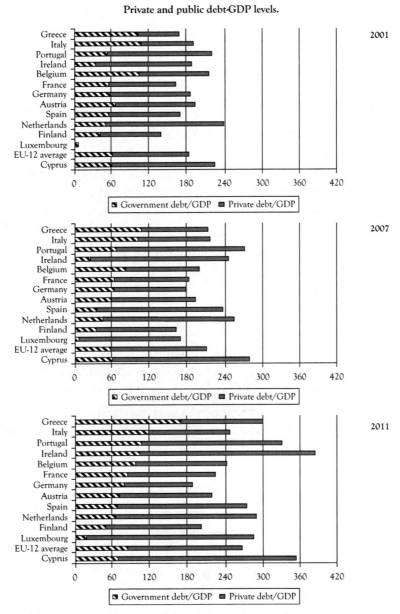

Figure 10. Government and private debt relative to GDP in 2001, 2007, and 2011.

Banks stopped lending in an effort to shore up deteriorating balance sheets, worsening economic conditions and creating a debt–deflation spiral, further destabilizing banking systems and increasing public expenditures and debt.

As the IMF noted in their OECD Economic Outlook in May 2011, problems in the Eurozone emerged as public finance burdens were willingly increased under faulty assumptions regarding the positive economic circumstances enjoyed in the mid-2000s:

> *Fiscal consolidation … looked successful, but – as has been a recurrent theme in the OECD's economic history – failure to attain sound underlying public finances was masked by very favorable cyclical developments. Fiscal rules (e.g. the European Stability and Growth Pact) failed to provide incentives to encourage the build-up of a sufficient reserve in good times. The implications of rising private-sector imbalances for the sustainability of public finances were ignored and forecasts of underlying public budgets were too optimistic. A possible correction in financial asset and real estate prices was not factored in and implicit fiscal liabilities were not taken into account.*[4]

Instead of convergence, structural imbalances in trade had led the EU to become a troubled debt alliance that left northern countries financing southern neighbors' consumption of northern goods and simultaneously helping to fuel property bubbles and expanding public sectors. As productivity improved in the northern countries relative to the south, southern economies became relatively less able to generate income and became more reliant on greater debt. Clearly, this fragile partnership would be in danger if credit conditions ever worsened, but in the mid-2000s concerns of such risks were greatly downplayed. This was another symptom of the great miscalculation worldwide that led to the financial crisis of 2008. After that crisis, a tipping point was created with respect to worldwide risk tolerance levels, and with the Greek revelations of 2009 what had been a virtuous European circle became the current crisis. Growth in southern economies stopped swiftly and northern creditors found they were holding a bag of potentially very bad debts. Those bad debts could have potentially catastrophic consequences both economically and politically for the Eurozone should debtors decide not to pay them. These potential consequences have shaped the response of creditor countries during the Euro crisis as southern states have requested bailouts to avoid such defaults. Strict conditionality and the need to recover debts where possible has made bailout deals difficult for recipient states and required significant public-sector contractions to avoid such outcomes, with predictable political consequences in these nations.

Country-Specific Structural Imbalances

The most troubled countries in the Eurozone have all been affected by some or all of the structural imbalances previously outlined, however, circumstances of the crises in each have been unique. As of mid-2013 five countries have required bailouts from the Eurozone, IMF, and the EU, collectively referred to unofficially as "the troika" in the media. The degree that symptoms of Eurozone imbalances had been present before 2008 for each of these five countries (Greece, Ireland, Portugal, Spain, and Cyprus), along with Italy is summarized in Table 1. The GIPSI countries have been the source of most concern during the Euro crisis, and Cyprus represents the first country to require a bailout as a direct result of crisis events in other countries, specifically the debt write-down of Greek debt held privately in 2012.

Greece

Greek revisions to national debt figures after a new government was elected to office sparked the beginning of the Euro crisis in October 2009. The causes of this revision, however, were years in the making. The required

Table 1. Structural Imbalances Among Troubled Countries, 2001–2007

Country	Productivity Decline Relative to Northern Countries	Increasing Trade Deficit	Housing Bubble	Declining National Savings	Increasing Debt– GDP Ratio
Greece	✓	✓	✓	✓	✓
Ireland			✓		
Portugal	✓	✓		✓	✓
Spain	✓	✓	✓	✓	
Italy	✓		✓		
Cyprus	✓	✓	✓		

Source: Eurostat, OECD, and author's calculations.

restatement of the government's fiscal position revealed that for years previous Greek governments had hidden massive debts from the rest of the EU. Greece's estimated government deficit for 2009 was more than tripled, revised from a previous 3.7% of GDP to 12.5% shortly after the new government took office. By April 2010, new EU figures suggested the deficit was even larger—nearer to 14%.

The causes of the large deficits were many. Primary among them has been a swollen public service sector and an ineffective and inefficient tax collection system. Public servants, once hired, had jobs that were constitutionally protected and granted for life in Greece. Originally intended to ensure the public service would be immune to political pressures, this rule had instead caused successive governments to offer government jobs in exchange for political support. From 1970 to 2009 public-sector employment increased fivefold, creating a powerful political constituency of public-service workers and families of over 700,000 people. Public-sector employment growth over this period was 4%, while during the same period private-sector employment grew at an average growth rate of less than 1%. Public-sector wages had climbed to a level almost 50% greater than in private-sector earnings and accounted for 27% of total government expenditures. OECD estimates indicated overstaffing levels in the Greek public sector of over 50%. In the decade from 2000 to 2009, wage and social program expenditures in Greece rose by 6.5% while revenues increased by only 5% annually. The result was an ever-widening government expenditure deficit.[5] From 2004 to 2009, according to documents submitted to the EU by the Greek Ministry of Finance, "output increased in nominal terms by 40%, central government primary expenditures increased by 87% against an increase of only 31% in tax revenues."[6] Over the period of Greek membership in the euro from 2001 to 2007, the average government deficit was 5.7% of GDP and the Greek debt–GDP ratio was 102.5% (Table 2). With respect to taxes, tax evasion remained a long-standing problem and one that little was done to correct.

Greece's large, inefficient, and expanding public sector, growing at four times the rate of the private sector ensured productivity growth was undermined, undermining its trade competitiveness. Since the euro was implemented as the common currency in circulation, Greece has recorded the lowest labor productivity in the union of the EU-12 countries, while also

Table 2. Maastricht Criteria Levels by Country Group and Selected Countries

| | Debt-GDP | | | Deficit-GDP | | | Inflation | | |
	Average Annual Debt-GDP Ratio (%)			Average Annual Deficit (−) or Surplus (+) to GDP Ratio (%)			Average Yearly Rate of Consumer Price Change		
	2001–2007	2008–2012	2012	2001–2007	2008–2012	2012	2001–2007	2008–2012	2012
Greece	102.5	143.6	156.9	−5.7	−11.1	−10.0	3.4	2.9	1.00
Ireland	29.2	85.1	117.6	1.0	−14.6	−7.6	3.3	0.4	1.0
Portugal	62.5	96.3	123.6	−4.3	−7.0	−6.4	3.1	1.9	2.8
Spain	46.1	61.8	84.2	0.6	−9.1	−10.6	3.2	2.3	2.4
Italy	105.1	117.9	127.0	−3.2	−3.9	−3.0	2.3	2.4	3.3
Cyprus	65.7	65.1	85.8	−2.5	−4.6	−6.3	2.4	2.8	3.1
GIPSI	69.1	100.9	121.9	−2.3	−9.1	−7.5	3.1	2.0	2.1
South	79.1	104.9	122.9	−3.1	−7.7	−7.5	3.0	2.4	2.4
North	55.0	64.2	69.9	−0.4	−2.2	−2.1	1.9	2.2	2.9
EU-12	60.8	79.7	91.6	−1.2	−5.3	−4.60	2.5	2.2	2.5

Source: Eurostat, May 2013.

experiencing the highest inflation rate. The effect of these outcomes has been to ensure Greek labor productivity and trade competitiveness have remained worst among the original Eurozone countries and its trade deficit the widest. Additionally, from 2005 to 2007 Greek home prices grew at an average rate of 8.5%, and the real estate and consumption bubbles in Greece reduced private savings while increasing private and public debt loads. Debt was sustained by the very large financial inflows, necessary to sustain the country's persistent trade deficits, which averaged 12% in this period as shown in Table 3. While Greek economic growth had been among the strongest of the Eurozone countries in the period before 2008, averaging 4.2% annually, the world financial crisis of 2008 was especially destabilizing to the Greek economy, which has historically been strongly dependent on its shipping and tourism industries. The recession caused by the effects of this crisis began in the third quarter of 2008 and reduced Greek economic output by 0.2% that year, and a further 3.5% in 2009, straining Greek public finances further as social program costs escalated.

The government's own revelations regarding Greek financial mismanagement resulted in an almost immediate series of credit-rating downgrades on Greek sovereign debt. Greek 10-year bond yields rose from less than 4.5% to over 8% in the period from October 2009 to May 2010, a level almost triple the yield paid on German bonds. In April 2010, Greek 2-year bond yields rose to over 15% and 5-year bonds exceeded 10%. Finding international financing of its debt service and operations unsustainable, the Greek government was forced to request a bailout from the EU and IMF on April 23. On May 2, 2010 the EU and IMF agreed to finance loans totaling €110 billion, granted for 3 years at an interest rate of 5.5%. In the following year it became clear that the terms of the first bailout were not large enough to maintain debt sustainability and a second bailout was required, eventually agreed to in spring of 2012, which, in addition to significant debt write-downs among private debt holders, also included renegotiated funding guarantees of an additional €130 billion, in addition to funds already allocated in the first bailout. In return for these bailout loans, successive Greek governments have agreed to significant reductions in public expenditure and enacted significant tax increases. They have also agreed to significant public-sector workforce reductions. These actions have simultaneously contributed to a recession that has been much deeper

Table 3. Economic Indicators by Group and Selected Eurozone Countries

	Real GDP Growth Average Yearly Change (%)		Home Prices Average Yearly Change (%)		Labor Productivity Euros Per Hour Worked at 2005 Prices		Trade Balance Average Yearly Current Account to GDP Ratio (%)	
	2001–2007	2008–2012	2001–2007	2008–2011	2001–2007	2008–2012	2001–2007	2008–2012
Greece	4.2%	-4.4%	5.3%	-3.0%	19.5	20.9	-12.0%	-9.7%
Ireland	5.1%	-1.2%	11.3%	-12.6%	49.1	57.0	13.4%	18.0%
Portugal	1.1%	-1.1%	.5%	1.5%	16.9	18.1	-8.5%	-6.0%
Spain	3.4%	-0.8%	13.7%	-4.3%	27.8	29.6	-5.0%	-1.9%
Italy	1.3%	-1.4%	6.1%	0.1%	32.2	32.3	0.4%	-0.1%
Cyprus	3.6%	0.2%	8.7%[a]	-3.5%	19.8	21.2	-2.2%	-5.5%
GIPSI	3.0%	-1.8%	7.6%	-3.7%	29.1	31.6	-2.2%	-0.1%
South	2.5%	-1.9%	8.6%	1.4%	24.1	25.2	-6.1%	-4.6%
North	2.2%	0.2%	5.2%	1.9%	44.3	46.4	5.7%	4.8%
EU-12	2.7%	-0.6%	7.1%	-0.3%	37.5	39.3	3.4%	4.1%

Source: Eurostat, May 2013, real-estate data from OECD, Eurostat, and GlobalPropertyGuide.com.
[a]Cyprus data only available from 2005 onward.

than anticipated initially by bailout partners, recording an average annual contraction in real economic output of 4.4% annually between 2008 and 2012. These conditions have caused significant political unrest and instability as unemployment has risen from an average monthly rate of 7.7% in 2007 to over 25% in 2013. As of summer 2013, the Greek economy had experienced 20 consecutive quarters of contraction and growth was forecast not to return for at least another year.

Ireland

From its entry into the expanded European Community in 1973, Ireland's economy began to transform itself. Historically one of the poorest countries in Western Europe, by 2007 on a GDP per capita basis, it was the second richest in the Eurozone, behind only Luxembourg. This turnaround earned Ireland the nickname "Celtic Tiger" in reference to the pace of its economic development and an apparent similarity to the so-called Asian Tigers: South Korea, Singapore, Hong Kong, and Taiwan. Causes of the economic boom that led to this turnaround have been attributed to several factors. Ireland adopted one of the lowest corporate tax rates in Europe. Membership in the European Community entitled Ireland to transfer payments from richer members within the community, accounting for as much as 4% of GDP, and these "cohesion funds" were invested in education and infrastructure. With respect to education, 35% of the transfer funds were allocated to developing human capital, an amount greater than the average of other recipient nations. The impact this had on the skills and education in the Irish workforce has often been credited for Ireland's attractiveness to the high-tech industry during the boom years prior to 2008. Subsidies also encouraged high-tech industry to locate in Ireland and by the 2000s Irish high-tech manufacturing had led to significant trade surpluses with the rest of the world and Europe. Favorable location and relatively lower wages were also often cited as factors in Ireland's economic success.

Growth in Ireland from 1983 to 2008 was unprecedented in the country. Annual growth rates of real GDP from 1984 to 2000 averaged 6.3%, while from 1996 to 2000 they averaged an astounding 10.3%. During the period of the euro from 2001 to 2007, real GDP growth continued at a still very high 5.1% average pace, despite a period of relative easing during the early 2000s due to the "dot.com" bubble bursting and information technology slowdown in the United States and elsewhere. As shown in Table 2, this robust growth was much greater than that in the other 12 original members of the European currency union; however, as experienced in several other developed economies in the mid-2000s, growth was in large part propelled by a property and housing bubble. High rates of economic growth allowed Ireland to run persistent budget surpluses, reducing its government debt–GDP ratio from over 90% to under 40% in the decade of the 1990s alone. Debt–GDP ratios continued to fall through 2007 and averaged 29.1% from 2001 to 2007 (Table 3). Again this performance was among the best in the currency union, and by 2007 Ireland's debt–GDP ratio was bettered only by Luxembourg in the Eurozone.

Unlike other troubled countries in the Eurozone shown in Table 1, the only source of serious imbalance in Ireland's economy after the European monetary union began was the aforementioned real-estate bubble that began to inflate in the early 2000s. Rates of home price increase exceeded 14% in 2003 and 2006 and averaged 11.3% between 2003 and 2007, propelled by Ireland's economic growth elsewhere in the economy, foreign investment, and easy credit. During the mid-2000s bond yields on Irish sovereign debt were often lower than that paid on equivalent German bonds, traditionally the benchmark rate to which other countries' debts have been compared. Growth in high-tech manufacturing, corporate relocation to Ireland and high levels of foreign investment also encouraged house price increases. The bursting of the U.S. real-estate bubble in 2007, however, coincided with that in Ireland and the Irish banking system was soon in crisis. Banks in Ireland as in the United States had financed much of the long-term real-estate investment using short-term borrowed credit and as concerns mounted regarding banks' ability to repay these loans, Irish banks faced an illiquidity problem. In that year, as the Irish economy fell into its first recession since 2003, and between 2007 and 2009 unemployment more than doubled. To stabilize the struggling banking system now struck by significant quantities of nonperforming real-estate loans, the Irish government issued an unlimited guarantee backing six of its national banks in an attempt to open credit markets for them. The Irish government also implemented deeply unpopular social spending cutbacks in an attempt to reverse a budget deficit that exceeded 7% of national output, the first deficit since the 1980s. Concerns regarding bank illiquidity rapidly turned to insolvency concerns as the recession worsened and more loans began to default.

By the end of 2008 the government had to bailout Anglo-Irish Bank, worst hit by the property collapse, taking a 75% ownership stake. This single bank would eventually lose over €34 billion, almost half of its investments and a loss equivalent to almost 20% of Irish GDP the year it was taken over. As conditions in the Irish economy continued to worsen in 2009 and unemployment continued to climb, conditions among Ireland's major banks similarly worsened. In September 2009 the country created the National Asset Management Agency, a "bad bank" in which the Irish banks' nonperforming assets were allowed to be transferred in an effort to stabilize their books, and for a second year the Irish government also offered an unlimited bank guarantee to back these institutions in an attempt to again open credit markets to Irish financial institutions. Credit market conditions, however, only worsened after Greece announced the first of its deficit revisions in November 2009, and Irish 10-year sovereign bond yields, which had averaged only a half percent premium over German bonds in 2008, climbed to a level 60% greater than the yield on comparable German notes. By the end of 2009 the Irish budget deficit was 13.9% of GDP and the Irish economy contracted by over 3%. By mid-2010, Irish 10-year bond yields were double those of Germany's, and in September 2010, the Irish government had to guarantee Irish bank obligations for a third year. The nation's debt–GDP ratio had combed from 25% in 2007 to over 90% in 2010, and with bank liabilities now worth over 30% of Irish GDP, the Irish government requested a bailout from the IMF and EU and on November 28, 2010 was granted an €85 billion rescue package. Throughout 2011 and 2012, Irish debt conditions have continued to deteriorate and at the end of 2012 the nation's debt–GDP ratio was more than 116%, increasing by more than four times in 5 years.

Portugal

The creation of the euro did not coincide with high growth in every participating country. From the inception of the European monetary union the Portuguese economy was persistently among the weakest in the Eurozone. Sluggish growth did not improve after the euro was introduced, and growth of real GDP averaged 1.1% from 2001 to 2007, lowest among the original Eurozone countries. Burdened by a large and inefficient public sector, low productivity throughout the economy, ongoing trade deficits averaging over 8% of GDP occurred from 2001 to 2007. Despite these conditions, inflation rates in Portugal during this period were also among the highest in the Eurozone, again undermining the country's ompetitiveness. The only positive aspect to Portugal's growth during this period was the fact that unlike the other countries shown in Table 1, it was the only one to escape a significant real-estate bubble.

During the decade of the 2000s following the implementation of the euro, government deficits were also excessive, averaging over 4%, and resulting in government gross debt–GDP ratios climbing in excess of 60%. Both deficit and debt ratios persistently exceeded Maastricht guidelines required of Eurozone countries, but despite threatened sanctions Portugal was not penalized under the EU's SGP rules. Sovereign bond yields were not significantly impacted by this economic underperformance, with interest rates on Portuguese 10-year bonds averaged only 0.17% more than German bonds from 2001 to the end of 2007. Without more serious financial or EU pressures, policy efforts were not forthcoming to motivate improvements in Portugal's competitiveness after the euro was implemented, leaving it very susceptible to the market shocks that would follow. Though no single crisis would befall its economy, the imbalances caused by uncompetitive productivity and trade, an oversized public sector, and ballooning debt and deficits would eventually cause financial markets to turn on the country.

As the worldwide economy worsened in 2008 and 2009, the Portuguese economy also slowed, falling into recession at the end of 2008. Deficits rose to over 10% of GDP by 2009, with government debt–GDP ratio rising to over 70% in 2008 and over 80% in 2009. In late 2008, Portugal's financial system also faltered as weak economic conditions forced the state to nationalize one of its largest banks after a banking scandal and severe losses. At the end of 2009, following the Greek deficit revelations, 10-year bond yields on Portuguese debt began to reflect investor concerns regarding that country's debt sustainability. A second bank also fell victim to management scandal and in early 2010 was liquidated by the Portuguese central bank. By the end of 2010, Portuguese 10-year debt approached yield levels of 7%, a level 4.5% higher and over two and half times the rate on comparable German debt. With Portuguese debt yields at record highs and unemployment over 11%, in April 2011 Portugal approached the IMF and EU for assistance and was granted a €78 billion bailout package.

Since 2010 the economy of Portugal has only worsened to 1.6% in 2011 and a further 3.2% in 2012. Growth was not forecast to return to the economy until 2014. Unemployment has risen from 11.2% at the start of the crisis in late 2009 to levels approaching 18% in 2013. Austerity measures required as part of bailout conditions appear to have reinforced the negative headwinds facing the economy and political instability has risen as the government has struggled to maintain support through trying economic conditions.

Spain

Much like Ireland, Spanish growth for much of the period immediately after the inception of the euro was among the strongest in the Eurozone. Also like Ireland, for a significant portion of this period, strong growth in the country was buoyed by a significant home price bubble. Growth in Spain from 2001 to 2007 averaged 3.5%, well above the rates of most of the original twelve euro countries, spurred on by public construction and home-building booms. The high growth rates fueled by the building boom, however, masked underlying structural problems in the economy. Trade deficits ballooned in this period. Unemployment rates also remained high relative to other states in Europe with unemployment throughout the boom remaining at levels over 8%. Public expenditures increased significantly, propelled in part by massive and inefficient public works projects throughout the country. Despite these expenditures though, strong economic growth allowed government budgets to remain in surplus and the debt–GDP ratio fell to levels well below most other countries in the Eurozone, achieving a level of 36.3% in 2007. As in Portugal, economic reforms were deferred, and productivity improvements did not keep pace with northern competitors. With wage and inflation rates in part reflecting housing prices and in part strong wage gains across the economy, overall Spanish trade competitiveness was persistently challenged and large trade deficits worsened. By 2008 the 3-year average trade deficit had climbed to 9.5% of Spanish GDP, a level almost three times that seen when the euro went into circulation in 2001.

In late 2007 the Spanish property bubble burst, as it did in Ireland and the United States. Within months, unemployment rates rose from levels near 8% to over 14%. The Spanish banking sector, which had supported real-estate financing and the financing of large public construction projects in large part through its *cajas*, smaller regional savings banks whose boards and lending decisions were often influenced by local and regional politicians, was severely impacted by this turn of events. The bursting of the housing market bubble had left many of these institutions in desperate financial circumstances. Lending contracted at many of these institutions as once more, as seen in other countries after the world financial crisis of 2008, banks contracted lending in an attempt to shore up their balance sheets. Worsening credit conditions magnified weak economic conditions. In addition to mounting social program costs caused by the severe recession underway, government expenditures began to balloon as stabilizing the Spanish banking sector required massive infusions of new capital.

Unlike Ireland and Portugal, as the recession deepened following the crash of the national construction and real-estate boom, failing banks were initially not nationalized but instead were bailed out by national authorities. Few banks were closed and instead authorities chose to support the *cajas* sector by merging several of the most impacted institutions into larger banking entities through consolidation. The largest of these consolidations occurred with the creation of a single new entity renamed Bankia. Such consolidations have not proven successful. While the worst performing loans from these consolidated entities were transferred to a national bad bank in an attempt to improve their balance sheets, rising delinquencies and rapidly worsening economic conditions have resulted in continuing losses.

Due to concerns that the banking crisis in Spain could quickly grow in cost and with similar repercussions for the government as the banking crisis in Ireland had, 10-year bond rates on Spanish debt began increasing in 2011. Spain, however, provided a concern much larger than the previously

troubled countries. With an economy almost twice the size of the combined economies of Greece, Ireland, and Portugal, a bailout of similar proportion to those already undertaken would be too large—bailout facilities
previously created such as the European Financial Stability Facility (EFSF)
and later the European Stability Mechanism (ESM) were not large enough
to cover the potential liabilities a Spanish failure might entail, yet a default
in such circumstances could create financial market chaos and the end of
the common currency. In Fall of 2011, these fears, combined with deteriorating conditions in the Spanish economy and persistent weakness in its
banking sector caused the ECB to take the controversial step of intervening
in markets for Spanish debt, buying limited amounts of Spanish bonds on
the secondary market in an effort to reduce these interest rate increases,
now in excess of 3% above German rates. Despite these efforts conditions
in Spanish banking markets only worsened through the latter part of
2011 and early 2012.

By early 2012, continuing Spanish banking losses resulted in greater
and greater resources required to prop up the Spanish banking sector. In
May 2012, Bankia, the largest holder of real-estate loans with an estimated
portfolio in excess of €38 billion, announced new losses and it rapidly
became clear that a new and larger bailout of the institution would be
required above and beyond previously negotiated aid in excess of €4 billion.
The Spanish government took the reluctant step of effectively nationalizing
the institution in early May in an attempt to stabilize Spanish financial markets but share prices in the institution and the rest of the Spanish banking
sector collapsed, worsening an already bad situation. In late May a €19 billion
state-funded rescue package was negotiated to maintain Bankia's solvency.
Credit rating agencies rapidly downgraded not only Bankia but much of the
Spanish financial to junk-bond status, effectively eliminating any access of
most institutions to private credit. With financial market conditions rapidly
deteriorating and the probability rapidly rising of the entire Spanish banking
system failing, the country requested aid from the EU to recapitalize its banking system. In June 2012 European leaders announced approval for loan
guarantees up to €100 billion. Recognizing that EU and Troika funds were
not available to cover Spain's sovereign debt, the Spanish bailout attempted
to avoid affecting sovereign bond markets by financing the banking system
directly and not through the national government. This effort it was hoped

would stem the pressure on Spanish sovereign debt rates by avoiding Spain's accumulation of additional debt and the perception of greater default risk, leaving the country's ability to access international credit intact.

Overall, problems in the Spanish economy have remained among the most severe in the Eurozone. The collapse of the construction sector in 2007 has pushed unemployment rates to among the highest in Europe, with unemployment rates reaching levels over 26% in 2013, and youth (less than 25 years of age) unemployment rates near 60%. Sovereign debt–GDP levels, once among the lowest in the Eurozone have more than doubled in 4 years and neared 90% by the end of 2012. Recessionary conditions are not anticipated to abate until 2014. Unlike other southern economies, the Spanish government has a firm majority in the state national assembly and though beset by financing scandals that threaten several government officials, the country is less likely to be afflicted by the political instability caused by economic conditions that threatens neighboring countries.

Italy

Like Portugal, Italy has also experienced slow growth throughout the decade of the 2000s, averaging annual rates of growth from 2001 to 2007 of only 1.3%. The third largest economy in the Eurozone after Germany and France, Italy was allowed to enter the currency union with a level of debt much greater than originally envisioned by its architects, with a debt–GDP ratio in excess of 110% in 1999 when the euro first began to be used. Deficit levels were also at or above Maastricht Treaty limits throughout the period from 2001 to 2007, however, unlike Portugal, Italian deficits were structural in the sense that they reflected slow economic growth and were also driven by debt service. While entrance into the common currency has not resulted in strong economic growth since 2001, it has been beneficial in one sense. By 2007 debt restructuring permitted by the lower sovereign debt rates available after the euro was introduced allowed Italy's debt–GDP level to be reduced to 103% from over 113% in 1999. These same low interest rates, however, also created an escalation in housing prices as they have in several other countries. Unlike other states though, this challenge did not cause inflation to rise relative to levels in the rest of the Eurozone as they had in Greece, Ireland, Portugal, and Spain.

Italy's trade deficit remained slightly positive throughout most of the first decade of the euro, and even since 2008 has been nearly balanced though relative productivity compared to northern Eurozone states has declined.

Overall, while the implementation of the euro has not improved Italy's economic condition, the country has few of the other structural imbalances that have proven damaging to other GIPSI states during the Euro crisis. Concerns with respect to Italy's economy have centered around its relatively large debt level and the cost to service it. While weak economic performance did not improve greatly after adopting the euro, consistent with its Maastricht obligations Italy did manage to reduce its debt load. Unfortunately by 2009 these debt levels had again begun to increase as the worldwide recession of 2008 also caused deficits in Italy to increase. Since 2009 the country's gains in debt–GDP have reversed for this reason and by 2013 had risen to over 126%. The size of Italy's sovereign debt–GDP makes the country very sensitive to sovereign debt rates and since the failure of Lehman Brothers Bank in the United States in Fall 2008, the country's bond yields have averaged over a percent higher than German 10-year bonds, a level more than 25% higher what Germany pays creditors. Since 2010 this spread has grown to 2% or more. This has created significant competitive disadvantages for firms in Italy, particularly in the north where productivity levels are otherwise equivalent to its northern competitors, but credit costs can often be twice as much. The result has been continuing weak economic conditions and high unemployment, with jobless levels over 12% for the general population by 2013, both of which have created challenges to Italy's government budget where austerity measures have been implemented in part to ease concerns in international debt markets. Due to the size of Italy's economy it is understood that, like Spain, it cannot be bailed out as resources for a bailout on such a scale would be unavailable.

The greatest challenge facing Italy is reversing the decade-long malaise its economy has experienced. Reform of its rigid labor markets and increased austerity measures meant to stabilize government revenues have been very controversial and met with great resistance. Political instability has been the result, threatening to undermine any attempt at creating reforms to help improve growth and government budgets. Of troubled countries, interest rates on sovereign debt yields have remained the lowest, however they still remain elevated at levels almost triple the rates paid by Germany and almost double those paid by France.

Cyprus

A small island economy dominated by a Greek heritage, Cyprus joined the common currency in 2008 and accounted for only 0.2% of total Eurozone output that year. In comparison, of the EU-12 countries that comprised the European monetary union, the next smallest economies (Portugal, Ireland, and Finland) are each almost 10 times larger in relative size. Prior to its membership in the euro, Cyprus enjoyed high growth but also high inflation in the early part of the 2000s. Inflation rates were in part driven by a real-estate bubble where prices rose at over 8% per year. Since joining the currency union, Cyprus has also become an off-shore banking center, particularly for Russian depositors eager for access to Europe due to its proximity and cultural ties to Russia dating back to the communist era. By 2012, the banking sector in Cyprus has accumulated deposits in excess of eight times the island nation's GDP, which has in part driven a widening trade deficit and maintained price increases in the housing sector. In addition to banking, Cyprus' economy is also strongly dependent on tourism and shipping, and this has left its overall economy susceptible to symptoms of the world financial crisis in 2008 and the European financial crisis afterward.

The financial crisis in 2008 and the collapse of the Greek economy in 2009 onward had a significant effect on Cyprus's banking system. Cypriot banks were active in Greek real-estate markets and the recession in that country has left its financial system with significant levels of nonperforming loans. The local recession also hurt its banks as worldwide shipping and tourism slowed after 2008. Efforts to support the banking sector and costs of the mounting recession has in part caused the nation's sovereign debt–GDP ratio to rise from under 50% prior to 2008, a level comparatively low relative to other Eurozone states, to levels near 90% by 2013. Due to the nation's small size and illiquid sovereign debt market, it has had difficulty in accessing international credit to support its growing government deficits and instead turned to bilateral loans with countries such as Russia to support its expenditures.

While Cyprus's structural problems revolve primarily around its out-size banking sector, housing and property price appreciation similar to other southern countries and its close ties to the Greek economy, Cyprus debt situation has been devastated by two events in particular since 2011. The first has been the fallout of high energy prices and a lack of electricity reliability since 2011 that have challenged its growth. This was caused by an explosion at a Cypriot naval base in July 2011 that resulted in the destruction of a power station that produced approximately half of Cyprus's electricity. Several weeks followed of rolling blackouts across the country, and since the disaster the country has had to import power at considerable expense. The cost to repair the station was estimated to be over €20 billion, or over 10% of its GDP in that year. The cost of the electricity imports and blackouts to economic output have been large and significantly contributed to the nation's recession experienced in the last half of 2011 and 2012.

The second event contributing to Cyprus's economic problems since 2011 has been the severe economic downturn in other southern European countries since the Euro crisis began, especially in Greece, Cyprus's largest economic partner. In particular, efforts to bailout Greece have had dramatic and unintended consequences on the Greek banking system. When private bond holders were required to take cuts to their holdings in excess of 50% as part of Greece's second bailout package, Cypriot banks, which had bet heavily on Greek sovereign debt, found a significant portion of their assets immediately devalued. The resulting impact on the balance sheets of these banks required an intervention by Cypriot authorities to stabilize the financial sector in the country, but due to its size relative to Cyprus's output this required external aid. The Cypriot government had depended on Russian aid previously during the Euro crisis, supported by a €2.5 billion loan made in January 2012 to cover government expenditure obligations and maturing debt. The loan, however, did not include unanticipated needs to recapitalize the Cypriot banking system following the Greek bailout. In June of 2012 Cyprus requested bailout aid from the Troika and in 2013 the details of this aid were finalized. Aid conditions were severe, and have resulted in significant political anger against both the newly elected government that holds a narrow coalition majority, and against the wider EU.

Overview

In summary, the creation of the Eurozone has turned out to have serious flaws resulting from the fact that it is a monetary union without a strong fiscal union. Long-term stability of the currency union required strong institutional restraints necessary to achieve the sound fiscal footing. The Maastricht Treaty requirements were expected to create these conditions—once the Eurozone was created many believed fiscal integration would then follow. Fiscal pacts, however, are politically messy. While convincing countries to give up the control of national currencies had been difficult, the idea of ceding national fiscal sovereignty to a supranational organization was even more so. With so many countries and varying national ideologies, historic fears and even national prejudices still existing in the union, attempts to achieve such a fiscal union never began. With strong economic growth occurring anyway, the pressure to make such politically difficult decisions faded, but the flaws in the design of the Eurozone still remained. Worse, politics also undermined adherence to Maastricht requirements and the institutional brakes meant to ensure debt sustainability in the union were undermined.

Despite these problems, proponents of the currency union reasoned adoption of the euro would create the political breathing space to allow necessary structural reforms to be achieved. Strong economic growth among many Eurozone countries after the adoption of the euro also seemed to suggest that, at least among poorer countries, an economic convergence was occurring. Unfortunately, economic growth occurring in this period was not driven by productivity improving investment or market reforms, but by expanding public sectors, consumption and property bubbles. What seemed like growth that would lead to convergence across economies was really just temporary growth induced by greater credit access. This access was in part propelled by trade imbalances between north and south occurring in the Eurozone.

Economic convergence in the Eurozone required not only strong growth, but also underlying productivity and competiveness improvements to avoid structural imbalances. Achieving such improvements would require difficult internal decisions in many member countries to dismantle uncompetitive institutions that undermined their productivity, including reductions in bloated public sectors, breaking guild control of large sectors of the economy resistant to reform, and removal of public subsidies and barriers to entry in some sectors. These were politically contentious issues, and as labor unrest and riots in Greece, Italy, Portugal, and Spain over austerity measures introduced throughout the Euro crisis have shown, it is very difficult to reform economies where people have historically relied on such institutions. Without such reforms, however, convergence cannot occur. The lack of movement toward such reforms, particularly in less-competitive southern countries, created and maintained significant economic imbalances. These imbalances with respect to trade and credit flows weakened economies and contributed to the emergence of the European financial crisis that has since caused serious unemployment and hardship not only in southern and GIPSI countries but also in much of Europe.

In the long term if the European common currency union is to be preserved, the flaws of the Eurozone will have to be addressed so that such imbalances cannot be allowed to develop again. Doing so will require not only addressing the causes of the fiscal and trade imbalances present in the Eurozone, but the institutional structures that are necessary to allow the Eurozone's currency union to become stable as well. Though, as Mario Draghi described in 2012, the European currency union bumblebee was able to fly despite its apparent violation of economic theory, to continue the bumblebee will now have to learn to fly according to those rules.

CHAPTER 6

Misperception of European Risk, Market Reactions, and Policy Response: A Timeline of the Euro Crisis

Introduction

The world financial crisis of 2008 created a focus on fundamentals. The experience, one still ongoing reminded the world that details matter, whether the details involve the quality of mortgages being used as underlying assets in mortgage-backed securities during the U.S. financial crisis, or the organization of a currency union and the underlying structure of the economies involved during the Euro crisis. In many ways the world before 2008 was one dominated by optimism, and optimism made it easier to ignore messy details of all sorts, including the structure of the European monetary union, its underlying trade and credit flows, and its banking and debt composition. As ECB President Mario Draghi noted in July 2012, like a bumblebee, the currency union flew even though it should not have been able to. Since 2008 though, markets and policy makers have been much less willing to optimistically assume the bumblebee can fly just because it did in the past. How and why it flies now matter and markets must be convinced the union can continue. This has been the omnipresent worry throughout the Euro crisis—can the monetary union actually survive? The timeline of the Euro crisis has, if nothing else, demonstrated this new reality, and how skeptical and questioning markets have become relative to the period before 2008 when the monetary union in Europe seemed to soar despite its underlying problems.

One lesson of the U.S. financial crisis in 2008 was that a crisis in a single sector of the economy can unleash consequences that affect the entire international financial system, especially when conditions of high leverage and debt exist. Leading up to 2008, early warnings concerning real-estate markets in the United States and elsewhere were shrugged off by analysts and policy makers alike with an optimistic assessment that even in a worst-case scenario their collapse would not seriously affect the whole economy. What became understood after the events in the United States was that the web of debt built on top of the real-estate sector could in fact destabilize the entire international financial system. "Leverage," or the accumulation of debt was the key, as debts were used to create assets, in this case mortgages, and those assets were then used to collateralize more borrowing. As long as confidence remained that all the underlying debts were good, the process of leveraging continued and drove more economic activity as lending begat the ability to borrow more. When confidence vanished, however, lending also vanished and total debt had to be reduced to match the new supply.[1] More often than not that debt reduction occurred through default and the results were much more painful than most policy makers and analysts had anticipated as economic activity contracted throughout most of developed world.[2] After 2008, financial market depth and breadth, interlocking webs of debt and their potential effects on the larger economy would no longer be ignored.

These lessons were not lost on markets when in late 2009 the election of a new Greek government brought new focus on European sovereign debt. In Europe, the debt of Greece and other Eurozone countries had also been leveraged into something much larger. The mistake was, not unlike the assumptions made regarding mortgage debt in the United States, that sovereign debt in the Eurozone was risk-free, or nearly so. During the mid-2000s, the tight convergence among Eurozone country bond rates that occurred suggested markets believed all member countries posed similarly low risks of default, even those member countries that had previously been considered the least dependable. Reinforcing this assumption, international credit agencies also assigned Eurozone country bonds investor-grade ratings.[3] Such an interest rate convergence was also consistent with a belief that the fiscal strength of stronger northern economies like Germany's would always support the previously less-dependable peripheral ones in the south if a crisis threatened their solvency. In hindsight, such market beliefs were clearly questionable, the first through an accumulation of history and the second due to the rules of the EU itself, which were meant to limit the liability among nations for other's debt. Greece's revelations caused markets to reconsider their assumptions and, as in the United States, this change in outlook was immediately felt in credit markets. The Euro crisis had begun.

In some ways, the experience of European leaders during the first years of the Euro crisis could be compared to the famous five phases of grief discussed in psychology. The Euro crisis had come as a shock and now threatened to end the currency union that had been the culmination of so many years of difficult European integration efforts. The first reaction to the crisis was one of denial. Leader's reactions during the earliest months of the crisis were broadly similar to those seen during the period when Europe implemented its fixed exchange rate system during the 1980s and 1990s, and market pressures emerged to destabilize those rates. Two decades earlier, market pressures were also predicated on analyses that suggested country-specific fundamentals did not support targeted exchange rate outcomes. During these earlier exchange rate crises, destabilizing currency market pressures built up when it became clear the fixed exchange rates in place could not be supported given market conditions. In the Euro crisis two decades later, interest rates began to climb when sovereign debt markets realized the presence of previously unrealized default risk in particular countries. Fears in both instances then appeared to become self-fulfilling as market pressures worsened. Denial of the problem and a lack of action allowed market confidence in both cases to worsen, eventually resulting in severe crises in both cases.

Denial also affected the willingness of European leaders to accept the causes of the situation in late 2009. Overwhelmingly, European leaders initially blamed the crisis they now faced on the U.S. financial crisis, and saw events in Europe as caused by events in U.S. financial markets, ignoring fundamental problems in their own economies. Where European blame was due, it was assigned to failures of governance, on irresponsibility in Greece, for example, and not the larger architecture of the Eurozone. Leaders' outlooks were also clouded by overly optimistic projections of rapid recovery in Europe then underway in 2009. IMF officials similarly were overly optimistic regarding economic conditions in Europe and Greece, and underestimated the effects that the onerous austerity conditions they recommended would have across the Eurozone.[4] The prevailing viewpoint in 2009 argued the crisis would be over by 2012 with growth occurring by then even in Greece.[5]

Anger, bargaining and depression, the classic second, third and fourth stages of grief followed. Anger was manifest across Europe once it became apparent denial was no longer possible, and that significant and costly actions would be required. Anger was everywhere, with Eurozone leaders and residents of creditor countries unhappy with Greece initially, and resentful of Ireland and Portugal afterward as bailouts became necessary, while people in aided nations, frustrated at their own governments and rapidly worsening economic circumstances, became angrier at the terms of their aid. Many across the Eurozone also seemed to resent the currency union and previous efforts at economic integration for the situation they now found themselves in. The bargaining that had to follow promised much but in each bailout the costs were often undersold, while bailout efforts oversold their prospects for success. Bargaining also was ongoing in creditor nations as countries worked internally to find domestic acceptance actions needed to resolve the crisis and protect the currency union from the threat of a sovereign default. The inevitable result appears to have been depression, which manifested itself in many ways. Emotionally there was disappointment that the hopes the currency union had embodied seemed frustrated. Economically, a depression would turn out to be the appropriate term for the conditions that would soon exist in each of the aided countries, and even some that had not sought aid. In some economies emotional depression would turn to despair as conditions steadily worsened.

The final stage of grief, acceptance, might characterize the point at which Eurozone policy makers began to realize effective actions would require deeper changes than those contemplated in the first 2 years of the crisis. Policy efforts in reaction to the crisis, when finally undertaken, initially attempted to treat only the symptoms of the crisis. These actions were two pronged: the ECB attempted limited interventions to stabilize the sovereign debt markets of troubled nations, while the IMF and EU nations, primarily those in the Eurozone, financed bailouts in an effort to restore confidence in sovereign debt markets that had evaporated with the crisis.

This strategy was repeatedly attempted, first in Greece, then Ireland and Portugal with only limited and short-lived success. Only when it became apparent that such repeated efforts would not work in late 2011 did leaders turn to more difficult policies, ones that would address the underlying structural problems of the euro. Reforms would be required not only in troubled countries but also in creditor nations and changes would demand problematic sacrifices of sovereignty by both groups. Significant and far-reaching political reforms would also have to be made by nations regarding their fiscal practices and the structure of the banking system if market confidence were to return over the longer term. Policies to manage the crisis would also require new, much stronger and more controversial ECB actions to be implemented if sovereign debt markets were to be stabilized in the short-term, restoring financial and banking stability in the Eurozone. To preserve the euro, the architecture of the Eurozone would have to be modified in ways that could not even have been contemplated 2 years earlier.

Timeline of the Crisis

A simplified timeline of major events in the Euro crisis from late 2009 through mid-2013 is shown in Figure 1a,b. The figure identifies changes in long-term sovereign debt rates (typically 10-year bonds) across selected Eurozone nations, showing how these rates changed as events in the Euro crisis occurred. As the crisis worsened more and more countries saw their rates rise, signaling declines in market confidence that these countries could sustain their debts. The rising solid lines in the figure indicate how the confidence in GIPSI nations deteriorated over time as markets reassessed the likelihood of default in these countries given events elsewhere in the currency union. Contagion is also clearly evident as trouble in one country, for example Greece in the fall of 2009, soon spread to Ireland and Portugal by spring of 2010 lifting their rates, and then spread to Spain and Italy by the end of the year, causing their rates to diverge from creditor nations' in the core of the Eurozone. Creditor nations on the other hand, particularly Germany, sometimes found their rates falling as investors sought the safety of those assets understood to pose the least danger in the worst moments of the crisis.

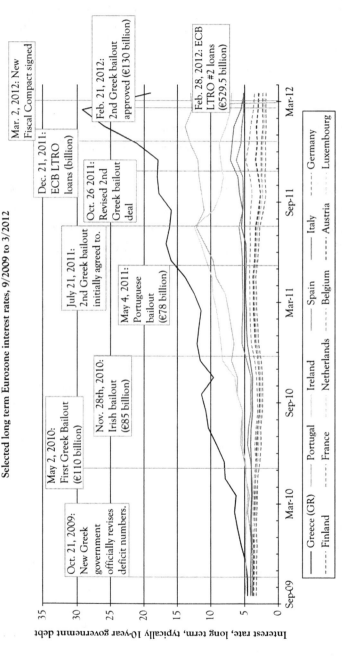

Selected long term Eurozone interest rates, 9/2009 to 3/2012

Figure 1(a). *European sovereign interest rates timeline: September 2009 to March 2012. Average monthly government 10-year or equivalent long-term bond rates. Greek interest rates hit a maximum value of almost 30% just as that country's second bailout was finalized. The high Greek rate reflected an expected write-down in Greek debt prior to the final agreement. Spanish, Portuguese, and Italian sovereign debt all hit highs just prior to the ECB's LTRO loans were made available.*

Source: Eurostat.

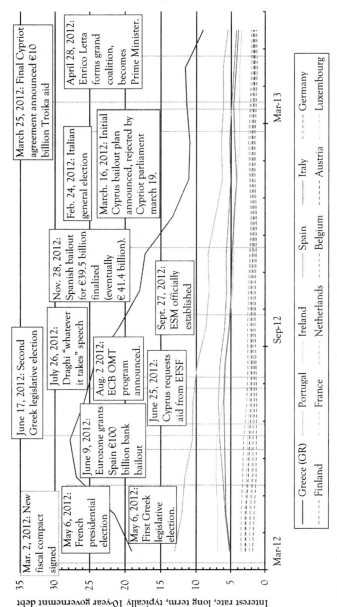

Selected long term Eurozone interest rates, 3/2012 to 5/2013

Figure 1(b). *European sovereign interest rates timeline: March 2012 to May 2013. Average monthly government 10-year or equivalent long-term sovereign bond rates. Greek, Spanish, and Italian bonds all reached maximum values in summer 2012, just before resolution of the Greek election and the ECB's declaration to do "whatever it takes" to support the euro. Afterward, rates declined through the remainder of 2012. By summer of 2013 the EU-12 countries' rates had returned to levels not seen since the start of the crisis.*

Source: Eurostat.

Using these sovereign debt rates, the crisis can be seen to have worsened throughout the period from the first Greek debt revelations in late 2009 through late 2011. The progression and intensity of the crisis can be followed by the levels of GIPSI interest rates relative to those in the core countries (shown by broken lines) and this intensity can be mapped to the policy actions and reforms undertaken in the Eurozone in response to these movements. The crisis hit a climax in spring of 2012, when, after very difficult and prolonged negotiations, a final agreement regarding the Greek bailout was reached. This was followed by a short period of calm before political turmoil gripped the Eurozone as an unresolved election in Greece threw the currency union once more into a period of high uncertainty. Uncertainty levels remained high for the rest of the GIPSI nations through this period as well until the Greek election was resolved and several policy actions were taken by the Troika in mid-June, and most importantly by the ECB in July 2012. After August 2012, all sovereign debt rates have declined to levels last seen in March 2010 near the beginning of the crisis, which has led some observers to declare the worst of the crisis has now past.

In analyzing the Euro crisis as it has unfolded, policy reactions by the Troika can be separated into three chronological phases. These phases can also be grouped into two distinct stages. These are described in Table 2. The first two phases represent stage one of the crisis and represent an evolution of policy efforts to deal with the crisis as it worsened during its first 2 years. These two phases also represent a set of policy responses that attempted to work within the existing structure of the Eurozone and EU Treaty framework where possible. Actions were mainly an attempt to gain control of the crisis without significant reform or change in the structure of the currency union and its system of fiscal governance, and consisted of three "bailouts," agreements in which the Eurozone, EU, and IMF provided liquidity in the form of loans and loan guarantees to Greece, Ireland, and Portugal to allow them to meet their debt obligations, thereby avoiding potential sovereign defaults. The ECB during this period also engaged in efforts to reduce pressures on sovereign debt rates. It did so through limited efforts to purchase the sovereign debt of troubled nations in secondary markets. The ECB's bond-buying efforts were limited in part by political disagreements in the Eurozone regarding the legality of such actions under EU treaties.

The original policy response to the Euro crisis, restrained as it was by attempts to work within the system of the EU, eventually proved ineffective, resulting in a new approach being needed. This shift in approach defined the beginning of the second stage of the crisis. In this period, the most effective policies adopted to control the symptoms of the crisis, namely the sovereign debt rates of GIPSI nations, have been the result of ECB action. These actions have redefined the long understood principle that the ECB remain a mostly passive actor, primarily maintaining the day-to-day workings of the EU's currency union and its banking system. After late 2011, the ECB's stance changed significantly with respect first to the level of support it offered the Eurozone banking system and then in its willingness to intervene in sovereign debt markets when in late July and August 2012 it pledged to "do whatever it takes" to maintain the euro. This change in the degree of ECB activism in 2011 coincided with both a continued worsening of the crisis that demonstrated more significant actions were needed, and the apparent realization by both Eurozone leaders and markets that a change in approach was necessary if the crisis was to be overcome. It also coincided with a change in leadership at the ECB. In November 2011, Jean-Claude Trichet, the ECB's president throughout the first 2 years of the crisis stepped down after a 5-year term, to be replaced by Mario Monti.

The actions of the ECB in the period since 2011 have served to stabilize markets to a degree that was not seen prior to this change in approach. The ECB's efforts have proven much more effective in improving bond market conditions than previous bailout efforts, creating the breathing space necessary to make changes to the EU's structure that would not have been politically impossible before the crisis. The stability such actions created has allowed EU leaders in the Troika to engage in sort of a policy "one-two," using ECB actions to reassure credit markets in the short term, while allowing political leaders to consider a wider set of actions and treaty reforms meant to improve the long-term structure of the Eurozone. EU actions have primarily focused on changes to fiscal policy making in the union intended to create stricter adherence to Maastricht conditions regarding debt and deficit stability, and more recently changes in the structure of the banking system of the EU. Both efforts might also be seen to have begun the greater political integration the currency union was originally missing. The following sections provide a narrative of the crisis timeline, attempting to explain policy outcomes in the context of events as they occurred from 2009 to 2013.

From Financial Tremors to Political Crisis, Policy Reaction in the First Phase of the Euro Crisis

While the Greek election results of October 4, 2009 signaled changes in Greece, few would have imagined how profound those changes would be. In the weeks following the election, the new Greek government found revisions were necessary regarding the previously Greek deficit, which was more than tripled overnight from 3.7% of GDP to 12.5%. It would soon be revised even higher. Debt to GDP in the country would also be revised upward significantly but announced statistics were almost meaningless. It was clear Greece's debt was much worse than previously thought and worse it appeared to be the case that no one was really sure how large it was. Suddenly, the safety of Greek debt was very uncertain. The Euro crisis had begun. As described in Table 1, the first policy phase of the European financial crisis began in late October 2009 and can be described as lasting until July 2011. During this time, policy was primarily reactive as European leaders struggled to both comprehend the crisis and adapt to rapidly changing financial and economic conditions. As Greek revelations undermined confidence in Greek debt in late 2009, concerns arose regarding how a potential default could affect the currency union. Behind closed doors, leaders in Europe were both taken by surprise and angered by Greece's admission that it had systematically understated its debt and deficits over the past decade, leaving their response to the resulting consequences flat-footed.[6]

Market uncertainty increased as, sensing this indecision, creditors became uncertain any aid would be forthcoming should Greece find it was unable to meet its debt obligations, leading to a rapid deterioration in Greek bond rates. European leaders' initial responses to the resulting crisis were not reassuring, as they primarily attempted to maintain market confidence through a series of optimistic assessments that Greek (and later Irish and Portuguese) debt problems could be dealt with internally through market reforms. Markets, however, were not about to be swayed by such

Table 1. Stages of Euro Crisis Policy Response

Stage	Phase	Dates	Important Events
Stage 1: Working within existing EU/Eurozone Framework	Phase 1: Credit Guarantees and Bailouts	October 2009 to July 2011	• Greek Bailout #1 (May 2010) • Irish Bailout (November 2010) • Portuguese Bailout (May 2011)
	Phase 2: Bail-ins and Haircuts	July 2011 to December 2011	• Greek bailout #2 (July 2011 to February 2012)
Stage 2: Modifying the EU/Eurozone Framework	Phase 3: ECB Market Liquidity Efforts And Monetary Union Structural Reform	December 2011 to Spring 2013	• ECB LTRO loans 1&2 (December 2011, March 2012) • The Big Bazooka: ECB programs to support sovereign debt in secondary markets. (July to August 2012) • Implementation of Fiscal Compact (January to March 2013) • Implementation of a banking union efforts (September 2012 to present)

rhetoric. They became much more driven by what they perceived to be market fundamentals—country-specific economic conditions. The new Greek government had promised fundamental and wide-ranging reforms to the tax collection and government expenditures in response to deteriorating conditions in its sovereign bond markets, but these promises to reverse the course of their sovereign debt crisis were not considered credible. As market conditions worsened in the early spring of 2010, Greek debt was quickly realized to be too large to remain sustainable. Meanwhile, Eurozone leaders struggled to create the political will necessary to support Greece.

Leader's hesitation to respond to the financial crisis caused by Greece was also caused by the backlash experienced in many European countries to the possibility their resources might be called upon to stabilize Greek finances. In Germany in particular, the reaction against such aid was vocal. Having struggled with the increased debt levels and slow growth caused by German reunification and having done so without external aid, Germans argued that the principles of independence and self-reliance were paramount. The Eurozone was intentionally designed with prohibitions against joint liability being created across countries as the common currency was implemented. To aid a country, especially one that had "cooked its books" to appear as if it were following Maastricht Treaty rules it was argued, would only encourage moral hazard, allowing Greece to avoid the consequences of accountability for its own decisions and poor governance.[7]

Poor governance had been Greece's problem. Since the introduction of the euro, as interest rates fell, growth in Greece had been debt-driven, particularly in the public sector. Unsustainable increases in the size and pay levels of the Greek civil service had been driven by political incentives as successive Greek governments had used such changes to gain political favor. Simultaneously, Greek pension programs had become increasingly underfunded as entitlements became more generous while publicly provided social benefits also expanded. The state had also assumed greater liability for debts accrued by public enterprises as their borrowing grew over this time.[8] To aid Greece under such circumstances, it was argued in Germany and elsewhere, would be tantamount to rewarding such poor governance, and worse, it would not correct the problem.

As credit market conditions continued to worsen for Greece in early 2010, however, leaders in Europe realized they had to act. Worsening the situation, Europe had no experience in managing a sovereign debt crisis within one of its own member nations, and the optics of soliciting aid from the IMF, the agency most often tasked with managing aid to countries in such crises, was considered politically embarrassing. Europe was a continent used to providing aid, not requesting it.

Despite the distaste leaders had for aiding Greece given the source of its problems, despite concerns regarding moral hazard and the EU's prohibitions against the concept of joint liability across countries, and even despite electoral resistance to the idea of a Greek bailout, there was really no choice. Default by Greece could create a chaotic and unpredictable situation in financial markets, and Europe's financial institutions were not ready to face another serious shock so soon after the world financial crisis of 2008. The facts of the situation were clear by early 2010: Greece would definitely need external aid if it were to avoid default and the amount of aid needed was large and would be very politically difficult to raise internally. Lacking experience to deal with such a situation and needing all the resources it could muster, European leaders eventually turned to the IMF to coordinate and contribute their eventual aid program.

The resulting European/IMF response, the first of the European bailouts, arrived 6 months after the crisis had begun. The bailout plan unveiled in May 2010 by the Troika would cost €110 billion, or almost half of the Greece's entire GDP from the previous year, and in addition to the financial aid, rested on three pillars that would define the general framework of the bailouts to follow. First, the plan required fiscal reductions. Greece would be required to immediate implement a severe and difficult austerity program. This program would aim to reduce Greece's fiscal deficit by 14.5% of GDP by 2014, a huge reduction by international standards. Deficit reduction would be accomplished by a series of expenditure reductions in social benefits and pension payments along with cuts in public works and services, and through tax revenue increases. Second, the plan attempted to create financial market stability. The Greek banking system would be supported by a dedicated set of funds to support it, avoiding a banking sector collapse and providing the liquidity necessary to support an eventual economic recovery. Finally, the plan outlined a program of structural reform. Greece would be required to reduce or eliminate labor market protections, and implement productivity improvements meant to allow the economy to return to growth and to allow an improvement in its external trade balance. IMF projections optimistically suggested that, while the scale of aid was unprecedented and conditions imposed on Greece severe, application of a bailout under these terms would allow growth to return in Greece by late 2012.

The bailout was also accompanied by a pair of additional actions meant to protect Europe from the fallout of the Greek crisis. The ECB began a limited intervention in the secondary markets for Greek bonds in an attempt to help stabilize its sovereign debt rates. Intervention also began in Portuguese and Irish markets as events in Greece had led markets to consider the debt sustainability of these countries as well. To prevent Greek market instability from spilling over to other European nations, Europe also embarked on creating a financial firewall to protect the rest of the European financial system from the risks Greece posed. Along with the announcement of the Greek bailout in May 2010, a significant new Eurozone mechanism, the EFSF was also announced, creating a temporary

€500 billion 3-year lending facility meant specifically to address the debt crisis and any potential needs of other countries should conditions worsen and additional bailouts be necessary.[9] They would be.

While Europe hoped the actions taken with respect to Greece would arrest the crisis, market contagion only worsened as concern spread to additional countries in the currency union, resulting in two additional bailouts being necessary for Ireland and Portugal. Confidence in European sovereign debt had been irreparably impaired. As in Greece, markets anticipated the need for bailouts in these countries months before authorities admitted their necessity. Again delays occurred for the same reasons as experienced for Greece, while the severe terms of the Greek bailout caused Irish and Portuguese authorities to defer aid as long as possible in hopes of avoiding similar conditions being imposed on them. Eventually though market conditions caused pressures on both countries to become intolerable as rising sovereign rates made maintaining financial stability within both countries impossible and debt sustainability unmanageable. As Irish sovereign bond rates increased to levels twice those of core countries in the Europe, in November 2010 Ireland was forced to agree to an €85 billion bailout made necessary by the fallout from the collapse of its real-estate bubble 2 years before. Similar bond rate increases caused Portugal to seek a €78 billion aid package in May 2011, a bailout made necessary by a recession, high debt levels and a recent banking crisis. Both the Irish and Portuguese bailouts were again financed jointly by the IMF and EU through its new EFSF and were conditional on each country pledging to take on fiscal expenditure reductions and structural reforms requiring onerous austerity measures.

Bailouts were intended as a final solution meant to restore market confidence. Credit guarantees from northern countries were meant to ensure debt obligations would be honored for troubled ones. In return, strict austerity programs in aided countries, characterized by sharp reductions in government expenditures for pensions, income support and social programs, state asset sales, and reductions in public-sector workforces, were meant to ensure northern taxpayers would be repaid. Austerity programs were also meant to appease critics in countries financing the bailout that profligate expenditure practices had been reformed, especially in bailed out southern economies. If northern economies were to risk their own treasure it would not be for nothing, the result would be permanent reforms to repair troubled economies thereby preventing future crises. For bond markets the strict austerity and conditionality required in each bailout was meant to signal reform and budgetary changes to ensure future debt stability, which it was hoped would eventually allow credit markets to reopen for these countries.

Nevertheless, market pressures continued. Bailout measures, as significant as they were totaling almost 50% of the combined 2009 GDP of the three aided countries, had not restored market confidence, nor had they reduced the market uncertainty they were intended to reverse. The progression of interest rate increases followed by bailouts, followed by concerns arising in a new country can be seen in the pattern of interest rate increases shown in Figure 1a,b. In each case, a bailout in one country that was intended to arrest the crisis only caused market concerns eventually to focus elsewhere. Markets were not to be impressed by the truly massive scale of European aid that had been pledged, and instead seemed more concerned by the frictions in implementing these policies. The denials and delay caused by political skepticism and populist anger in creditor countries that impeded the Troika's efforts to resolve the situation speedily only focused attention on which countries were likely to also require relief next, and whether the currency union could withstand these continual demands for aid.

Long before European leaders acknowledged the problem, markets also became aware that the dynamics of aid were leading to troubling patterns of political instability. Contributing countries' electorates rapidly began to suffer from bailout fatigue as expansive and expensive credit guarantees were unsuccessful in stemming market pressures and resistance to further aid efforts began to build. In southern countries political pressures were also rising. The costs of austerity measures meant to improve debt sustainability caused angry publics in Greece and Portugal not only to blame their own politicians, but also created tremendous resentment toward their northern EU neighbors who were seen to have forced such conditions in return for relief. In both creditor and debtor nations it appeared many people were asking if such help was worth the cost, and markets became more and more wary that Europe would stand behind its currency union.

The primary concern for European leaders in the crisis, however, remained Greece. Interest rates there had continued to rise despite the first aid agreement and subsequent efforts as markets correctly reasoned the resources pledged in the first bailout were inadequate. As it became clear a second Greek bailout would be necessary, it also became clear markets demanded greater guarantees than previous policy efforts had provided. Rising political instability in Greece also damaged the country's outlook. The government seemed to be losing control and its public support earned in elections less than 2 years before was rapidly melting away. Large and sometimes violent demonstrations were commonplace as citizens protested rapidly worsening economic conditions. Riots in the streets of Athens demonstrated the vehemence felt in Greece against the market reforms northern nations demanded in return for aid. The Greek government, in the face of such opposition, appeared unwilling and unable to deliver the promised restructuring in state obligations and taxation programs its bailout pledges demanded and rapidly fell behind those deadlines.

The progress and policy efforts of the Euro crisis had not improved many observers' outlooks for the currency union and in some ways had worsened it. Austerity programs were problematic in Greece and elsewhere they appeared to only create greater recessions in troubled countries, worsening state revenues, and potential debt sustainability. In southern states they stoked political crises that were making reform efforts nearly impossible in Greece and very difficult in Portugal. Far from soothing market conditions, bailout efforts, as massive as they had been, and efforts to stabilize sovereign debt markets and financial systems had failed to improve the symptoms of the crisis. It was clear more would need to be done and a change in approach might also be necessary.

The first phase of the crisis had focused on attempting to stabilize sovereign debt market uncertainty by avoiding default. To accomplish this, the sovereign debt obligations of bailed out countries had been transferred from private creditors to northern creditor-nation taxpayers, making them liable for southern countries' debts. As it became clear additional resources would be needed to support Greece, it also became clear that northern taxpayers were increasingly unwilling to increase that country's credit line, and that to attempt to do so would only endanger the domestic survival of the political leaders supporting such a deal. Simultaneously, austerity programs in Greece appeared to only create a deteriorating situation in that troubled country, worsening state revenues and potential debt sustainability while undermining its political stability.

If a new solution was to be found, it would be difficult to increase the liabilities of northern taxpayers to cover the southern obligations alone and there was little more the southern public could or was willing to contribute to their own aid. If the crisis was to be resolved, it would now also require new resources to be called upon and impose sacrifices on those who had not yet borne a cost. It would require a reduction in the obligations held by private debt holders. Moral hazard also applied to lenders. They had made risky loans and if their loans were protected by bailouts what was to stop them from making such risky loans again. Lenders too would have to be made responsible for the risks they had undertaken in making the now troubled loans to Greece.

Phase 2—Bail-ins, Haircuts, and Worsening Political Conditions

Despite the credit guarantees and austerity programs imposed on Greece, Ireland, and Portugal, conditions in bond markets had gradually worsened for each of these countries. Adding to EU leader's concerns, the banking system across the Eurozone was being rapidly weakened and now showing the strain caused by bond market conditions, the creeping recession now spreading over Europe and rising uncertainty regarding the euro. As markets again turned their attention to Greece, it became clear that initial efforts to stabilize Greek debt levels had failed and that new plan was necessary. Assumptions made over the previous year for creditor and aided countries had proven far too optimistic—growth was not returning to the Eurozone and outcomes in aided countries were proving far worse than originally forecast.

Austerity measures, social unrest, and political uncertainty had plunged the Greek economy into a far worse recession than the IMF and EU had expected.[10] Similar concerns, although to a lesser extent, also appeared in Ireland and Portugal. These recessions, combined with the uncertainty that now lay like a gray cloud over all of Europe was also resulting in worsening economic conditions throughout the Eurozone. Lack of improvement in the crisis, forced European policy makers to admit the crisis would not to be short-lived and more drastic and difficult actions than those already pursued would be necessary if they were to navigate through the storm now upon them. Plans were made to shore up existing policy efforts, implementing a permanent Eurozone firewall in 2011 through treaty reforms creating the ESM to buttress the temporary EFSF, which was to expire in 2013. The ECB also increased efforts to contain interest rate increases in sovereign debt markets through an expansion of its intervention efforts. As conditions worsened in 2011 new ideas were also considered, specifically consideration of the possibilities some form of joint liability across nations might offer to curb the crisis. Additionally, creditor losses became a serious policy consideration. Phase 2 of the crisis represented an evolution and expansion in those policies begun in Phase 1. It also marked a period in which Eurozone countries paused to consider their commitment to the monetary union. And in this period they determined that private-sector creditors would have to contribute.

In late spring and early summer of 2011, protracted negotiations were continuing in Athens and Brussels regarding the potential expansion of Greek aid. Bailout-fatigue, however, was worsening both in the halls of power and on the streets of creditor nations, particularly the largest of the creditors, Germany. Critics of expanded aid, both the original actions and any expansion in aid, claimed these efforts violated the terms of the Maastricht Treaty, specifically the prohibitions against countries taking on liability for another country's debts. Such arguments fell on deaf ears, with policy makers though, as bailout agreements passed national parliaments and were upheld in German constitutional courts. Detractors also found fault with ECB actions, arguing they were prohibited by rules against directly financing a member country's debt. Criticism remained vocal as opponents of aid saw both bailouts and ECB market interventions as contraventions of EU treaties in principle if not technically.[11] For many, bailouts implied the breaking of a moral principle, one in which debtors should be solely responsible for their own obligations and the consequences of not meeting them.

Moral hazard concerns were not limited only to the governments receiving aid. In the first phase of the crisis moral hazard concerns had been focused on the public sector, with bailout terms meant to ensure aid was not seen as rewarding poor governance. In the second phase of the crisis attention turned to moral hazard in the private sector. Bailout actions to date had imposed burdens of debt and austerity on citizens within the affected countries, and also on the taxpayers in the creditor nations who financed the aid packages. Each of the three original bailouts had transferred the risk of default from the original financial creditors who had bought the bonds to the taxpayers of nations financing the rescues. Buyers of the bonds at the center of the crisis had not shared in any costs of the bailouts.

As resistance to greater bailout aid grew, so too did pressure to include creditors in the costs of such efforts, including them in what has been referred to in official documents as "private sector involvement" or "PSI" in bailout agreements. Unofficially, these efforts have been referred to as debt "haircuts" or bail-ins—those who owned the bonds would now suffer some losses in return for having the rest of the original investment preserved. This idea had been considered previously, but only became official policy when formally announced as part of a new Greek bailout, the first outlines of which were announced in July 2011.[12] Supported by the IMF where the practice was common in IMF-sponsored bailouts elsewhere in the world, the ECB and some EU members of the Troika had resisted the idea during the first phase of the crisis arguing the threat of private-sector losses could further destabilize markets, undermining the purpose of aid efforts. Reducing debt, it was also argued, would cause additional moral hazard by rewarding aided governments with reduced debt loads. Moral hazard could work both ways, however, for debtors and lenders and given additional resources were needed to stabilize Greece as part of a larger agreement, such concerns were over-ruled. In an important precedent, it was determined additional aid to Greece would include private sector write-downs on a portion of the debts outstanding. This important policy decision, however, was only the first in a lengthy negotiation to resolve the second aid package for Greece.

The question of additional aid for Greece also created more existential dilemmas for leaders in both creditor nations and in Athens. Given the fact that Greece would require greater support to remain solvent, creditor nations faced a deeper dilemma. Without additional assistance, Greece faced default. Fallout from such an event would still pose significant risk to Europe's financial system, especially to the largest creditor nations France and Germany whose banks still had the greatest exposure to Greek debt. But additional aid also risked domestic political fallout from electorates now tired of pledging national resources to support other countries. Electorates and leaders in creditor countries, particularly Germany, had tired of the possibility of continued calls for aid. As it became clearer the crisis would be a lengthy one, the question began to arise whether it might not be better to reserve such resources for repairing the cost in individual national economies of what might be inevitable, a Greek default. The Eurozone had to decide whether it was committed to keeping Greece in the currency union. Similarly, Greece would have to decide whether it was committed to the conditions staying in the Eurozone required. It would be this question that would dominate the next 8 months of the crisis.

The second phase of the crisis marked a period of significantly greater uncertainty as the politics of continued aid worsened. When the initial framework of a new Greek bailout agreement was announced in July 2011, sovereign debt markets were initially calmed and bond rates began to fall, but as negotiations dragged on into Fall of 2011 between the Troika and Greece, it appeared questionable whether there was a politically will to find any solution at all. In Greece, austerity protests worsened. Speculation began to mount regarding whether the Greeks would elect to default and leave the euro to avoid accepting the greater austerity conditions additional aid would require. Targets regarding tax collection and public workforce cuts in Greece continued to be missed. In creditor nations, frustration began to characterize leaders' reactions to suspected Greek unwillingness and inability to deliver promised reforms and deficit reductions demanded in the first bailout. Negotiations bogged down and recriminations in both Greece and creditor nations became more common.

In the background, bond rates began a relentless rise across the southern European states as concerns worsened regarding Spanish and Italian debt, especially given the new policy of bondholder losses that had been invoked. Urged by Europe and the United States, Spain and Italy began pre-emptive austerity programs of their own, seeking to reverse rising deficits before they were forced to by markets. In an effort to stabilize the situation in these sovereign bond markets, the ECB also expanded its Securities Markets Program (SMP) begun in May 2010, increasing purchases of

Spanish and Italian bonds in August 2011 despite objections from Bundesbank officials in Germany. To observers it was becoming unclear if the willingness to preserve the monetary union was even present among some of the policy makers tasked with preserving it. Complicating matters further were emerging political crises in several troubled countries.

By mid-September, consensus among Eurozone members appeared to be breaking down. As conditions worsened in debt markets for troubled countries, the European Commission, the executive body of the EU suggested that collectivization of the European debt was necessary. Several proposals emerged to create Eurobonds, bonds that could be swapped for individual nation's debts and backed by the entire Eurozone. The purpose of such actions would be to explicitly back the debt of troubled nations by the collective resources of the entire Eurozone and the strong credit ratings of northern states, thereby restoring confidence that default would be avoided in markets. Germany, among other countries, was staunch in its opposition to such proposals, arguing that such actions would not only violate the terms of the Maastricht Treaty, but would also create moral hazard in aided countries, reducing the pressure to enact difficult economic reforms necessary to increase productivity.[13] Internal politics in Germany was also influential as it was feared extending Germany's commitment would lead to political crisis in that country. France publicly backed Germany in this response and eventually the proposals were quietly dropped.

Still, despite the defeat of Eurobond proposals, sharp divisions between Germany and the EU were still apparent over the expansion of EU efforts to resolve the crisis. Germany and other northern creditor states such as Finland and Austria pressed for the adoption of long-term reforms in the Eurozone, focusing on the need to enshrine fiscal reforms across Eurozone nations to ensure fiscal rectitude. Pundits suggested this approach was akin to prescribing a healthy diet to a patient in the midst of a heart attack. The European Commission and the ECB continued to focus on more short-term considerations, arguing the most pressing policies needed were those that would address the difficult financial market conditions. Critics of these policies argued they did not address the causes of the crisis or that they violated EU rules. Such policy conflicts became especially apparent in late summer 2011 at the ECB when Jürgen Stark, a German member of the Executive Board and chief economist at the ECB resigned in opposition to the ECB's decision the month previous to begin buying Spanish and Italian debt in an effort to reduce interest rate pressures on those countries' bond rates.[14]

The austerity costs of the previous bailout agreements led to a political backlash in Portugal and Greece, and additionally in Spain and Italy where austerity efforts had also been undertaken to reduce pressures in their own sovereign debt markets. Across southern Europe, protests and more violent confrontations became more common as austerity policies now gripping these countries affected more and more people. In Greece, support for Prime Minister George Papandreou's government was quickly eroded. Negotiations over the new bailout continued into Fall despite the apparent agreement the previous July. As fiscal targets were missed, Eurozone creditors demanded greater cuts. Greeks argued the reason targets had not been met was in part due to the effect austerity was having on their economy, which had plunged into deep recession. As usual, northern creditor nations responded by invoking the familiar argument that such efforts encouraged moral hazard. Both sides appeared unwilling to compromise but only one had the resources. The golden rule of finance would soon be invoked—"he who has the gold makes the rules," but as might be expected this reality created resentments that only made reaching a solution more difficult.

Economic crisis had now clearly turned into a political crisis. Internal political problems in troubled countries beyond Greece, specifically Spain, Italy, and Portugal where austerity was deeply unpopular, resulted in widespread civil unrest. Political indecision was apparent among Eurozone members as approval efforts for the newest Greek rescue package dragged on through September and October. Internally, Chancellor Merkel easily won a confidence vote over extension of the second Greek bailout, but the difficult debate in Germany underlined the political tightrope even she was walking despite her tough stances at European negotiations. It was still unclear whether the EU would actually deliver the new aid promised the previous July, or even future installments aid promised in the first bailout and so necessary to avoid a Greek default. Despite the fact that a Greek default would almost certainly result in a financial crisis across Europe, EU member countries appeared to hesitate in their efforts to quell the situation. Concern began to mount whether there was even commitment to do so among member nations in the Eurozone. By late summer speculation was loud regarding whether Greece would be forced to default and leave the euro. Additional speculation began to consider other possible outcomes including whether countries in the north of Europe, those with the strongest economies might choose to leave the currency union given the political unpopularity of the bailouts.

Eventually Greek negotiations culminated with an eleventh hour deal in late October, one that outlined a new bailout agreement between the Troika and Greece. While greeted with approval in most of Europe the deal was met with outrage in Greece for the additional austerity measures it imposed. Faced with greater opposition than had been expected domestically, the Greek Prime Minister appeared to back away from the deal, suggesting that acceptance would require a national referendum. European leader's response was immediate and incredulous. Papandreou's reversal seemed only to underline Troika concerns the Greeks were not willing partners in the aid efforts being made to avoid a Greek default and by extension to protect the euro. The suggestion of a bailout referendum was eventually withdrawn but the damage was done. The Greek government's indecision was punished—it fell in a vote of no confidence in the first week of November. With Greek opposition parties unwilling to be associated with controversial bailout discussions and the public now blaming establishment politicians in both parties for the troubles the country found itself in, little political support could be found to take the reins of power since doing so would require administering painful bailout commitments. The result was the imposition of an unelected technocratic government charged with implementing previously agreed to bailout terms and negotiating a new agreement. It would serve until new elections could be held the following spring. Bailout conditions remained unresolved, but public anger in Greece only worsened as many people there felt democracy had been suspended.

Simultaneously, while the drama of the Greek negotiations and government's failure dominated the news, the Italian government fell. While ostensibly committed to reducing their debt level, the Italian government had also not implemented promised reforms. In what appeared a populist bid for support, Prime Minister Silvio Berlusconi began to question the austerity calls the Troika were making in exchange for aid elsewhere. Again the Eurozone was taken by surprise as Italy was expected to cooperate in presenting a common front for Europe as negotiations continued with Greece. Opponents of the Italian government took advantage of the political unpopularity of the sitting government and engineered a successful vote of no confidence over its inability and unwillingness to implement market reforms, leading to Berlusconi stepping down. Once more, however, opposition parties were unwilling to take the reins to implement what were certain to be unpopular policies. The ruling government was replaced by a technocratic one, with a mandate extending to the next election in 2013. It was to be led by a former European Commissioner, Mario Monti, who was seen as a willing partner in attempting to stabilize the crisis. As in Greece, the new government's charge was to implement austerity measures and market reforms necessary to maintain the country's perceived debt sustainability, which had been eroded both by a worsening recession and rising bond rates. Again those bearing the costs of austerity wondered whether democracy had been suspended and whether their interests were being sacrificed for those elsewhere.

Political dramas continued across southern Europe. The government of Spain fell a week after the Italian government did. Deeply unpopular, the sitting government was defeated in a landslide over its management of the economy, and was widely blamed for both the recession that had occurred after the Spanish real-estate bubble had burst in 2007, and the more recently for austerity measures implemented to appease sovereign bond pressures. By the end of November 2011, the tally of political victims included three more governments falling in less than a month, and including the defeat of the Portuguese government after its bailout in May 2011, the governments of all of the southern periphery countries now at the center of the crisis had been replaced. Including the resignation of the Irish Prime Minister and fall of his government in January 2011, also precipitated by the economic crisis and reaction to austerity conditions the country was forced to accept as part of its bailout, in less than a year the crisis had taken down all five GIPSI governments.

By mid-December 2011, sovereign bond rates continued to increase across GIPSI countries. Most troubling, Italian and Spanish rates were now approaching the same levels that had instigated bailouts elsewhere. It was understood that in the case of these countries the resources in the Eurozone did not exist to offer similar aid to its third and fourth largest economies. The combined sizes of the economies of Greece, Ireland, and Portugal represented about 5.8% of total output in the Eurozone in 2011, but Italy represented an economy almost three times larger, making up 16.8% of Eurozone output. Using IMF figures from September 2011, Italy's total public debt was over €1.9 trillion—larger than the combined annual economic output of 12 of the 16 other nations in the Eurozone and dwarfing the collective liabilities of Greece, Ireland, and Portugal, which totaled €693 billion in the same period. Spain, while smaller than Italy, still represented an economy over twice the size of previously bailed-out countries and over 11% of Eurozone output. While Spain's debt–GDP ratio was more manageable, just under 70% in late 2011, the value of that debt was still over €730 billion. In late 2011, the Eurozone was stretched politically to support the bailouts already incurred. If Italy and Spain were to become unable to support its debts in private markets, resources in EU would not be large enough to simply create another bailout—if these countries failed; the European monetary union would too. Two years after the crisis had begun and despite the allocation of billions of euros to protect it, the Eurozone seemed more fragile than it had ever been.

During the period from November 2009 to December 2011, market uncertainties had worsened as policy reactions proved inadequate, often ill-timed and ineffective. Far from improving, economic conditions deteriorated across the Eurozone. Bailout actions meant to save the euro had become deeply unpopular in both aiding and aided nations. The Greek bailout continued to remain unresolved and whether Greece would be allowed to default was still uncertain. Even if defaults were not to occur, private creditors holding Greek debt were uncertain how large a haircut their assets might be expected to experience in any new bailout agreement. Actions by the ECB and Eurozone leaders to arrest the crisis had been constrained by their own domestic politics and the perceived limits of the treaty conditions under which the Eurozone operated. The continued decline in market confidence as exhibited by a relentless rise in interest rates for most countries using the euro, combined with a decline of the euro on world currency markets caused policy makers to begin to consider how the rules governing the monetary union could be changed to encourage a renewal of market confidence.

Phase 3—Expanding Market Liquidity, Structural Reforms, and the Big Bazooka

The first example of the new approach to policy a desperate EU would finally take in a bid to gain control of the crisis came in late December 2011. By Fall of 2011, it was apparent previous policy actions had done little to arrest the crisis as bond-market conditions had continued to worsen and were now affecting the Spanish and Italian whose size made them too large to bailout. On December 21, 2011 the ECB embarked on a new effort to free-up credit markets in the Eurozone. These markets had frozen as political and economic conditions worsened in the Eurozone. Banks in troubled GIPSI economies, in particular, were known to have significant amounts of debt due early in the new year, and credit markets had almost dried up as financial institutions anticipated the credit scarcity this would cause. To address this problem, the ECB unexpectedly allowed banks across the euro area access to 3-year low-interest loans, referred to officially as the Long Term Refinancing Operation (LTRO). These loans allowed banks to refinance the debt obligations coming due and avoided what appeared to be an impending financial crisis. They also allowed financial institutions the ability to earn income by using the low-interest loans to purchase higher yielding sovereign debt in their own countries, which reduced pressures in sovereign debt markets as well. A second round of loans was offered in February 2012 and together the two actions poured more than €1 trillion into Eurozone banks, allowing the ECB to engage in a massive effort to restore liquidity to Eurozone financial institutions and by extension sovereign debt markets.

Because financial crises cause banks to become illiquid—banks become unable to borrow due to market fears regarding their solvency—fears tend to become self-fulfilling. Banks fail as they cannot obtain financing to cover their debt obligations despite the fact that they may be fundamentally sound. The potential to arrest such crises had been known since the 1870s when Walter Bagehot wrote *Lombard Street*. That account described how a central bank, acting as a lender of last resort, could arrest financial crises by providing massive quantities of liquidity into financial markets.[15] Such actions, he argued, reverse the expectations causing the crisis by restoring liquidity, thereby restoring faith in the financial system and allowing it to function again. The potential effectiveness of such policy has been shown in numerous financial crises since, including in the United States in 2008.

The injection of new liquidity the ECB's actions represented immediately caused market concerns to ease and Eurozone sovereign bond rates to decline. The action was not one that had been expected, as traditionally the role of the ECB had been perceived to be passive, and in the past even relatively modest interventions in sovereign debt markets had been controversial. Under new leadership after Mario Draghi had succeeded the former ECB President Jean-Claude Trichet, and with the Eurozone clearly in need of a new policy approach, the ECB signaled its willingness to break with old assumptions and also that it was now willing to expand its actions as necessary to ease conditions. The LTRO actions succeeded in reversing the upward trend in Italian, Spanish, and Irish debt that had occurred in the previous quarter. As 2012 began to unfold, for the first time in over 2 years market conditions began to ease. This allowed the Eurozone some much needed breathing space to develop longer term policies.

Throughout the period from 2009 through late 2011, EU policy to stem the Euro crisis had focused on stemming immediate issues. Policy was primarily concerned with reacting to sovereign debt problems in markets with bailouts and later bail-ins, and developing a firewall to shield additional countries should the contagion in sovereign debt markets spread. The ECB's actions signaled of a new EU approach and a break with previous policy thinking. The second stage of the crisis would now focus on exploiting the ECB's ability to manage symptoms of the crisis in sovereign debt markets while EU leaders began to focus on addressing the long-term structural problems that had contributed to the Euro crisis occurring.

The first structural change leaders embraced was one spearheaded by Germany to establish debt brakes on member states' budgets. This was accomplished by the creation of a new "fiscal compact" in which Eurozone nations agreed to enact national legislation requiring limits in national debt and deficits, thereby ensuring the debt conditions that had contributed to the crisis would not occur again. The details of this effort began in late 2011 and were finalized in early 2012. The new rules were meant to ensure Maastricht convergence conditions were better adhered to. Specifically, the compact required Eurozone countries to implement constitution-level laws requiring they adhere to Maastricht limits and further, that structural deficits not exceed one-half of 1% of a country's GDP. They also mandated debt reductions if a country's national debt–GDP ratio exceeded the Maastricht maximum of 60%.[16] Exceptions would only be allowed in special circumstances and would require approval of the European Commission. Required treaty changes ensuring these new rules came into force occurred between March and December 2012 and the agreement came into force in January 2013.

The ECB's LTRO actions also allowed the Troika a period of calm in which to complete a comprehensive new Greek aid plan in February 2012 and to address the shortcomings of the first aid package. Worth €130 billion, the package included significant austerity conditions, and required additional structural reforms and privatization of government assets. The agreement also included strong conditionality, specifying the Greek actions required in the agreement to be implemented before funding payments could be released. These would require additional tax revenues, public sector employee reductions, and additional expenditure cuts. Bail-out funds would be disbursed to a kind of international escrow account to ensure they were used as specified and only if conditions were met. The agreement also formalized a bail-in, the private sector write-downs announced the year previous and the negotiation of which had proven very difficult. The final negotiations of these haircuts as they were often referred to, had been in part responsible for the months delay in reaching a final Greek agreement. The new deal imposed losses on private sovereign debt-holders of 53.5% on the face value of bonds held using a debt-buyback financed by the EFSF. Overall, the agreement decreased Greek debt by an estimated €110 billion, and allowed the plan to lower the Greek debt–GDP ratio from a forecast level of 198% to 160% in 2012, and the projected ratio to 120.5% by 2020.[17]

In March 2012, still taking advantage of the calm in markets, the Euro-zone also finalized the implementation of its permanent bailout fund, called the ESM. Meant to replace the EFSF that was due to expire in June 2013, this fund would provide permanent ability in the EU's architecture to address financial crises of the sort that beset the currency union after the Greek surprise of 2009. The ESM was initially allocated a lending capacity worth €500 billion, and temporarily increased the Eurozone's total bailout facilities to over €800 billion, at least until the EFSF was to be terminated in just over a year.[18]

By the end of the first quarter it had begun to seem like the crisis may have reached a turning point. The momentum following the breakthrough in conditions the ECB's LTRO operations had enabled seemed to allow EU leaders to finally get ahead of the crisis, as they enacted both structural reforms with the fiscal compact, and addressed new policies meant to shore up previous efforts with the new Greek bailout package and the finalization of the ESM. EU leaders seemed to be regaining a feeling of confidence even if such confidence was not yet returning to European economies. Clouds, however, still remained on the horizon.

As 2012 marched on into the second quarter those clouds slowly became more ominous, and the period of calm that characterized the first few months of 2012 began to worsen. Two political changes would soon shatter the previous calm like a thunderclap. In April 2012, the French presidential election resulted in the need for a runoff as France's incumbent President Nicolas Sarkozy failed to secure a majority of votes, nor even to place first among the election's 10 candidates in voting. Sarkozy and Germany's Chancellor Angela Merkel, leaders of the Eurozone's two largest economies had maintained a carefully coordinated policy front during the first 2 years of the Euro crisis, and had used their combined political and economic power to guide Eurozone policy since the crisis in Greece first began.

The efforts of the two countries' leaders had been very effective. For Germany, French support helped secure the tough positions Merkel preferred regarding austerity and debt reduction. It also allowed Germany to shield itself from being perceived as setting the terms of EU policy unilaterally. While Europe recognized its wealthiest country held the greatest say, having France on-board gave the impression of a more conciliatory process. For France, the partnership had allowed the country to preserve its national pride, as the country could claim to be at the center of EU decision making. Sarkozy's leadership and style, however, had been controversial in France and the Euro crisis and domestic events throughout his term both undermined his support. In a runoff held the following 5th and 6th of May, after a very hard-fought campaign Sarkozy was defeated by the socialist-party candidate François Hollande, whose party was not allied Chancellor Merkel's policies. The political alliance that had been most influential in guiding European policy since the currency crisis had begun was now broken, leaving Germany influence as dominant voice of Eurozone creditor countries obvious. It also created additional uncertainty regarding the direction of future policy. Previously, with the leaders of the Eurozone's two largest economies in agreement, policy making had been more predictable than it might otherwise given the structure of the EU's governance. Now markets worried that the Eurozone could potentially find itself dangerously split if the leaders of France and Germany pursued alternative agendas.

This major change in the leadership of the EU came on the same day as legislative elections in Greece. Widely viewed as a *de facto* referendum on the second Greek bailout and Greece's willingness to remain in the Eurozone, the results of the election were inconclusive and no party was able to create a ruling coalition. Voters, clearly frustrated by the crushing recession brought on by Greece's near-default, and deep austerity measures imposed on their economy by the subsequent bailout, punished their mainstream parties and turned instead to populist and anti bailout candidates, leaving the Greek Parliament unable to create a ruling government. The specter of Greek default, though to be banished from the Eurozone only 2 months earlier, had suddenly reemerged. Results of the election underlined concerns Greece might not have the capacity or willingness to abide by its most recent bailout agreement, or the willingness to commit to measures that avoided default. Uncertainty rushed back into markets and speculation whirled that what became known as "Grexit," a Greek exit from the currency union, might be imminent. A 6-week period of uncertainty followed, and sovereign debt rates for Greece shot back up to levels of almost 30%, heights last seen just before the Greek bailout in February had been negotiated.

Market tensions remained high awaiting the outcome of a second election 6 weeks later. The result was a narrow victory by parties supporting the bailout, allowing a thin majority coalition government to be formed. While the results of the second election were widely interpreted as confirming Greek willingness to remain in Eurozone, the lack of a result in the first election had proven costly, delaying the implementation of bailout reforms required in the second agreement reached 3 months earlier. The delay caused by the 6-week electoral delay had left Greece far short of the debt targets the country needed to meet to receive the bailout aid promised in its February agreement. Given how aid was now disbursed to Greece, it was now unclear whether the second bailout agreement could remain in effect. The narrow but favorable election victory in Greece had not exorcised markets' rediscovered default concerns.

Political changes were not the only challenges the Eurozone faced in fateful late spring and early summer of 2012. A third test of the Eurozone also presented itself, even before the second Greek election was resolved. During late spring of 2012, while political attention was centered on Greek and French elections, Spain faced a banking crisis as loan losses stemming from that country's real estate and construction crash in 2008, coupled with a brutally deep recession and unemployment rates above 20% left its banking system in crisis. By late spring it became clear the country would need a significant recapitalization of several of its largest banks. Despite ongoing efforts over the past 2 years to restructure the Spanish banking sector, problems had not been resolved. Loan failure rates had worsened and the country found itself in a position in which it could not sustainably finance the required resources needed to stabilize its financial system. As these conditions became apparent, concerns regarding the continuing threat of a default in Greece, and now a financial crisis in Spain had a contagious effect on sovereign debt markets, causing bond rates for Portugal and Italy to soon begin to climb. As fears increased, funds began to be withdrawn from GIPSI nation banks and transferred to safe-haven countries, particularly Germany, once more leaving financial markets in southern Europe facing a liquidity crisis.

Less than 3 months earlier it had seemed the worst of the Euro crisis might have passed and that Europe might have turned a corner, but the calm that followed agreement on the second Greek bailout and ECB's LTRO loans now seemed more like a distant and pleasant memory. The relative calm Europe's markets had experienced in the Spring of 2012 had not signaled a turning point in the crisis, but had instead been more like the eye of a hurricane—it had not signaled the end of the storm but merely a pause before its imminent return. Within a period of 2 months, European sovereign debt markets and the continent's banking system moved from conditions that were better than they had been in 2 years, to their most serious test yet as three simultaneous threats had now emerged to threaten the currency union.

Conditions were also different now from what they had been in years past. The banking crisis and economic conditions in Spain made the need for a bailout apparent. Unlike what had occurred during earlier bailouts though, Spain, as the fourth largest economy in the Eurozone, found it commanded significant bargaining power over the terms of its bailout due to its economic size. To its credit and in its favor, the country had implemented significant austerity measures previously and its government had publicly committed to important structural reforms. Also, while its debt relative to GDP was rising quickly, it was not yet at levels like those seen in previously troubled countries. The problem facing Spain and the Eurozone was how to deal with the banking crisis there without creating a sovereign debt crisis as well. In the past, for example in Ireland, a similar banking crisis had caused the government there to be forced to assume the costs of recapitalization, which increased its debt level to heights considered unsustainable in private markets and leaving Ireland no choice but to request aid from the EU and IMF. In the case of Spain though, given it was a much larger economy, Europe could not afford such a sovereign bailout from a political or financial perspective.

The Eurozone could also not afford to let Spain fail. Given uncertainty created by political conditions in Greece and the threat of contagion a Spanish financial crisis failure could create in Europe, especially in Italy, the Eurozone changed its bailout strategy from that followed in past agreements and designed an aid package in which the burden on Spanish sovereign debt would be minimized. The agreement reached in principle a week before the second Greek election created a guarantee to finance up to €100 billion in aid specifically to support a Spanish bank bailout. While details were still to be determined and negotiations continued through the month, by end of June Eurozone leaders had decided to allow aid to be delivered directly to banks and not the government, thereby potentially avoiding an onerous increase in Spanish sovereign debt and the type of austerity conditions previous bailouts had required under the Troika.[19] In principle this, it was hoped, would ease sovereign debt market pressures.

Still, the agreement to offer Spain credit guarantees and the resolution of Greek elections did not quell market concerns, and sovereign bond rates remained high. Worsening the situation, on June 25, Cyprus also requested bailout aid. Since its entry into the Eurozone in 2008, the Cypriot banking industry had boomed as an offshore banking center with total deposits accumulating to a level seven times Cyprus's GDP. The banking sector had also accumulated significant amounts of Greek debt and the recent Greek bailout agreement, which included significant private-sector write-downs, had severely destabilized Cyprus's banking system, prompting the request.[20] The amount of aid this would entail, an estimated €10 billion, was considered very minor relative to previous packages, but given conditions—the uncertainty still surrounding Greece, Spain's banking problems, Italy's worsening debt rates, and now Cyprus's request for aid, concerns began to mount that the Eurozone could not avoid a system-wide financial crisis and imminent set of sovereign debt crises in the region. Such an event would overwhelm the Eurozone's financial firewall made up of the ESM and EFSF bailout funds. Given such concerns, many began to wonder if the currency union faced failure. The euro's exchange rate tumbled against major currencies to levels not seen since the start of the crisis and a virtual bank run began across Eurozone economies, particularly in southern states, as deposit holders attempted to transfer their wealth out of the Eurozone or into safe-haven economies, especially Germany.

Facing record volatility in both currency and sovereign bond markets, and a severe liquidity crisis that was spreading across the European banking system, the ECB was once more forced to act in an unprecedented way, and at the end of July 2012 it unleashed what the media dubbed the "big bazooka." Abiding by its mandate to maintain the stability of the euro, in a well-publicized speech the ECB's President Mario Draghi promised to do "whatever it takes" using the ECB's unlimited euro resources to stabilize the situation.[21] This statement, while only a comment in an otherwise seemingly innocuous speech describing the currency union's recent experiences, was immediately understood to imply the ECB now stood willing to enter sovereign debt markets in an unlimited way.[22] Actions would no longer be limited, as they would have been in previous programs to protect sovereign interest rates.[23] Calling on its potential to be a lender of last resort, the central bank had finally signaled it was willing to do what many had argued it should since shortly after the Euro crisis had begun. The ECB had threatened to use its unlimited power to purchase Eurozone sovereign debt as necessary to stabilize markets.

The initial announcement had an immediate impact on markets, which began to stabilize after having reached record levels for Spain and Italy. A week later the ECB formalized "whatever it takes," unveiling its Outright Monetary Transactions (OMT) program, outlining the conditions and procedures under which the ECB would intervene in sovereign bond markets. The announcement stated that in cases where a country had applied for a bailout, and agreed to the conditions under which the bailout was made, the ECB would be willing to purchase an unlimited quantity of government bonds on the secondary market to reduce interest-rate pressures. The roles of the ECB and the Troika were now clear. The Troika would define the conditions under which bailouts were made. Once these were agreed to the ECB would then stand ready to ensure interest rates were maintained. In principle, a bailout agreement should now resolve any future questions regarding a country's debt sustainability. Eliminating such concerns also implied the euro's stability was far sounder. As long as a country abided by the terms of its aid agreement the risk of default would be removed. Following this announcement bond market conditions immediately began to ease. As shown in Figure 1a,b, except for a brief period in March 2013, rates for troubled countries began a rapid decline, approaching levels not seen since the early months of the crisis. Given this turn of events one could argue that since the ECB's announcement the original Euro crisis has ended. This did not become clear until several months of declines in sovereign bond markets and the stability of the European financial system returned as destabilizing deposit flows began to slowly reverse.

The return of confidence to the European financial system was aided by additional policy efforts in Fall of 2012. Buttressing the ECB's efforts that summer, the European Commission and ECB followed up on previous policy promises and released initial and long-anticipated plans for a banking union that September. The reforms, while still subject to further negotiation, were far-reaching. In principle, the banking union outlined would release individual countries from the responsibility to support their own financial systems in times of crisis, breaking the so-called doom loop.

The ECB would now be the sole regulator of major banks in the Eurozone and as such would have the power to support them directly should recapitalization ever be necessary. This reform would permanently allow the link between financial crises and sovereign debt crises to be broken, adding an element of stability to the Eurozone that had been missing since its formation. After this announcement Spain's bank bailout terms were also finalized in November with €39.5 billion in aid being made available in 2012 to capitalize its banking system, and an additional €1.9 made available in February 2013. While €100 billion had been initially approved for Spain's bailout, the additional funds were no longer needed—a testament to turnaround that had occurred in market conditions in only 6 months.

The steady downward trend Europe has enjoyed in its sovereign debt rates, and the steady increase in confidence that has been felt across its banking system continued throughout the remainder of 2012 and then through 2013. By Fall of 2013 the European Financial crisis appeared to be well on its way toward resolution. Even two new setbacks in early 2013 did not derail the recovery in sovereign debt markets.

In February 2013, Italian parliamentary elections resulted in no clear electoral winner. Mario Monti's bid to turn his previous appointment as prime minister into an elected one suffered a significant defeat. Italian voters, frustrated by his government's austerity programs on top of a decade of slow growth, turned to populist candidates and protest parties, many with no clear agenda and who secured a significant portion of the vote. These results made the formation of a government very difficult, creating significant market uncertainty. Due to the size of Italy's economy there was great concern that should Italy abandon austerity programs in place, markets could react negatively and swiftly given the country's high-debt level, plunging the continent back into crisis. After repeated attempts a weak coalition government eventually formed in late April. The fragile government headed by Prime Minister Enrico Letta, a relative newcomer to Italian politics adopted as its policy agenda the creation of economic stability. Implicit in this it appears the governing parties have agreed to ensuring Italy's membership in the euro but under terms that benefit the Italian people. The result of the political maneuvering necessary to form a government has been to slow austerity measures previously adopted and to focus on economic growth by addressing the continuing and severe recession in Italy. After the new Italian government formed, sovereign bond rates in GIPSI countries resumed their previous decline and by summer of 2013 had again reached new Euro crisis lows.

A second event in the early months of 2013 also failed to leave any lasting impression on the improving trends in European financial markets. Cyprus, whose government had requested EU aid in late June 2012 had continued to negotiate the terms of a bailout through that Fall. In late November the Troika's terms were made public and as in past aid programs, severe austerity measures, cuts in public jobs and salaries, pension and benefit cuts, and tax increases were mandated. The value of the bailout package would be €17.5 billion, with €10 billion financed by the Troika funding and the remainder through Cyprus's restructuring and austerity efforts. Final agreement on the bailout, however, did not take place until March 2013 to accommodate a Cypriot federal election in which a change of government took place. What followed as negotiations over a bailout resumed was an unfortunate set of policy errors during a 2-week period that March.

The initial plan agreed to by the Troika and the new Cypriot government in March 2013 included a bank holiday to allow a tax on all existing bank deposits to finance Cyprus's share of the bailout, in addition to a series of other austerity actions and reforms. The tax was to be levied on all deposits, even those not in troubled banking institutions and regardless of deposit size. A political backlash resulted in Cyprus as many people in the island nation felt betrayed that deposits they thought had been guaranteed and safe were subject to losses to finance the bailout costs, especially in banks not in trouble. The government, caught by surprise at the degree of anger its agreement had created then, backed away from the deal, catching the Troika off guard. On the island, political deadlock resulted as the island's political parties struggled to define a strategy. The result was a financial crisis in the country during which all banks remained closed for a week and financial transactions were severely limited. Eventually after more negotiation a new deal was worked out that imposed a tax only on deposits over €100,000 but the damage was done. The package was accepted by the Troika and the Cypriot government but the week-long stalemate caused an immediate economic impact on the island and the economy dropped into a severe recession. Still while these dramatic events were occurring, sovereign bond markets seemed to barely notice with financial markets in the core of Europe suffering only increased volatility while events took place.

Had either the Italian election or the Cypriot crisis occurred a year earlier, their effects likely would have been far worse in sovereign debt markets, demonstrating the resilience the currency union had regained. Although the severe symptoms of Europe's financial crisis that so defined it from 2009 through mid-2012 continue to fade away, there will certainly continue to be unexpected financial problems to sort out as time goes on, and policy mistakes cannot be ruled out. The conclusion of the Cypriot bailout in March 2013 demonstrated this point, but tellingly its effects seemed more a tempest in a teapot than a return to the hurricane conditions on the continent. The financial healing process has begun, but the economic consequences of the crisis will require a long and protracted recovery.

Timeline Epilogue

Arguing that the crisis is now over may be controversial to some. It may instead be reasonable to argue a new phase in the Euro crisis is beginning. Problems certainly are not yet solved, but whether conditions now constitute a crisis is a matter of judgment. A crisis implies an immediate threat. The conditions the Eurozone faces are now long term. Most pressing are economic conditions in the area. The fallout of a years-long financial crisis is a deep economic recession, particularly for GIPSI nations at its center. Unemployment rates in Spain and Greece exceed 25% as of this writing. Youth unemployment rates in these countries are over double this level. Unemployment rates in Ireland, Italy, Portugal, and Cyprus exceed 10%. Even the healthiest creditor nations have seen growth slow to zero. The currency union must benefit all countries within it, and this will require political reform at the national and supranational levels. Pressures for such political change are now evident. There will also still be financial problems to sort out as time goes on, and policy mistakes cannot be ruled out. The conclusion of the Cypriot bailout in March 2013 demonstrated this point, but tellingly caused only minor effects in sovereign debt markets.

As outlined, the policy response to the Euro crisis can be seen as following three phases as defined previously in Table 1. In the first two phases, policy was slow in implementation, often optimistic in its assumptions and short term in its nature in that it focused on addressing country-specific problems. In part, this was due to the fact that the Eurozone had little experience dealing with financial crises in its member states, the cause of which was seen at the time to be due to external events and poor governance, not the architecture of the currency union itself. Focus in the early years of the crisis tended to be on protecting bondholders from default and concerns with respect to public sector moral hazard, imposing the costs of bailouts on the citizens of aided countries, while indirectly transferring default risks onto the taxpayers of creditor countries. Policy actions also attempted to limit the financial market contagion to troubled countries in an effort to protect the banking and financial sectors of the wider Eurozone. It can be argued that these policies also were to a degree self-serving as they tended to protect the financial sectors of the largest Eurozone economies, those economies that had underwritten the large debt buildup in troubled countries prior to the crisis and who therefore had the largest exposure to the default risk troubled countries presented.

The second phase of the crisis might be defined as the period after which private-sector lenders were included in bailout costs. Bailout actions had been politically costly in creditor countries and therefore an incentive was created to limit the additional liability any future bailouts presented to these countries' taxpayers. To expand the liability for future bailouts and because time had passed, which allowed financial systems in creditor countries to adjust to the risk the Euro crisis posed to them, the second phase of the crisis included private creditors in bailout costs or "haircuts" to private-sector lenders. This group had previously been protected in the first phase of the crisis by the assumption of default risk by creditor country taxpayers. This created arguments about fairness—why should taxpayers be indirectly bailing out wealthy financiers who should have known the risks they faced when they originally made their loans? This argument implicitly acknowledged the moral hazard that bailouts created not only for governments in aided countries who had run up large debts, but also for those who enabled the borrowing practices that had led to the crisis. Defining the first two phases of the crisis together as stage one of the crisis, this period focused on avoiding default and attempts to stabilize sovereign debt markets. The actions taken in the first stage of the crisis were, however, largely unsuccessful in reversing market conditions and did little to address structural reforms. Actions taken worked within the original rules of the currency union to solve it.

The second stage and third phase of the crisis occurred when policy makers, seeing that actions to address the crisis working within the existing rules and practices of the Eurozone had not worked, then attempted to address the crisis by changing the system. Policy efforts now attempted to change the structure and operation of the Eurozone and its institutions to address structural problems in the currency union, while the ECB, to address both extreme market conditions and the threat very real threats these now presented to maintaining the currency, took unprecedented actions that would previously have been very controversial. In combination, the Eurozone structural reforms announced since December 2011, and the ECB's actions to use its unlimited power to provide liquidity to the banking and sovereign bond sectors as needed have finally reversed what had been, prior to the summer of 2012, a steady worsening of financial market conditions in the Eurozone.

Overall, the combined policies of the Eurozone and ECB have significantly altered both the policy rules of the Eurozone and their interpretation. Eurozone reforms, specifically the implementation of the Fiscal Compact as a first step toward a greater fiscal union, and the beginning of banking union negotiations, combined with restructuring reforms across the currency unions least competitive countries have the potential to repair serious architectural flaws in the currency union and add to its potential stability. The ECB's use of its power to provide almost unlimited amounts of liquidity similarly contributed to improving stability and its promise of additional actions should they be needed, as long as they remain credible, also eliminates concerns the euro will one day fail.

Since December 2011 the actions of the ECB and Eurozone suggest at least an implicit acceptance that the Euro crisis was caused by flaws in the design of the original monetary union. These actions have not, however, solved all the problems facing the currency union. As the crisis affected countries asymmetrically, very challenging conditions now exist across many countries. In some, unemployment rates are now at or approaching

Depression-era levels. To address this state of affairs will require significant additional reforms and actions, not only by those who have been asked to reform throughout the crisis, but also by those who have set the policy-reform agenda. Accomplishing both a fiscal and banking union will require ceding sovereignty to the EU from the capitals of Europe. Ironically, success in checking the Euro crisis may now have created a new form of new moral hazard among policy makers. Without the threat of a crisis, policy makers may attempt to avoid politically difficult but still needed reforms. The lack of an immediate threat may also reduce the incentive for creditor countries to engage in actions or aid that would help reverse current economic conditions and restore growth in the most troubled nations union, a problem that is now the union's greatest challenge.

PART IV

Moving Forward

Introduction

Effective treatment of the Euro crisis, like a serious disease, has proven elusive through much of the crisis. Bailouts, grinding austerity, bail-ins, and even treaty reforms did not seem effective in reversing the worsening conditions in bond markets through much of the crisis. The only effective treatment has appeared to be the ECB's actions, actions some might have considered a last resort. Not once but twice hefty doses of liquidity have been administered to the Eurozone, and twice they seem to have rejuvenated what appeared to be a doomed patient. In each episode, the ECB's actions have proven effective in reversing worsening market confidence, and have also bought time in which other policies have then been able to act. Still, while final success seems closer, it remains to be seen whether the crisis has been overcome. Past respites have proven transitory, as they did in 2012, and so could the current one. Further, economic conditions are now so serious in the Eurozone they present a new set of problems that could be as serious as those that began the crisis. What remains to be seen is whether Europe's long fever has finally been broken, or whether conditions will worsen as eventually another relapse occurs. The longer the calm remains in European markets, the more the Eurozone's condition moves from critical to chronic, and the more important it will be that the opportunity presented by this calm is not ignored. The danger, therefore, has not yet passed and the greatest risk the currency union may now face could be one of complacency.

Moving forward will first require an assessment of the damage caused by the crisis. This damage has not only been due to its direct effects but also from those of the policies used to treat it. Austerity has had effects far more severe than expected and moving forward it will be necessary to determine if the appropriate balance between austerity and growth policies is in place or whether some adjustment needs to be made. The latter is almost certainly the case. Secondly, reforms begun during the crisis must continue if they are to repair the flaws in the currency union that contributed to causing it. This will require completing reforms already initiated and a careful consideration of the flaws in the monetary union that led to the crisis to determine if more still needs to be done. This may entail politically painful compromises in some countries to accomplish, but the consequences of not acting could be a return to the conditions recently overcome. Finally, while the original crisis seems to have passed, a new political crisis threatens to take its place. The latter may be much harder to treat. The need for additional policies—new treatments to heal the savages the Euro crisis wrought on many of the economies of Europe is still present. The question is whether Europe has the willingness to face these challenges and how it will move forward.

CHAPTER 7

Where Are We Now?

While conditions in sovereign debt markets in the summer of 2013 were the best they had been in 3 years, the same could not be said for most of the Eurozone's economies. Assessment of conditions now that the crisis may have turned, of the effects of the crisis and of policies taken to fight it, will need to be evaluated to determine what more can be done to improve the situation, and whether the willingness exists to embark on further actions. One question that can be asked is whether the price of the policies used was worth it—is the Eurozone better off than it might have been had nothing been done or had euro been allowed to fail?

To determine the answer to that question requires an estimate of outcomes as they would have been had the currency union collapsed. While such estimates are too complex to hope to predict exactly, many predictions were attempted to try to determine the possible losses such a collapse would cause. One such estimate is shown in Table 1 as an example. It examined how each of the EU-12 countries would have been impacted by the collapse of the monetary union given conditions in late 2011 and early 2012. While affecting countries differently, the predicted consequences were grim for each country considered. In GIPSI countries the average decline in economic output 2 years after the breakup of the Eurozone was estimated to be 12.5%, and among the other seven nations the average decline was predicted to total 9.9%, or four times what would normally be considered a severe recession would cause.

The stark differences and damages caused by a breakup of currency union were reflected in other measures as well. Unemployment would be even more severely impacted than output, rising by an average of 20% in GIPSI nations and 10.6% in the remainder. Employment outcomes reflected in particular the labor market rigidities present in the Eurozone—the fact that labor released in one sector cannot be quickly absorbed in another due to rigid wages and closed professions. Differences

Table 1. Potential Economic Impacts of a Eurozone Failure (Spring 2012 Estimates)

Country	Change in Output	Change in Unemployment	Change in Inflation Rate
	(Change 2 Years After Last Year of Euro)	(Change 2 Years After Last Year of Euro)	(Relative to Last Year of Euro)
Greece	−15.4%	+23.8%	+18.6%
Ireland	−8.9%	+19.4%	+9.5%
Portugal	−14.9%	+18.0%	+13.1%
Spain	−11.0%	+26.7%	+12.9%
Italy	−12.3%	+12.3%	+10.3%
Germany	−9.2%	+9.3%	−0.9%
Austria	−9.7%	+8.6%	+0.8%
Finland	−8.4%	11.7%	+0.8%
Netherlands	−10.8%	+8.8%	+0.7%
France	−11.6%	+15.9%	+1.2%
Belgium	−10.4%	+11.8%	+1.1%
Luxembourg	−9.3%	+8.4%	+0.8%
GIPSI average	−12.5%	+20.0%	+12.9%
Non-GIPSI average	−9.9%	+10.6%	+0.6%
12-country average	−11.0%	+14.6%	+5.7%

Source: ING, Der Spiegel.[1]

in these rigidities have also been very important in understanding the regional disparities that have occurred during the crisis as countries with more open labor markets have been far less affected than others.

Predictions also showed inflation would differ by country. In GIPSI nations, the re-adoption of national currencies would result in precipitous declines in exchange rates relative to levels during the time of the euro, and were estimated to lead to rapid increases in the costs of imports, causing very high inflation. In stronger Eurozone countries, price effects were forecast to be much more moderate as these countries were projected to experience far less exchange rate effects. Trade balances would remain strong, bond market outcomes would be less severe and these stronger economies would be better able to manage their currencies to stabilize domestic price shocks. Depending on the country, exchange rates in countries less troubled by the crisis, the northern and central creditor countries, would vary little or actually appreciate; quite the opposite to that effect experienced in GIPSI nations where price changes would be severe.

Results in Table 1 can be compared to the actual outcomes that have occurred during the crisis to get some sense of both the success and cost of policies implemented in the Euro crisis. Economic outcomes during the crisis were previously presented in Table 2 of Chapter 5. They are also presented in more detail in Figures 1, 2, and 3. Consideration of actual outcomes relative to the predictions of outcomes had the currency union collapsed suggests that policy efforts have allowed the economies of some countries to avoid the potentially devastating recessions a monetary union failure could have caused, particularly those creditor nations in northern and central Europe. Aided nations, however, particularly those in the south have not fared as well. GIPSI economies that were either forced to implement severe austerity measures as a condition of their aid or, like Spain and Italy, did so defensively, have experienced severe recessions. In some cases

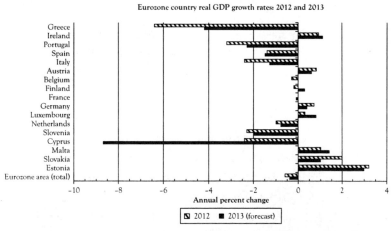

Eurozone country real GDP growth rates: 2012 and 2013

Annual percent change

☒ 2012   ■ 2013 (forecast)

Figure 1. Eurozone countries' real GDP annual growth gates in 2012 and 2013. Growth slowed to its lowest levels in many countries in 2012 as the crisis reached its worst point. Only one country was forecast to grow at what would be a normal growth rate in excess of 2% in 2013, and the Eurozone as a whole was forecast to endure its second consecutive year of contraction by the end of 2013.
Source: Eurostat.

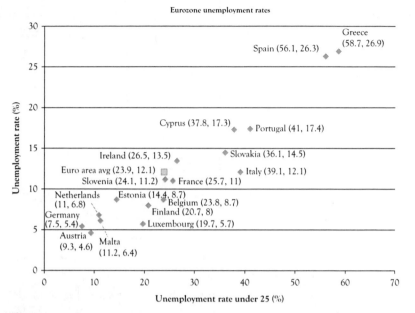

Figure 2. Eurozone unemployment rates (June 2013). Data labels identify the country and its respective youth (under 25 years of age) and overall adult unemployment rates, both seasonally adjusted. In most countries rates are far above what would be expected at full employment, and in several countries they are at depression levels, especially in Greece and Spain. On average, almost one in four youth willing to work in the Eurozone are unemployed. In Spain and Greece it is over half, with over one in four people in the overall workforce unemployed. Source: Eurostat.

the recessions that have occurred are almost as harsh as the predicted outcomes countries were attempting to avoid had the euro failed.

The severity of the recessions some countries have faced can be seen in the growth and unemployment outcomes that occurred in 2012, the worst year of the crisis. Figure 1 describes the growth outcomes in 2012, and EU forecast outcomes for 2013. Output across the Eurozone in 2012 contracted at an annual rate of 0.6%, and the recession was forecast to carry on into 2013 with a contraction continuing at a 0.4% pace.[2] In the subgroup of 12 countries originally making up the Eurozone when the euro went into circulation and who combined contribute over 98% of total Eurozone output, the 2012 contraction was worse than the Eurozone as a whole. Among these countries the growth rate averaged negative 1% of GDP at annual rates in 2012, and was further forecast to fall another 0.6% the following year.

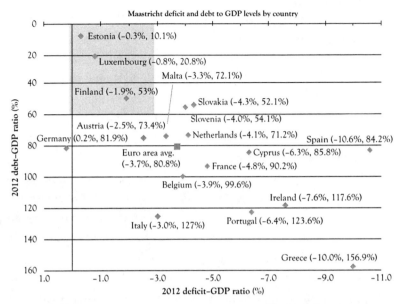

Figure 3. Eurozone countries' debt and deficit to GDP levels (2012). Poor economic conditions in 2012 due to the Euro crisis took a toll on Eurozone deficit and debt levels. Only six countries in the currency union were meeting their deficit target defined by the Maastricht Treaty, and only five were able to meet their debt–GDP requirement. The shaded area indicates where both criteria are met—only three countries did so in 2012. This outcome suggests the tradeoff facing the currency union. Either the Eurozone will have to relax its Maastricht requirements or significant additional austerity will be necessary for most countries to reach these goals soon. Clearly, additional austerity could threaten to worsen economic conditions at a time when most countries' economies are already weak.

Across these countries, however, economic outcomes varied significantly. The worst outcomes have not unexpectedly occurred in southern states. In Greece where the worst contraction experienced by a major economy has occurred, a decline of 6.4% of output was observed in 2012. Another 4.2% decline was expected in 2013, resulting in a reduction of over 10% of the economy's income in only 2 years. Since the crisis began in 2009, the Greek economy has shrunk by approximately 25%. Other southern Europe countries have also been hit hard by the crisis. Cyprus's economy fell by over 2% in 2012, and after their banking crisis and Troika-financed bailout, was predicted to decline a further 9% in 2013. Serious declines in economic output also occurred in Portugal, Italy, and Spain in 2012 and were expected to continue in 2013.

At the other end of the spectrum, 7 countries of the 17 in the Eurozone experienced positive growth in 2012, but where growth has occurred it has not usually been strong. Among the largest economies, Germany barely saw any growth in 2012, recording an increase in output of only 0.7%, while France recorded no growth at all. For comparison, in the United States growth in 2012 was 2.2%, highlighting how the crisis has worsened outcomes in Europe relative to similar developed economies elsewhere. Ireland has been an apparent bright spot in the crisis, where post-bailout growth has been positive and growth in recent years reversed a serious decline previously. The country returned to growth in 2011 after receiving its Troika-sponsored aid package, but conditions in that country have still been far from booming as the previous 3 years had seen a cumulative contraction of over 8% of output, leaving its unemployment rate at the highest level seen in decades. Furthermore, growth figures in that country are deceiving. Demand still continues to contract, and a labor exodus has resulted in many of the most talented workers leaving for opportunities elsewhere. Mortgage failures continue to occur in the housing market, leaving banks weak and construction moribund over half a decade after the crisis began in that country.[3] In the Eurozone, even what appear to be positive numbers often mask severe problems, a reflection of the toll the crisis has taken.

Unemployment outcomes across the Eurozone are shown in Figure 2. As one might expect given growth figures, unemployment rates were generally very high across the monetary union and followed a worsening trend as the crisis has continued. In June 2013 the unemployment rate across the euro area was 12.1%, a record high reflecting several years of contraction in most countries. Worse was the unemployment rate for those less than 25 years of age, where rates across the Eurozone had climbed to 23.9% and were in double digit levels in every Eurozone country but Germany and Austria. Again the experiences of countries were widely different. Conditions were worst in Greece and Spain where the unemployment rate in each country was over 26%, and for those less than 25 years of age, rates had risen to near 60%. Among the other GIPSI nations, Portugal and Ireland were suffering with unemployment rates in the teens and Italy had recorded an unemployment rate over 12%. Youth rates ranged from 26.5% in Ireland to 41% in Portugal with Italy nearing 40%.

For policy makers, youth unemployment rates are potentially the most worrisome economic outcomes of the crisis. The crisis has clearly had a differential impact on the peoples of Europe, both geographically and also demographically where a disproportionate share of the cost has fallen on young people. The potential implications and political fallout such a lost generation might have on the continent in the future are of grave concern. Overall, even if growth was to return to Europe quickly, the amount of unemployment now present will take years to clear out of labor markets, with costs in potential output, earnings, and in depressed demand remaining high for years to come. The costs to future productivity will likewise be high as prolonged periods of unemployment undermine future human capital and depreciate people's skill sets. Clearly, such conditions could also sow the seeds of political discontent and social instability.

Slow growth and high unemployment have taken their toll on the fiscal positions of Eurozone countries too. Debt and deficit levels have spiraled as economic contraction has reduced tax revenues and increased social program costs across the Eurozone. These outcomes are shown for Eurozone countries as they stood in 2012 in Figure 3. Compared to precrisis levels (shown for debt in Figures 9 and 10 in Chapter 5) the impact of the Euro crisis is clear. By the end of 2012 only three countries could claim to meet the basic treaty obligations the European monetary union requires—maintaining deficit levels under 3% of GDP and gross debt levels under 60% of GDP as defined by the shaded area of the figure. The remaining 14 nations were well outside these requirements, and will remain so for some time. Collectively these 14 countries experienced average deficits of 5% relative to GDP in 2012. Overall, the debt and deficit in the Eurozone situation has significant implications for the area's ability to address growth and unemployment challenges moving forward.

Overall, conditions remained very weak across the Eurozone as of 2013. Output contractions that have occurred since the Euro crisis began have been severe in almost all countries, and in most of those countries lucky enough to avoid such outcomes, growth has been slow. Unemployment remains high in almost all countries, especially among those less than 25 years of age. Deficit and debt levels also remain elevated, higher than Maastricht conditions allow in almost all Eurozone countries. Economic contraction has had the added effect that it has worsened debt–GDP ratios for several countries, especially GIPSI nations.

This set of conditions presents a dilemma for European policy makers. If countries wish to expand output through stimulus to support growth, they will worsen debt and deficit conditions when most countries are already well outside their targets ranges. Furthermore, this option is not even available to the worst-hit countries as the very worst countries all have been recipients of bailouts and cannot expand debt and deficits as per the terms of these agreements. In almost all cases these countries also would not have access to credit markets to finance such stimulus anyway.

Given the size of its economy, one option that has been suggested is that Germany attempt to stimulate its economy. The argument goes that such efforts would increase demand for exports from other European countries, improving their economic performance and lowering their unemployment. In effect, Germany could drag the continent out of recession, much like a tow truck could drag a stuck car out of a ditch. Increased German wage inflation caused by such efforts would also have the added effect of improving other countries' relative wage and export competitiveness, further improving conditions in Europe. Such actions would be in Germany's interest given it has not been experiencing very strong growth throughout the crisis. Germany, while outside its Maastricht target range, faces the lowest sovereign bond interest rates of any European country, therefore such debt financed growth would be possible and could be supported at rates lower than any other country would have to pay. German policy makers, however, have not welcomed such suggestions.

Relative to the projections the estimated effects of a currency union breakdown would have as shown in Table 1, conditions remain better to date than what they might have been. In the case of Greece and Spain, however, one might argue that conditions are not much better. This suggests that overall, and even despite the very weak economic conditions that exist across the continent, policy makers have been able to avoid the consequences of a failure of the European monetary union at lower cost than what might have been caused had the euro failed. The cost of the crisis though has been very high indeed for almost all members of the Eurozone, and prospects are expected to remain weak into the future.

CHAPTER 8

What Happens Next?

The potential impact that a failure of the European monetary union could have is complex to predict. This impact has likely been made worse over the past crisis due to additional uncertainty caused by policy mistakes. Despite significant policy actions, European sovereign debt markets continued to sour until the ECB took definitive action in summer of 2012. The fact that the original Greek deal was not large enough, that growth in aided countries and the Eurozone was continually overestimated, and that the effect of austerity was repeatedly underestimated undermined world confidence in the EU's ability to come to an effective policy solution to avert an eventual Greek default or the collapse of the monetary union. Each time policy actions did not lead to a solution to the crisis, investors' risk aversion to European debt increased, tightening credit conditions throughout the Eurozone, turning fears into expectations, and then causing those expectations to become self-fulfilling. A long-term solution to the Euro crisis will require the original architectural problems of the currency area to be addressed. Specifically, economic problems in the design and competitiveness of countries in the currency union that contributed to destabilizing financial flows will have to be repaired. Additionally, political and social structures will have to change.

What Should Be Done? Reforming the Eurozone's Economic Architecture in the Long Run

The economic architecture of the Eurozone needs to change in three fundamental areas if the problems that contributed to causing the Euro crisis are to be avoided in the future. The first of these is a redesign of the banking system. The Euro system was designed to preserve sovereign control of each country's banking system and to create a strong and independent central bank, the ECB. To accomplish this, the regulation of each national banking system was left to each country. The lack of strong oversight in some countries, however, led to significant problems building up in the mid-2000s. Banks in Ireland and Spain both accrued significant portfolios of risky real-estate debt that later led to banking crises in both countries. In Cyprus, the banking system accumulated assets greater than eight times the country's GDP, and then found itself undercapitalized when investments made in Greek bonds incurred heavy losses. Even in Germany, banks, including large international institutions like Deutsche Bank were allowed to operate with very low levels of capital, allowing the firms to potentially threaten that country's financial system.

National banking system crises have been pivotal in the evolution of the Euro crisis, leading to bailouts being required in Ireland, Spain, and Cyprus. Breaking the "doom-loop," as the linkage between banking system crises and sovereign debt crises have been called, will require several changes to the Euro-system's structure, changes that began to be initiated in September 2012.[1] These reforms have been referred to as the creation of a European "banking union." Creation of such a union will require three new elements to be instituted in the existing Euro-system structure: a single common supervisor and set of banking standards across all banks in the EU, a well-defined resolution process to determine how illiquid and insolvent institutions will be dealt with, and a common deposit protection scheme covering all EU deposits.

The first of these new standards is to be accomplished by having the ECB take over the regulation of all banking systems in the EU, and imposing a common set of operating standards across each. The common rule-book will ensure that the pressures of bank competition do not result in the worst regulatory practices becoming standard practice, a concern in the past. Furthermore, a single regulator will ensure that similar banking problems in different nations are addressed coherently and consistently, avoiding the buildup of destabilizing problems in some countries and not others. Such a change will reduce uncertainty among regulated banks, and avoid problems seen in the past when domestic political incentives reduced the willingness of national regulators to deal with banking problems.

A single resolution mechanism is also intended to create consistency and greater certainty across the Eurozone by instituting a common set of practices by which troubled banks are shut down or recapitalized. Critical to this process is the determination of how such recapitalization might be funded to avoid such actions triggering a national sovereign debt crisis—the "doom loop." One suggestion is to allow the ESM to directly inject capital into banks, thereby transferring the liability incurred by such actions to the greater EU and not the country in which the problems occur. The argument against using funds not financed by the state to recapitalize banking systems has been one of moral hazard. Little incentive would be created for careful regulation if someone else's funds were available to be used to finance the costs of a failed bank. For this reason, it is important that the creation of such a fund be accompanied by the replacement of national regulators with a single common one. Under a common EU-wide regulator, common EU-wide funds used for such recapitalization purposes would be less susceptible to creating such moral hazard. In June 2013, common EU resolution rules were initially agreed to, which included allowing the official use of ESM funds for bank recapitalization.[2]

The final reform necessary to create a banking union is a common bank deposit insurance system. In the past banking insurance guarantees have been the responsibility of individual nations. This, however, can create concerns if a country is believed to be unable to insure all deposits due to its sovereign debt position. Such fears would lead depositors in times of financial crisis to withdraw their funds and transfer them to banks in countries perceived safer, thereby weakening already troubled banks and exacerbating the situation in troubled countries. A common banking insurance scheme funded by a single pool across all of Europe would undermine such withdrawal incentives. Financing such a system could be financed by a tax or levy on each bank proportional to their deposit base and guarantee all deposits in the EU up to some limit.[3] The idea of creating a common deposit insurance system, allowing the ESM to be used to recapitalize troubled banking systems directly, and imposing a common regulator over all European banks has been controversial.

Opposition to implementing the reforms needed to create a banking union has been driven by two concerns. The first is the unwillingness of some countries to relinquish sovereign control of their own banking systems. The second has been the concern regarding the principle of joint liability. Funding common pools to be used for bank recapitalization or to finance a single deposit insurance scheme across the EU could result in the funds required for either action to be greater than the funds contributed by the nation where the crisis occurred. This then creates a concern regarding the prohibition of joint liability in the EU as it would impose the liability for bank failures in a single country to be spread across all currency union members. As noted above, concerns regarding moral hazard that such joint liability creates could be reduced by the creation of a single system-wide regulator, but such a regulator creates national sovereignty concerns. Creating a banking union requires imposing both joint liability and a reduction of national sovereignty and therefore has been difficult to generate agreement on. The issues of moral hazard and sovereign national banking systems make it clear that all three reforms in the banking union must be made simultaneously and also demonstrates that each may be difficult to generate agreement on.

The second economic flaw in the Eurozone construction prior to the Euro crisis was the existence of structural imbalances between countries, which resulted in destabilizing credit and trade flows. As shown in Chapter 5, countries in the currency union had radically different levels of productivity and labor market flexibility, which resulted in significant differences in the competitiveness among countries using the euro. These competitiveness differences then resulted in destabilizing trade flows, which in turn helped finance the credit bubbles that affected several countries. To address these imbalances requires changes to country's labor markets. For example, regulations that limit access to specific occupations and protect wages and employment must be reduced. Such reforms, however, are politically very difficult since they remove protections from industries with significant political influence. As noted in previous chapters, while markets were booming and growth was high in the mid-2000s there seemed little political incentive to take on these difficult and unpopular challenges. Since the Euro crisis began though, bailout terms in each aided country have required that reform occur to improve their competitiveness and eventually economic growth. In the short run, however, such stipulations have been very unpopular as they have resulted in wage decreases and greater wage and employment competition. This unpopularity is also apparent in the observation that those countries not forced to make such reforms through bailouts, such as France and Italy, have been very hesitant to do so.

The implementation of the Fiscal Compact implemented in 2012 has in part accelerated some labor market reforms. The compact, which requires countries to submit budgets to the EC for approval prior to implementation at the national level, allows exceptions to debt and deficit requirements only under specific conditions. In the EU this has been done using conditionality—for example, deficit targets have been relaxed in exchange for competitiveness reforms. Such was the case with France in 2013. The problem, however, has been that such conditionality imposed from Brussels has allowed national governments to suggest unpopular reforms have been imposed by the EU, casting the existence of the currency union as a cost to national sovereignty and undermining support for additional economic and political integration.

Difficult reform in national competitiveness could also be created through external incentives. One such incentive that has been suggested could occur through the creation of a free-trade agreement between the EU and the United States. Preliminary negotiations for such a pact began in early 2013. Trade reforms, including the removal of tariff and non tariff barriers between the two partners, have been estimated to offer considerable economic benefits. The benefits, however, depend in part on the relative competitiveness of countries within the Eurozone given the common currency used by all. The potential benefits of opening a deeply integrated free-trade zone (reducing both tariff and non tariff barriers) between the EU and the United States has been estimated to create an average increase in per capita incomes across the entire EU of nearly 5%. In troubled countries this increase would be even more significant, increasing per capita incomes by an average of 5.4% across southern countries and 5.7% across the entire GIPSI area.[4] Not only would the creation of a deep trade pact between the EU and the United States potentially be a stabilizing influence on the Eurozone by creating additional economic incentives to maintain and improve competitiveness, but it could also create an additional benefit. Such a deal would create an additional incentive to commit to the European Union.[5] The trade pact under consideration only includes EU nations. Membership has its advantages and having negotiated such a trade deal could ensure that member-state support for the EU is maintained.

The third area of reform needed to address the economic architecture of the Eurozone is creation of a fiscal union. A fiscal union would harmonize the fiscal policy of countries across the currency area, and thereby reverse some of the problems in the current design. The first step toward this goal was in the adoption of Fiscal Compact during the crisis. The original Maastricht convergence requirements were meant to stabilize debt and deficit levels to ensure these would not destabilize the currency area, but for various reasons previously described, these conditions were relaxed during the early years of the euro's introduction. The ratification of the Fiscal Compact in 2013 strengthened the enforcement of these requirements and implemented further mechanisms by which destabilizing fiscal policies can be avoided. This alone, however, is not enough. Greater fiscal prudence and coordination in the long run is essential to ensuring a similar crisis to the one that began in 2009 is avoided in the future. Actions have yet to be taken to move closer to this goal. Some possibilities include the imposition of a comprehensive EU or Eurozone budget which would define overall deficit levels. Such a budget would clearly move a significant share of financial decision making to Brussels and for that reason the discussion again is very difficult as it implies movement toward greater political integration in the Eurozone and lessens national sovereignty over fiscal issues.

Greater fiscal accountability and coordination could, however, open the door to greater shared liability in the currency union. While politically unpopular, increases in sharing the financial burdens of the Eurozone could prove stabilizing. Germany's opposition during the Euro crisis to the idea of Eurobonds, bonds that could be used by troubled nations to access credit by allowing their debt to be backed by the entire EU, was premised in part on the basis of moral hazard. The slogan often heard was "greater responsibility and accountability before shared liability." Creating increased fiscal responsibility through tighter fiscal harmonization could open the door for the sharing of liability for debt. The creation of additional accountability could reassure those countries currently skeptical of joint liability that controls existed to avoid the effects of moral hazard. Looking forward, as the economies of southern Europe try to recover, access to credit markets could greatly help that recovery. The existence of at least limited amounts of jointly backed debt could be very helpful in creating growth through the stimulus offered by infrastructure improvement programs and other actions.

The difficulty in implementing many long-term reforms in the Euro-zone is that they often involve greater political integration and a reduction in national sovereignty. The increase in political integration required across Eurozone states implied by proposals to implement a tighter fiscal union and banking is been significant.[6] For example, such plans would encom-pass the banking union already described but would also encompass even greater centralized fiscal control in Brussels. The ultimate fiscal union would create a single fiscal budget within the EU, including a single Euro-zone finance minister and a single comprehensive revenue and expenditure program across the currency union. The ceding of national sovereignty to Europe to accomplish this is not likely. Conceptually, however, a move-ment toward common fiscal programming would be very useful. Harmo-nization of unemployment, social, and pension benefits across the Eurozone could avoid the fatally destabilizing effects such programs had in southern countries, such as Greece and Portugal, where pension liabil-ities began to undermine debt sustainability. Expensive and relatively gen-erous social benefits programs in Italy and France created fiscal drags in those countries too. Germany's Angela Merkel has often quoted three key statistics in her argument that Europe needs fiscal reform—50% of the social benefits in the world are paid in Europe, which generates only 25% of the world's income and is inhabited by only 7% of the global population. Such a generous social safety net is difficult to sustain, and Europe may have to consider the cost and affordability of such programs in the future if they are to be preserved or modified. Standardization of such programs across states is one possible reform.

Such harmonization would also create additional benefits. First, pro-gram reform could enhance labor mobility across Europe. While officially the Eurozone allows open immigration, restrictions regarding pension, health, and other social benefits payments to immigrants have been imple-mented to deter such mobility. The problem has arisen from the existence of significant differences in the level of benefits offered in each country. With differential benefits levels, incentives have been created to avoid leav-ing countries with higher packages while causing those with more generous programs to institute controls on those immigrating to their countries to avoid "benefit shopping" by migrants. Harmonization would avoid the incentives caused by differential benefits levels and create greater incentives for labor mobility based on fundamental differences in labor market conditions. Secondly, benefits harmonization could enable the creation of transfer payment systems across the Eurozone. Common unemployment and benefits systems across the Eurozone would facilitate the possibility of a federal transfer system of payments as used in many countries. As noted previously in the chapter discussing optimal currency areas, transfer systems offer a means of creating greater stability in currency unions. Such a system could also enhance political cohesion across the peoples of Europe by creating common benefits for being a member country. Eventually, such a common benefit system might become synonymous with "being European." This could have long-term political benefits. During the Euro crisis, it may have been very difficult for a 60-year-old worker in Germany to empathize with the conditions faced by Greek workers, knowing many could retire at age 55, while they would have to work at least another 5 years. It is also understandable why as a condition of the bailouts, reforms imposed on Greece included increasing the retirement age. This was not well accepted in Greece where workers who had expected to retire soon now found they would be working for several more years. It is not unlikely that in Greece this has contributed to feelings of animosity toward the peoples in creditor countries for requiring this reform.

Overall, the swift adoption of greater political integration to achieve fiscal coordination is unlikely; however, the opportunities such changes could create one day would be useful to keep in mind. For now, however, the Fiscal Compact a banking union and the potential of utilizing external agreements to create incentives to improve competitiveness are likely to be the only meaningful changes that are likely to occur in the near term to address the Eurozone's original architectural problems.

What Else Could Be Done? Reforming the Eurozone's Economic Architecture in the Short Run

Although creating a fiscal and banking union and improving the Eurozone's competitiveness would address long-standing flaws in the design of the currency union, making it more resistant to destabilizing effects like those posed by the Euro crisis, they would do little immediately to help the poor economic conditions now affecting most of Europe.

Given the economic conditions described in Chapter 7, the Eurozone now faces a dilemma. Creditor and aided nations alike face weak economic conditions. Because of the common currency, troubled economies cannot simply devalue their currencies to stimulate their economies through greater exports. Clearly, if treaty obligations were to be strictly followed in the future, significant austerity would be required in the countries where deficit and debt outcomes exceed Maastricht guidelines. Alternatively, even if treaty requirements were relaxed, given these levels of debt and deficit there is little fiscal space for many of these same countries to engage in any form of stimulative policy to reverse current growth trends. This leads to the most pressing short-run policy questions. First, to improve current conditions, should governments be allowed to relax Maastricht requirements to create space to allow additional expenditures intended to rekindle growth, or should they attempt to return government deficit and debt outcomes to those required by Maastricht? Fundamentally, this question is about policy effectiveness—is there a tradeoff between "greater austerity" and growth, or are these policies mutually compatible? Secondly, if there was a desire to stimulate economies, where would the funds for such efforts come from?

This first question reflects a long-standing policy debate in theoretic economics. Traditional macroeconomics would suggest that in times of recession, governments should not reduce their fiscal position. Among "Keynesian" economists, policy advice would go further and advocate the expansion of government expenditures and deficits when economic conditions are like those in the Eurozone. This was the reasoning behind the many stimulus programs across the world in the aftermath of the world financial crisis of 2008.[7]

In contrast, an opposite line of reasoning also exists; this one suggesting that governments cannot stimulate economic activity in any real or permanent manner and that government should only ensure stable economic finance, and that debt or deficit be limited to long-term efforts to increase capacity and capital that will otherwise not be provided privately in optimal quantities. Policy consistent with this viewpoint would hold that government finances must be put in order, and that a focus on lowering deficit and debt, or an austerity policy is necessary in Europe where government expenditures are far too large. This is an especially common view in some creditor countries, particularly those that have proven most fiscally conservative through the crisis—Germany, Austria, the Netherlands, and Finland. Some advocating this argument would go even further, suggesting just the opposite view to Keynesians, that additional austerity will not hurt growth and may actually encourage it by creating additional confidence in bond markets through a demonstrated dedication to fiscal prudence. Such increases in confidence then lead to expansionary effects in the private-sector economy, resulting in growth without increasing debt.

These two viewpoints, one advocating less austerity and more stimulative policies, and the other arguing just the opposite frame the political debate in the Eurozone since 2010. They also imply an important empirical question—what effect does austerity have on growth? Since 2010 there has been a sort of policy experiment across developed nations as countries collectively increased austerity in reaction to events in bond markets following Greece's revelations regarding its debt and deficit. Major economies that had previously been focused on economic recovery after the worldwide financial crisis of 2008 now had a new fear—too much debt and becoming "the next Greece" in the eyes of bond markets. The debate to stimulate or cut back occurred among global leaders at the G-20 economic summit meeting in Toronto in June 2010. On one side, American President Obama went to the summit with a plan to convince G-20 countries of the need for stimulus and a worldwide focus on job creation. At this meeting, however, he ran directly into the wall of debt fears that were the world's reaction to the new financial crisis in Europe. Britain's Prime Minister David Cameron, Germany's Chancellor Angela Merkel, and Canadian Prime Minister Stephen Harper's arguments for austerity carried the conference and world economic policy made a sharp U-turn, turning its focus to debt, not recovery. Governments rapidly began to raise taxes and decrease expenditure.

What has been the effect of these policies? While a simple association is not proof of causality, Figure 1 uses the IMF's online data since 2009 to summarize growth and austerity outcomes—each point shows a single country's austerity and growth outcome over this period. Of the 23 countries included in Figure 1, some were recovering or had recovered from the financial crisis of 2008 and associated recession afterward (like the United States), while some were still in recession or had slipped back into recession (like many of the countries of Europe affected by the Euro crisis). While

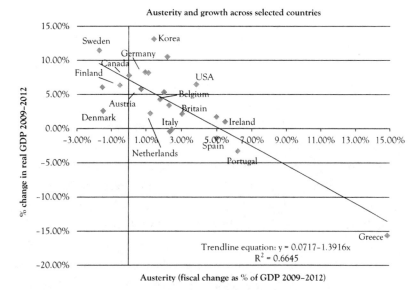

Figure 1. Austerity and growth across selected countries. The relation-ship between greater austerity (total combined increases in fiscal revenues and expenditure reductions) as a proportion of GDP is generally associated with a decrease in real GDP growth. Using a cross-section of 23 developed countries' data from 2009 to 2012, the trend-line shows that on average a 1% of GDP increase in austerity was associated with a 1.39% decrease in real GDP growth. Major Eurozone economies are shown by data labels above, along with selected other major countries.

Source: IMF Fiscal Monitor, October 2012 and World Economic Outlook Database.

recovering countries tended to see tax revenues increase after the recession because of improved economic conditions, the majority of the countries shown here reduced their fiscal position regardless of the state of their economies by some combination of increased taxes or reduced expenditures. On average across the countries shown, government austerity increased by 2.5% of GDP. The collection of countries shown includes 13 from the Eurozone where austerity increased by an average 3.5% of GDP. Austerity in the Eurozone ranged from a low of 0.5% in Finland (Finland's fiscal position increased as a percentage of GDP, the opposite of austerity), and GDP grew by 6.4% over the period to a high of 14.9% in Greece (Greece's government increased its tax revenues and decreased expenditure by an amount equivalent to 14.9% of the economy's output). At the same time Greece's economic output contracted by almost 16% over the 3-year period.

To estimate the implied relationship in Figure 1 between austerity and growth, a simple regression analysis was conducted, which is summarized by the trend-line shown in the figure. More austerity (from increased tax revenues, decreased expenditures, or both) as measured by the total change in a country's fiscal position as a percentage of its economic output between 2009 and 2012, is shown by moving rightward along the horizontal axis of the chart. A country's economic growth over the same period is shown on the vertical axis as the percentage change in GDP. As shown by the estimated trend-line's negative slope, on average an increase in austerity relative to GDP of 1% (increased taxes, reduced expenditures, or both) was associated with 1.39% decline in economic growth.[8] This suggests the data are supportive of a view consistent with Keynesian economists—that economic growth slows when government contributes less and takes more from the economy. From the data in this period there appears to be little evidence greater austerity is consistent with increased growth. More sophisticated analyses are also consistent with the results shown. The IMF issued a well-read report in late 2012 that detailed their analysis of the cost of austerity efforts on world economic growth.[9] They concluded that the effects of increased austerity across the world likely decreased economic growth significantly.

These results have important implications moving forward for Europe. First, they suggest less austerity would be better than more. To promote growth, especially in the economies most affected by the crisis, austerity demands may have to be reduced and in fact stimulus may be appropriate. Unfortunately, a natural question then follows; how would such a policy change be financed? There are few options regarding how this might be accomplished. Delivering aid in the form of grants or external stimulus could be one possibility. Development funds from the EU to finance productivity enhancing investment would be stimulative. The problem with this approach is where does the EU get these funds? Creditor countries have already financed several bailouts, and it is unlikely that there is the political will in these countries to further extend financing to the EU to fund such projects, especially to the extent that would be necessary to meaningfully increase employment and growth in the troubled economies of Europe.

Alternatively, troubled countries could finance their own stimulus. This again, however, leads to the same question—where will the funds come from? The troubled economies that might benefit most from such stimulus are exactly the countries unable to access international credit markets. Again this implies that creditor countries would have to be the source of funds since they are the countries with such access, and again, given the conditions in countries that have received aid, reducing austerity demands are unlikely to be welcome in creditor nations, nor are demands to extend credit further. Since creditor nations are unwilling to finance such aid directly, an alternative could be to share their credit ratings and credit-worthiness instead, allowing Eurobonds to be used. In this case troubled nations could gain access to international credit markets by having their lending guaranteed by creditor nations in exchange for strict limits on such borrowing and the use of such funds. Eurobond proposals, however, have fallen on deaf ears in creditor countries were there exists a deep resistance to such forms of joint liability. Overall, it would appear that at best some slowdown in austerity demands in existing bailouts is likely the most realistic means to deliver swifter recovery within the troubled countries.

A focus on troubled economies, however, threatens to lose sight of potential for economic improvement elsewhere. With respect to stimulating the most troubled economies in Europe, it is possible that stimulus in the least-troubled economies could be an effective recovery policy. Specifically, if the strongest economies were to take actions to stimulate their own economies internally, such growth could lead to two positive outcomes for those economies where recovery is needed most. First, growth in the strongest economies is likely to increase export demand from weaker economies. Increased incomes in wealthier economies could also stimulate tourism in southern economies in Europe, thereby further aiding growth. Secondly, strong growth in creditor economies is also likely to increase inflation in these countries, raising their wage levels in these countries. Such a change could further improve the relative competitiveness of weaker Eurozone economies, further stimulating their export growth. Stimulus in creditor economies would also have another advantage–it is likely to avoid the type of political resistance increasing financing to troubled countries would create. Since growth in creditor economies has not been strong, efforts to improve growth in these countries would likely be welcomed by many of their residents.

The problem of finding funds to stimulate troubled economies in the Eurozone was demonstrated by the EU's response in 2012 and 2013. In 2012, a "Growth Pact" championed by France was suggested as a means of balancing Germany's efforts to achieve the Fiscal Compact. In June 2012 it was announced the EU would allocate €130 billion to programs that would allow troubled economies in the Eurozone to recover. Unfortunately, this did not reflect any new funds being offered. Almost half of the announced funds were merely repurposed from existing EU regional development funds. Furthermore, the remaining funds pledged were contingent on private-sector contributions and would have to come from external private investment with the ECB providing limited loan guarantees. Of course, given conditions in the Eurozone, there was little private appetite to provide such funding. In 2013, an additional EU sponsored Youth Unemployment Initiative promised €6 billion in aid for unemployed in Europe. Given the scale of youth unemployment in the EU, however, such an effort was almost certain to be far less than is necessary to make a dent in the problem given the EU economy's €13 trillion size. Such efforts suggest the difficulty in defining meaningful policy under the Eurozone's current economic circumstances and such announcements appear to be made more for political effect than to accomplish meaningful change.

Overall, recovery in the short run is the most difficult economic policy-making task facing the Eurozone. Analysis of the data would support the argument that reduced austerity in troubled economies is necessary to improve growth, but it would appear from a practical perspective the willingness and ability to stimulate these economies directly are limited. Financing of such policies would have to come from creditor nations, nations, already suffering from bailout fatigue and who are unlikely to be politically willing to further increase their nation's economic liabilities to improve growth elsewhere. This includes efforts to extend credit indirectly through mechanisms such as Eurobonds that rely on a form of joint liability. Policies, therefore, are likely to be most politically acceptable if they focus on attempting to improve short-term recovery in creditor nation economies.

Such efforts could focus on increasing economic activity in the strongest Eurozone economies such as Germany's, for example, and then allowing this increased demand to raise export demand in more troubled economies elsewhere. In this way the stronger economies would pull the weaker ones out of recession through stronger growth. Furthermore, higher growth in stronger countries could result in greater wage growth in these economies, thereby increasing the relative competitiveness of troubled economies where internal devaluation has caused wage costs to fall. Such plans also have the additional benefits of being more politically acceptable as stimulus funds are used in the countries providing them.[10] Moving forward, it is likely that the political constraints faced by policy makers in the Eurozone are the most binding with respect to finding effective strategies to tackling the effects of the Euro crisis.

Addressing the Social and Political Architecture of the Eurozone

The depth and duration of Europe's crisis has primarily occurred for two reasons. One is that the scale of the problem is very large. It has involved the entire financial system of an area defined by 17 countries whose collective GDP is larger than that of the United States.[11] The second is that policy response has often appeared uncoordinated and slow. This is due to the significantly more complicated and restricted political and legislative environment of the Eurozone, where policy must be determined on the basis of consensus. Policy actions have required coordination of three separate entities: the EU, IMF, and ECB, or "Troika," which has introduced delays due to the multilateral bargaining necessary between each entity before a policy is enacted. Furthermore, defining the EU's position within these negotiations has required consensus among member states as the governance of the EU is constrained by the demand that the sovereignty of each nation be respected. In practice, this implies that in important matters affecting the entire EU, the unanimous support by all member states is needed for any policy decision. Since the leaders negotiating are not answerable to Europe as a whole but instead to the narrower interests of their own constituents, unanimity among EU leaders in turn implies national self-interests will often be traded off against the optimal policies for Europe. Each leader faces incentives to first consider the consequences of their actions not in terms of European-wide interests, but instead with respect to the reactions policies will have back home.

The problem of slow policy implementation and limited reform can therefore be defined as due to the incentives posed by currency union members' narrow self-interests within the EU system of governance. The lack of a strong Europe-wide federal system has caused individual states to pragmatically consider their own self-interest (and often more narrowly on the interests of their leader's own parties in maintaining their elected mandates) before the interests of Europe as a whole. In these circumstances, national leaders have been reticent to take the lead in the Euro crisis, in committing to bailouts or in developing comprehensive solutions for fear of their being seen as committing an unwilling domestic electorate to external obligations and liabilities not necessarily in their own limited interest. Furthermore, recognizing the delicate politics that exist within the leadership body of Europe, leaders typically refrain from putting other leaders in such a position publicly. Heads of state, who define Eurozone policy through their decisions on the European Council, were elected to represent their own interests, not the interests of Europe, and they have recognized and acted with this limitation in mind. European policy has therefore been slow to develop and more limited in scope due to these constraints.

In addition to political motivations, a second reason for the lack of speed and effectiveness with respect to EU policy during the Euro crisis has been the preferences of those countries with the greatest financial resources. Given that the crisis has required significant commitments of resources to support bailouts and credit guarantees, policy efforts have required the consent of those who would be the primary paymasters—the largest countries in the monetary union. Since the EU's bailout funds are financed by contributions by each member state proportional to their relative economic size, decision making and timing of actions have been determined by those countries with the most funding influence and economic means. For this reason, support by the leaders of France and Germany has been especially crucial to any agreement during the Euro crisis as these two countries represent over 47% of the total funding guarantees to the EFSF and ESM, the two main funds used to administer the crisis bailouts.

The need for the two wealthiest countries to back any policy deal has effectively granted both a financial veto for any given policy measure, especially when they have acted as a bloc. Combined with incentives to follow national self-interests, this constraint implies that overall the domestic interests of Germany and France play the greatest role in determining Eurozone policy. An example of this dynamic can be seen in the lack of success proposals for Eurobonds have found. These proposals, which have found support in several other countries in the Eurozone, faced vehement resistance in Germany because the electorate there saw such proposals as violating the prohibition of joint liability in the Eurozone and potentially very costly to their own country. For this reason, Eurobonds have never been considered seriously as a policy option. It is difficult to imagine that similar concerns in Luxembourg, for example, would have had the same effect on Eurobond proposals had France and Germany been on board.

Figure 2 illustrates the reason for France's and Germany's significant influence in policy making during the Euro crisis. Throughout crisis negotiations, three negotiating blocs have often formed. Germany and the northern countries (Austria, the Netherlands, and Finland) have formed the first bloc and control over 40% of the collective commitment to Europe's bailout funds and financial firewall, the EFSF and ESM. Germany alone represents over 27% of the commitment. These countries have typically called for the greatest fiscal responsibility in aided countries, resisting joint liability proposals and usually in favor of smaller less-costly aid packages. France and other countries (Belgium, Luxembourg, Cyprus, Malta, Slovakia, Slovenia, and Estonia) not in the GIPSI group have represented a second bloc accounting for another 27.7% share of commitments, with France by far the largest contributor within the group.[12] This set of countries has often acted as the balance of power between calls for more conservative policy making and calls for greater action. GIPSI economies could be considered a third bloc. While in theory GIPSI countries have a significant contribution to make to the financial facilities, in practice they have been the primary recipients of aid, thus their potential contributions have mattered less and their negotiating position has been weak. Effectively, it is the credit of the French and German blocs in Figure 2 that guarantee the financing of both the EFSF and the ESM, and within these blocs it is France's and Germany's concerns that matter most.

Clearly in a group of equals, two countries are likely to be much more equal than the rest. This has given the leaders of these two countries the greatest influence in policy setting since the crisis began. Recognizing this influence, through most of the crisis France and Germany have attempted

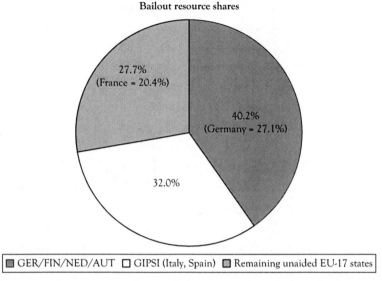

Bailout resource shares

27.7%
(France = 20.4%)

40.2%
(Germany = 27.1%)

32.0%

■ GER/FIN/NED/AUT   □ GIPSI (Italy, Spain)   ▩ Remaining unaided EU-17 states

Figure 2. Commitment shares of the two primary bailout facilities in 2012 across the 17 countries in the Eurozone. Northern countries led by Germany were committed to over 40% of the bailout liability. Of this, Germany represented 27% of the total and over two thirds of the resources in this bloc. Those GIPSI countries that had not received aid at that time (Spain and Italy) accounted for 32% of resources, and the remaining countries including France accounted for 27.7%. The blocs including Germany and France had the highest credit-worthiness and therefore bore the most implicit liability risk for future bailout actions. From this circumstance it is understandable how the leaders of France and Germany emerged as the two leading policy makers in the crisis.
Source: European Union, ESM treaty, Annex 1 adjusted assuming Ireland, Greece, and Portugal have responsibilities suspended due to their bailouts.

to coordinate their positions to ensure that both their interests are maintained. Overall, policy response in the Euro crisis has depended on the speed with which countries have been willing to commit to particular actions and, in particular, the interests of the two countries with the greatest means. Their willingness to support policies in turn has depended on their leaders' willingness to act. That readiness has not necessarily been determined by the perception of a threat to Europe's best interests but instead threats to the best interests of their own countries. This has then slowed the adoption of policies to address sovereign debt market instability and aid programs for troubled nations and often resulted in the scope of policies adopted being compromised once chosen actions are agreed to.

Power in the Eurozone comes from the pocketbook, and the pocketbook also grants the power to dictate the speed circumstances will be reacted to.

The influence of national self-interest and the need for compromise has also almost certainly contributed to policy mistakes. The implementation of costly austerity programs has been strongly supported by northern European countries, in part to reduce the contributions they faced in supporting bailout programs. As discussed previously, this has likely undermined economic recovery in aided countries and worsened the economic circumstances bailouts were hoped to improve. Similarly, the original lack of EU support to include private sector losses in the first Greek bailout likely stemmed, at least in part from the fact that French and German banks would have incurred the largest losses in resulting private write-downs and bond haircuts. In hindsight, this could be viewed as an example of a policy mistake caused by the narrower self-interests of the two largest countries negotiating policy as this unwillingness to allow private-sector losses only increased the eventual total cost of the Greek bailouts.[13] Overall, national self-interests is have resulted in aid programs that have proven too small, too slow, too costly or too harsh in their implementation, creating the conditions under which aid has been less effective than it could have been. Furthermore, the potential for policy mistakes and the difficulty in predicting policy outcomes due to the EU's need to achieve political consensus has contributed to greater uncertainty in financial markets during the crisis, which in turn has raised bond rates and made finance more difficult in troubled countries. This too has raised the cost of policy making in the Eurozone.

While the structure of EU governance has slowed policy making and increased the cost of policies implemented to control the crisis, it may also have undermined the political stability of the European monetary union as well. The Euro crisis has imposed significant hardships on millions of people in the Eurozone, which could in turn endanger the project of European integration by undermining its political support. Disaffected citizens in the currency union have become more and more disenchanted and disenfranchised by the European project and the fallout of this dissatisfaction can be seen in a decline in support for Eurozone membership as reflected in public opinion polling that has occurred since the start of the Euro crisis.[14] This decline in support has also been reflected in the rise in popularity and

electoral successes of anti-European integration parties in national elections. For example, Greek elections in 2012 resulted in the party Syriza
coming in a close second overall. Its platform was to reject the Troika's
bailout package and the party's leader had threatened to leave the Eurozone
during his campaign. Populist support for Syriza and the complete collapse
of support for the traditional Greek parties that had shared power since the
1970s was unexpected, and almost certainly reflected the overall frustration
of that country's voters and the bleakness of economic conditions in
Greece. The result has been a politically unstable coalition government and
greater uncertainty regarding the ability of Greece to meet bailout
obligations.

In Italy, frustration among voters over the economic climate there also
resulted in an antiestablishment party, The Five Star Movement, receiving
the greatest number of votes in that country's House of Deputies elections
in Spring of 2013, forcing a very difficult process of government coalition
building and a government with a very weak electoral mandate. Even in
Germany, the Alternative for Germany party entered elections in 2013 with
a platform of removing that country from the currency union. Its efforts
have elicited support from several influential pundits while simultaneously
creating a threat to split Chancellor Merkel's traditional conservative base.
This, in turn, has made it more difficult for Germany to compromise on
unpopular issues in crisis negotiations regarding a banking or fiscal union.
Overall, the leadership of the EU and Eurozone now suffers from a crisis of
legitimacy—growing populist interests reflect the fact that more and more
voters feel disenfranchised and alienated from their national political processes and consider their leaders as working for their own self-preservation,
not those of the voters who elected them. This, in turn, has created a climate of political instability, which has increased the difficulty in developing and implementing effective policy to deal with the Euro crisis.

Rising frustration with economic conditions has also had more insid-
ious effects on political stability and social cohesion in Europe. Within
countries where popular opposition to bailouts has been strongest, opponents of such policy actions have portrayed the situation as a morality
play—with clear heroes and villains. In Germany, for example, narratives
regarding the causes of the crisis have often involved stereotypes, especially
regarding the character and productivity of those living in Mediterranean

states. This has resulted in insinuations the crisis has in part been caused by these societies being profligate or "lazy." Such rhetoric has then increased demands by pundits in Germany for greater austerity in bailout negotiations, and harsher terms with respect to private creditors' losses. Such comments, repeated in the press and elsewhere, have then created a backlash in the countries referred to unflatteringly, affecting politics in Greece for example, where in reaction, Greek stereotypes of Germans have often included suggestions of Nazism. They have also characterized German support for greater austerity as unsympathetic, authoritarian, and mean-spirited and have undermined Greek support for the bailout agreements reached. Both in Germany in Greece, reaction to such politics has caused popular support for solving the Euro crisis to dwindle and has been in part reinforced past stereotypes, increased old and unfounded prejudices and increased the rise of populist impulses. Such stereotypes and references have also had powerful effects emotionally, and have affected internal politics profoundly, focusing them on perceived differences among the people of Europe or historic injustices. This has then created anti-European pressures, and a "crisis of cohesion." The economic crisis and efforts to stem it have resulted in politics that undermine the historic ideas and ambitions to create a greater Europe, which were the inspiration for much of the larger ideas of European political integration.

The fact that the Euro crisis has undermined the political legitimacy of the EU and the cohesion among the peoples of Europe suggests a third crisis being created—a crisis of faith in the idea of a united Europe. The ideas to achieve greater integration of Europe have over time been motivated in part by a desire to end the historic conflicts and perceived differences among peoples that have dominated European history. The focus on differences among people the Euro crisis has caused through references to unfortunate historic events and unfounded stereotypes and prejudices has worked to reverse this motivation, focusing people in Europe on their differences instead of their similarities. This in turn threatens to undermine the motivation to achieve greater political integration, something that is necessary to introduce the institutional changes necessary to address needed long-term reforms in the currency union.

Overall, the political crisis has caused a malaise to settle over Europe in which it is very difficult to find the motivation to press on with the process of European integration. Ironically, efforts to create a more integrated Europe, which culminated in the achievement of the common currency union may now, through the Euro crisis, have created conditions that threaten to reverse several decades of progress toward that goal. In the words of one observer "the only thing that Europe's countries have in common is growing anti-Europeanism."[15] If the European monetary union was meant to more closely integrate the peoples of Europe, this cohesion has been undermined by the incentives the crisis has created to focus on self-interest and differences among its states.

Possible Scenarios: Does Europe's Integration Continue?

Deeper European integration is necessary at the economic and political level to ensure the currency union is to become more stable in the future. Such efforts, however, will threaten to make nation states less important over time. Efforts to create a banking union and fiscal union have already begun a process in the direction of nation states ceding some economic sovereignty to Europe as a whole, but if the currency union is to become more resilient to shocks in the future it will require significantly more economic and political integration. Currently, the Eurozone's structure causes most decision making to be determined by national leaders in the European Council, a forum where the interests of Europe as a whole are subservient to the need to satisfy the domestic interests of each leader. Leaders wish both to preserve their own power and sovereignty and to maintain their grip on power thus they are unwilling to work on changes that undermine either. Given the organization of the EU's power structure, these incentives are likely most powerful for the leaders of the wealthiest countries having the greatest political power in the EU. Under these current conditions it is difficult to imagine significant reforms that create deeper political and economic integration being implemented in the Eurozone as the system provides little benefit or incentive to leaders to support change. In addition to leaders' motivations, it is also the case that the people of Europe are reticent about such changes. Given falling support for European integration across the union, any effort to increase such integration would almost certainly fail as the peoples of Europe seem especially wary right now of governance by a single, large super-state. Overall, it would seem there is little impetus at the governmental or social level for change to occur.

So how will Europe move forward and can it? With respect to the process of European political integration it appears two possible scenarios are possible. The first would see little or no change to the current political structure of the Eurozone over the next 5–10 years, beyond what has already occurred in the crisis. Such a no-change outcome is most likely to occur if the Euro crisis has truly hit a turning point and the worst of the economic and financial crisis has occurred. As has been apparent throughout the events of the recent past, change in the Eurozone has been motivated only when critical situations have arisen. Before the Euro crisis it would have been hard to imagine that the policy changes that have occurred since 2009 would have been possible. The implementation of the greater fiscal coordination and control across states and additional enforcement mechanisms of the Fiscal Compact, the creation of a Europe-wide bailout and firewall mechanism (the ESM) and the willingness of the ECB to overtly intervene in markets to stabilize bond markets through its OMT program all mark significant changes and evolution in the structure of the European monetary union that would not have been likely to occur without the motivating circumstances they were adopted in. Strong arguments regarding the need to avoid moral hazard, to respect national sovereignty, and to maintain the independence of the ECB would almost certainly have been invoked to stop such changes otherwise. Indeed these arguments have been heard during the Euro crisis when such changes were being discussed, but the potential consequences threatening Eurozone leaders when these actions were adopted overcame such opposition. Desperate times called for desperate measures and caused national attitudes to change remarkably quickly. Conversely though, it would seem without such desperation, such changes are much less likely to occur.

The political dynamics of the system are clear. Leaders, faced with a potential economic or political catastrophe, like the failure of the currency union would threaten, recognize that allowing such an event to occur would end their careers and likely the reign of their respective parties. It is difficult to survive the political backlash that follows when severe negative shocks occur. To avoid losing power and electoral support leaders must do all they can when presented with what appears an imminent catastrophe, with policies being adopted that, under normal circumstances, would not be. Similarly though, taking actions necessary to avoid the failure of the currency union requires changes to its political and economic organization and operation that are likely to be deeply unpopular within leaders' countries and similarly threaten leaders longevity in power. Again, the political incentives are to avoid such risks if possible. Faced with being "caught between a rock and a hard place," or being "damned if you do and damned if you don't," leaders take the only other course open to them to maximize their chances of their political survival—they postpone any action, hoping the storm will pass. This also explains why policy making has been slow and its effect often underwhelming when it arrived during Europe's monetary crisis. Only when catastrophe is seemingly inevitable are leaders willing to act to avoid an otherwise unavoidable outcome. When such inevitability is not present, no incentive for action is present either. Leadership necessary to induce change in such circumstances is a public good and underprovided at the European level.

It is therefore difficult to imagine additional steps toward political integration taking place without the impetus of an impending crisis. Calm, combined with the decision-making structure of the Eurozone and EU have almost certainly ensured no such evolution will be been politically possible. The increased political integration of the EU that has occurred over decades has happened in jumps followed by periods of little change. A sort of malaise has crept over the continent in part caused by the length of the recession now affecting most of Europe, and in part by a sort of policy fatigue that has set in after nearly 4 years of crisis. Given that significant change has occurred in a relatively short period of time and given political and negative public opinions regarding additional reform, as long as circumstances remain less than critical, it seems unlikely additional and significant political integration will occur.

What will motivate change in the future then is most likely an event that triggers a new beginning to the crisis, or a new crisis should the current one end. That may not, however, be sufficient to create additional reforms. The reforms now required involve imposing a more federal authority over Europe's member states, beginning with the planned banking and fiscal unions, and possibly in the future continuing with the harmonization of national programs leading to a mechanism that would allow federally administrated transfers across member states. The creation of a credible fiscal and banking union could also allow concerns in wealthier states regarding moral hazard to be reduced. Following these reforms, Europe and particularly Germany, where resistance is greatest, might then consider consenting to expanded provisions for joint liability across states including some form of Eurobonds. Such reform would narrow interest rates across the union in sovereign debt markets, spurring faster economic recovery and removing the internal competitiveness differences now present across the union. Such credit rationing has hobbled business growth in parts of the Eurozone, particularly the southern states of Spain, Portugal, Italy, and Greece.

On the political side, to ensure that increased centralization does not alienate the peoples of Europe, democratic accountability over the leadership of the entire Eurozone will also be necessary. As illustrated by Rodrick's Trilemma, difficult political reform must move toward elected supranational federal governance if voters are to feel some ability to affect policy directly. Voters need to believe their opinions can have political importance and impact, something the current structure of the EU undermines given its reliance on intergovernmental decision making. Because deeper political and economic integration will require treaty reforms and national referenda in some countries, such reforms could also take considerable time. Unfortunately, given the long list of reforms still needed, if change is motivated only by crisis, such reforms would be very difficult to implement in the midst of one. Not only would they be slow and difficult to effect procedurally, but as has been seen in the Euro crisis, worsening conditions have tended to reduce people's tolerance for "more Europe," not increase it, thus further shocks may not be enough to induce change either.

Given that a new shock or threat to the Eurozone may not be enough to encourage additional integration under the EU's current political dynamics, particularly if it occurs in the near future when policy fatigue and malaise seem to have drained the willingness to make more changes, the emergence of a "benevolent hegemon" may be necessary to guide such reforms. Charles P. Kindleberger, in his book *World in Depression* (1973) described how a benevolent hegemonic power, through its influence and direct powers, could implement large and sweeping policy reactions during a period of financial crisis by providing the public good of leadership in an otherwise unstructured world system of governance. Through its hegemonic influence and means, a single politically and economically dominant country could create the coordinating incentives necessary to effect policy across several nations. Such a country though, to be effective, would have to be willing to ignore narrow self-interests and instead be willing to take account of the interests of the financial system as a whole, including the interests of all participating countries. Kindleberger ascribed the lack of such a hegemonic power as the reason the Great Depression of the 1930s was so prolonged:

> *The 1929 depression was so wide, so deep and so long because the international economic system was rendered unstable by British inability and United States unwillingness to assume responsibility for stabilizing it in three particulars: (a) maintaining a relatively open market for distress goods; (b) providing counter-cyclical long-term lending; and (c) discounting in crisis .... The world economic system was unstable unless some country stabilized it, as Britain had done in the nineteenth century and up to 1913. In 1929, the British couldn't and the United States wouldn't. When every country turned to protect its national private interest, the world public interest went down the drain, and with it the private interests of all ...*[16]

His idea of the importance of such a hegemonic power and its ability to provide the public good of leadership and create order in an otherwise "anarchic international system" of world governance has since been adopted in the wider context of international relations and political science, and is known as the "theory of hegemonic stability."[17]

Leadership is lacking in the Eurozone because given its governance structure, leadership might similarly be considered a sort of public good. No country has the incentive to offer it. If a single state were, however, to consider the needs of the union ahead of its own narrow self-interest and provide that public good, greater political integration could occur. Such a country could then act like a locomotive of reform to pull the continent toward change. As the most influential country in the currency union, likely the only country capable of taking on such a role is Germany.[18] An example of this power was seen when Germany used its influence to drive through the Fiscal Compact in 2012. It is unclear though that Germany is willing and able to take on this role.

Such efforts would require careful diplomacy. To be effective, Germany would need a change in approach; to take on the role of a benevolent hegemon, a leader-state would have to be perceived as acting in the interests of the Eurozone and not purely its own, something many observers are not convinced Germany has done in the past. While the Fiscal Compact was sold as a policy to improve Europe's economic structure, it was also clearly in Germany's interest. Germany had already adopted many of its conditions. Furthermore, ensuring fiscal stability elsewhere lessened the likelihood German resources would be needed to correct previous fiscal errors somewhere else. To date, as exemplified by the Fiscal Compact and other reforms, Germany's efforts have focused on sticks, not carrots, which have not only seemed less benevolent, but created resentment among those states and peoples most affected. These sticks have also allowed Germany to become a convenient scapegoat when political interests within some countries have created the wish to avoid being held responsible for economic or policy outcomes. Casting blame on Germany, whether reasonable or not, has undermined the support that would be necessary in Europe even if Germany were to attempt to take on a greater leadership role. To gain greater acceptance for change across the Eurozone, any future leader-state will have to adopt policies that focus on cohesion and solidarity, and frame objectives in this manner over efforts based on discipline and sanctions. The difference is subtle and often more perceived than actual, but this is the nature of effective diplomacy. Leadership to accomplish greater European reform and integration will have to focus on what Europe can be for states, not the constraints a greater Europe would impose, which in turn would have the effect of creating support for Europe, not undermining it.

Given the above and for additional reasons, Germany is unlikely to take on such a leadership role. First, it is not likely given the domestic politics in that country, especially given the feeling among many Germans that their country has already spent too much to save Europe. There are also other reasons as well. Culturally since World War II, Germany has refrained from asserting itself as a hegemonic power on the world stage, due in part out of respect for historical mistakes of the past. It is also not clear Germany would be willing to give up the considerable power and influence it has in Europe now. Thirdly, the German perspective to European integration has reflected a focus on individual country responsibility and not joint efforts a more federal system would imply. Germany would seem to prefer generally that national resources be used for national interests, not shared among weaker states when necessary as a federal transfer system would imply.

The Eurozone's current structure already reflects Germany's apparent preferences in many ways given the dominant influence it has asserted in the reform process. The Fiscal Compact reflects fiscal controls Germany would prefer and has imposed on itself—a requirement for balanced budgets and strict controls on the expansion of government debt and deficit. The ECB was modeled after its own Bundesbank, and German influence is still very strong in that institution. Given the likeness of EU institutions to its own, and the influence Germany currently wields over the EU's governance, Germany's leaders are likely to be unwilling to take the risks of "leading from the front" attempting to move Europe toward a more politically integrated body, especially if such reform could entail moving away from some of the structures and principles that govern the EU now.

Even the incidence of a new crisis would not be likely to create incentives for a hegemonic power like Germany to attempt such changes. Only if leadership in Germany emerged that really was motivated to leave the legacy of a more united Europe are such incentives likely to be created.[19] Overall, Germany might be seen as a reluctant hegemony, one unwilling to provide the public good of leadership for cultural, political, and strategic reasons. Given this state of affairs, Germany in some ways resembles the United States that Kindleberger discussed in his description of why a lack of leadership was present in the Great Depression, and for that reason it is unlikely that Europe will see such a strong leader-state emerge.

So how does, or does greater European integration continue? It would seem that unless a crisis is imminent, further reform will be slow and incremental in coming, focusing on adjustments to reforms already begun. The question then is, if major reform is not coming and given Rodrick's analysis, is the current level of integration an unstable outcome?

Although intergovernmental negotiation over economic reforms can continue, it would seem the continued social alienation current EU political structures engender could eventually create a watershed moment when a buildup of demand for reform creates such change. Alternatively, such alienation could create the pressure to dissolve the current state of affairs and move away from the integration already accomplished. What sort of pressure builds may depend on whether economic conditions in Europe soon get better or worsen. It is unlikely that Germany has the willingness to provide the role it could in leading European reforms that would be necessary to motivate greater integration or to help control the destabilizing forces that might otherwise build up, thus the only likely scenario in which change occurs in the near future likely involves another crisis occurring when leaders realize change is necessary to avoid a new disaster.

Outcomes in a future crisis would be uncertain and strongly dependent on the economic and political conditions that preceded it. A future crisis could threaten to cause an eventual fracture of the current levels of integration already achieved or a crisis may be the only way a strong willingness to commit to a more integrated Europe could be created. It would seem then that how the European integration process continues will depend on the likelihood of a future crisis occurring, but such an event may or may not lead to a more integrated Europe.

What Happens Next?
From Status Quo to Doomsday in the Eurozone

Is it possible to divine what lies ahead in the Euro crisis? Gazing into a crystal ball is always fraught with risks. Recounted images are almost certain to be mere speculation, and often that speculation is shaded by the biases of the mystic reporting them. Economics has many failings and one is that its ability to predict what is yet to come is sometimes only slightly better than a carnival fortune-teller's, and some would argue potentially worse. It is a discipline that is far better at describing the past than divining the future and with that in mind what follows is offered very cautiously and with the utmost humility. All we can be certain of is that any prediction offered will be wrong in some way. Still, the fundamental nature of economic agents is that, if they are rational they are forward looking, taking the information at hand to determine their most likely future. It is the curse of being human to be continually compelled try to predict what is imminent and to almost as often be disappointed at the inaccuracy of our forecasts. While we may control nature in the present, the future is nearly always shrouded in a midst that is just out of our sight and often out of our control. Given these caveats, possible scenarios are offered describing potential outcomes in the Eurozone as the area moves on from its current crisis. None is offered in great detail and all are offered on the basis of current information and admitting the author's biases, recognizing that events not yet known will certainly render the conclusions inaccurate and possibly obsolete before any can occur.

Markets have calmed significantly since their worst periods of crisis in 2011 and 2012. This calm was most recently caused by the ECB's palliative actions in late summer of 2012—their implementation of the OMT program. The market sedating effect that program created has managed to persist despite an electoral stalemate in Italy and the near failure of policy makers to avoid default by Cyprus in early spring of 2013. Given the fact that markets seemed to have regained their confidence that the euro can survive and that aided countries are no longer a sure bet to fail, the most likely outcome of the crisis currently appears to be that sovereign debt markets will very slowly continue to improve for European economies. As this improvement occurs, the crisis will very slowly ease.

Reforms already begun will continue to move forward incrementally. An imperfect banking union is likely to form with national interests of some creditor countries, namely Germany slowing the process and compromising the agreement in the interest of greater sovereign control over aspects of banking system oversight, and to avoid the potential shared liability a full deposit insurance system would create. While imperfect, however, the resulting reforms will be an improvement over conditions prior to the crisis. In addition to the banking union, changes made to the fiscal union will create greater sovereign-debt brakes in the future. Outside of these efforts, however, it is difficult to imagine any additional integration occurring. As previously described, the combination of political incentives and public suspicions regarding greater European integration, along with a general fatigue caused by 4 years of crisis and the lack of any pressing need for countries to act will combine to create a malaise, one that undermines the motivation for any policy action greater than deemed necessary or already underway.

As markets stabilize, the most pressing issue in the Eurozone will be the economic situation in the countries most dramatically affected by the crisis—Greece, Spain, Portugal, and Italy. Their recessions are dragging down not only their own growth and employment but also growth and employment across the Eurozone. As sovereign market pressures recede the currency union will feel a greater political need to be seen to be addressing this situation for both moral and economic reasons. Mounting unemployment, particularly among youth threatens to become a dangerous political issue about intergenerational fairness that will also be difficult to ignore. As such concerns mount though, it is unlikely significant action will occur. Actions necessary to reverse economic trends in the near term would require less austerity. Such actions would then be labeled by many as undermining the policy reforms already taken to encourage greater debt control. For policy makers the trick will be to do enough to claim they are concerned and taking action, but not enough to appear to be compromising recently made reform deals and commitments to reducing debt levels. Accordingly, efforts will be made by European leaders to quell rising empathy for troubled countries by taking actions that have more optical than economic value, but again without doing enough to stir the anger of those opposed to such actions. This will likely mean that in leader's summits at the European Council, the EU will continue to trumpet agreements regarding the creation and use of "solidarity funds" to help youth unemployment, but these efforts will remain too small to have any significant impact, at least in the near term when it is most needed.[20]

The problem with reforms like the Fiscal Compact already implemented is that they implicitly bar any sort of stimulative policy that could be interpreted as undermining the credibility of fiscal reforms agreed to during the worst of the crisis. Policy makers' hands are tied, which in large part was the purpose of the Fiscal Compact to begin with. Stimulus cannot be funded nor fully supported because it would break these commitments, undermining their credibility. Serious stimulus would also cause concern among some policy makers and their constituents that the negative signal sent by such efforts would encourage moral hazard, weakening the resolve of weaker states to mend their balance sheets and continue efforts at institutional and labor market reform. Simultaneously, they would worry such efforts would also undermine the confidence of international sovereign debt investors in the currency union's seriousness regarding debt sustainability. As Paul Krugman has wryly noted, this is seemingly a "... form of Puritanism in H.L. Mencken's sense—*the haunting fear that someone, somewhere may be happy.*"[21] In fact, it is not the fear of happiness leaders' face, but the opposite. Anger among voters caused in reaction to any stimulative action, which in some quarters will never be seen as enough aid and in others as too much, leads to a political incentive to do neither. Barring significant changes in the politics of the Eurozone, policy regarding current recessionary output and employment conditions will be guided by caution and inaction. Leaders will do as little as possible while hoping things will improve in the interim.

This is a risky course. Not only does this risk a buildup of dissatisfaction as leaders are (accurately) perceived by the voting public across Europe as unwilling to take action, but it also implies recovery will be slow and difficult. The worst economies face a long road of hard reform amidst incredibly high levels of unemployment. They also face very difficult credit conditions. Banks, still reeling from the credit crises of recent years will continue to hoard cash to pump up their capital reserves and balance sheets, offering little business credit with which to support growth, much less spur it.[22] Poor business conditions have combined to make banks unwilling to lend and businesses unwilling to borrow and this has created little hope of an expansion in economic activity or employment occurring quickly. Furthermore, world conditions could worsen these already bad conditions. Recovery in the United States, and with it the threat of rising interest rates could create pressure on European interest rates to keep European yields competitive, increasing the cost of borrowing for businesses and nations. Credit conditions and the straitjacket of previous commitments to policy change made during the crisis will combine to make recovery difficult, painful, and slow. The threat politicians now face is that a perceived lack of action on the part of the rest of the EU and the Eurozone could set in motion a very negative political dynamic toward Europe in general, especially in the worst-hit countries. Weak or nonexistent recovery leading to greater dissatisfaction and frustration could cause political stability to worsen, leading to very weak coalition governments like those already in place in Italy, Greece, and even Portugal, and greater chances of political instability undermining not only economic recovery, but also any ability to accomplish greater European integration and reform in the future, even if there were a willingness to do so.

These conditions then create three possible outcomes that are listed in order of probability given the author's priors. The first scenario is straightforward. Conditions continue much like they appeared in the summer of 2013—very limited reform politically continues with incremental steps that focus on the Eurozone's economic apparatus and procedures without treating the real problem, which is that you cannot run a currency union made up of very different countries facing country-specific shocks without a federal system of transfers and centralized fiscal authority. Europe cannot have its cake and eat it too; it cannot maintain the system in place now if the goal is long-term stability. That said, the current system can persist a very long time with very slow change unless some major shock occurs. Then leaders will react as necessary, doing as little as they can given their concerns for national self-interest first caused by the structure of the EU's governance, especially the preeminence of the European Council in decision making.

Political discontent, like a rot could begin to set in and take its toll, especially in weaker countries. Europe in 2013 is sick, with a banking sector that cannot lend to support growth and a fiscal structure that cannot allow stimulus to create it either. Even Germany, widely regarded as the least negatively affected country during the crisis that finds itself barely growing at only a 0.2% annual rate. While European leaders will try to keep things together as they have throughout the crisis, without major changes because they have too much vested political capital in the current arrangement, the political instability caused by social disillusionment will make things very difficult. Political instability could worsen as unemployment mounts and economic stagnation persists. Stagnation will make room for more fringe populist parties stepping into the political vacuum disillusionment creates, parties with no vested political capital in the current system. This will make current leadership very unstable, and should such new parties achieve power, future changes unpredictable. This state of affairs leads to two possible different future scenarios, in decreasing subjective order of probability. Buildup of political dissatisfaction stemming from an apparent status quo could also lead to a continuum of intermediate cases between them.

The first alternative scenario is the occurrence of a policy mistake regarding Greece or a political breakdown within that country, that causes it to leave the euro. The most likely scenario involves Greece because it is by far the weakest country in the Eurozone and still potentially at the greatest risk of default. Coming into the crisis, Greece was a broken country. Its public institutions were very weak—it had very little ability to collect revenue, its public sector was bloated and protected, entitlement obligations were crushing and its political and economic system dependent on patronage. The events of the Euro crisis and ensuing recession have encouraged very significant reform in that country, but at the cost of great pain and dislocation. Debt levels even after remedial actions and bailouts still appear unsustainable under current arrangements. Greece finds itself in a situation where it is very likely to be unable to achieve Troika-set targets for reform and improvement necessary to maintain bailout funding.

This situation will require at some point in the near future a likely need for yet another new deal—with more haircuts on debt if it is to become sustainable in the long term. Since private creditors have already been cut to the bone with respect to reductions in principle and interest renegotiated under legal terms that limit additional losses after the second Greek bailout agreement, the need to restructure Greek debt yet again will imply public creditor entities in the Troika (other EU countries that have financed the previous bailout resources, the IMF, and the ECB) will have to accept losses. When this occurs such losses will create a serious political backlash in the northern countries, particularly Germany. Any new bailout that demands such losses will in response demand even tougher conditionality on Greece and its reforms in return for such action. This may then create the final political breaking point in Greece. While likely worsening the situation, a populist backlash will result in the fall of the government, replaced by one that either withdraws from the union or refuses to work under Troika conditions. Either outcome leads to default by Greece and its departure from the Eurozone.

Alternatively, the second scenario in which Greece leaves the Eurozone could be caused by a domestic political error that brings down the government and with it the commitment to reform necessary to maintain current bailout conditions. Current political instability and worsening political conditions in Greece leave any government there on a knife-edge in which any error or significant shock could topple it.[23] Such an error or miscalculation could cause Greece to choose to refuse current conditions under which the Troika would release funds to maintain its current bailout conditions, leading to a disorderly and sudden default and again an exit from the common currency. Regardless of whether such a political breakdown occurs due to internal or external pressures, Greece would either opt to leave the euro suddenly or be forced to, which regardless of outcome would lead to a significant new turning point in the saga of the Euro crisis.

Following either of the chain of events above, after the crisis caused by Greece's departure from the euro, Europe could be spurred to "double-down" on reform to maintain its remaining members and the stability of the currency, making far-reaching changes rapidly to ensure its own survival. As such a crisis would immediately drive up sovereign-debt rates, putting other weak countries in jeopardy and the health of Europe's financial system at risk, an almost certain and necessary response would require opening up facilities for Eurobonds or some other form of joint liability and transfers across the Eurozone to backstop the financial circumstances of the remaining weaker countries. Politically this would be difficult and the scale of changes required in a short time would be very complicated. The ECB would also be required to make good on the promise its OMT program to stabilize sovereign bond rates, and massive interventions in international markets would be required to prove its commitment to the remaining countries on the euro.

Assuming efforts were successful to stabilize the crisis after Greece's exit, the final outcome would be a system that, after the crisis, left sovereign debt markets across the Eurozone locked in a relationship of mutual reinforcement. Tighter fiscal reform necessary to allow such joint liability would in effect create a much deeper economic integration in the Eurozone. The cost of achieving such integration, however, would be a worsened set of recessionary conditions across countries. Greek conditions would also be much worse in the short term with access to international credit eliminated. Overall, in this scenario Europe achieves greater political integration through the crisis caused by a Greek departure, but at considerable economic cost.

The final possible scenario is caused by the same circumstances as that just described—a Greek exit. In this scenario, however, agreement to achieve greater integration is not possible and effectively the European currency union begins to "unzip" as the national departures from the euro begin to cascade. A Greek departure leads to a rupture in Germany and other northern states as losses mount to creditors in the case of a Greek default. One by one weaker countries end up in crisis brought on by worsening sovereign debt market conditions and worsening recessions the uncertainty this turn of events causes. Creditor countries refuse to backstop weaker ones as previous losses make new commitments to additional bailout liability toxic in domestic politics. The ECB cannot follow through on its promised OMT operations as countries cannot agree to remedial actions OMT actions require as a prerequisite for their use. The credibility of the ECB's promise to protect the euro is broken, and a run on banks across the Eurozone occurs much like what appeared to be beginning to occur in June and July of 2012. Portugal, Spain, and Italy withering under the pressure of mounting sovereign debt rates and capital flight from their countries to safer havens in Europe and elsewhere, resort to strict capital controls and the effective or eventual replacement of the euro with an alternative currencies.

What might be left after such a crisis could be a much smaller core of countries that included France and Germany using the euro due to vested political capital in the single currency, or a complete or nearly complete set of independent currencies as the previous common currency system broke down. Deep recessions follow and countries realize the risk, not the reward of a common currency system. Political and economic integration in Europe then takes a step backward as political and economic uncertainty overwhelms the continent. This is the economic-doomsday scenario governments fall, unemployment spikes, and Europe experiences a lost decade, which in turn has sharply negative consequences on the world economy.

All of the above is highly speculative and intentionally vague. The three potential scenarios outlined, however, suggest that the process of European integration is not certain to move forward and continue to evolve. Each of the above suggests a different leg of Rodrick's trilemma is a possible end point to the process of change now in motion. In the most catastrophic course of events, integration takes a step backward, moving to a state in which Europe returns to less integration, not more—a set of nation states overseeing unstable domestic politics. In the situation argued the most likely, the process of integration has hit a wall, one that is unlikely to be overcome unless another significant crisis arises or an unexpected champion leading a powerful state emerges to push past the current situation. In this case Europe remains in a state of deep economic integration and yet a nonfederal system of governance, which continues to alienate voters. The drawback of this state of affairs is that if current recessionary conditions continue, voter alienation is very likely to create a buildup of destabilizing political forces that eventually leads to a crisis and one of the two other alternatives argued. It may be the case that only a national departure from the Eurozone, for example, a Greek exit, can actually create the conditions that solidify commitment to the common currency, allowing the remaining countries in the currency union to jump to the next stage of political and economic integration—one necessary to ensure the stability of a common currency.

CHAPTER 9

From Forest Fires to Bumblebees and Hammers and Nails—Lessons from the Euro Crisis

So what have we learned from the Euro crisis? There are many lessons one can draw from the experiences of the Eurozone since 2009. Some have been enumerated in the previous pages. The purpose of this book has been to attempt to describe the complexity of the Euro crisis, what it is, why it occurred, and why it has been so difficult to treat for European policy makers. This too has been described previously. In concluding our investigation it would be too easy to declare how the Eurozone could have improved the worst impacts of the crisis or avoided them altogether with some simple policy prescriptions gleaned only with the aid of hindsight. Clearly, the currency union could have been better off had some countries not been included, some rules more strictly enforced, and some changes to institutions and mechanisms been implemented earlier—the list goes on of how mistakes now recognized could have been sidestepped were the opportunity to present itself again. Such comments, however, would be of little value. It is left to the reader to create such a list if they like, and the previous chapters, though not exhaustive should provide a good start. Reality moving forward, however, is more difficult. The Euro crisis occurred and the clock cannot be turned back on the many decisions and actions that contributed to it.

As defined throughout, this book has referred to the Euro crisis as the crisis in sovereign debt markets and resultant banking system crisis that occurred across the Eurozone after Greece's debt revelations in the fall of 2009. The result of this financial crisis has been a deep recession across much of Europe. While arguably the worst of the financial crisis is now over, the economic crisis it has left will take years to recover from. As noted in the past few pages, if the currency union is to return to health and avoid its past instability, policy options now must focus on rectifying flaws in the currency union's architecture to ensure that such outcomes do not arrive again, while also focusing on growth policies to improve economic conditions. Addressing the first of these tasks—repair of the common currency system's flaws has already begun. The first steps toward a true fiscal union were taken when the Eurozone nations agreed to cede some sovereignty to Brussels and abide by the increased limits imposed by the Fiscal Compact agreed to in 2012. More could be done here, but this was a start toward more effective debt brakes being implemented in the union.

The flaws in the Eurozone's financial system that caused crises in a nation's banking system to be directly transferred to its sovereign debt sustainability are also being improved. The doom loop can be broken by creating a proper banking union across the euro area. Creating such a union will require a single common regulator, operating under a common set of regulatory rules and applying common resolution mechanisms, and providing a deposit insurance system that applies union-wide. Again, Eurozone leaders are pursuing these objectives. The devil, as they say, will be in the details. Creating such a banking union requires an enormous amount of information and eventually the creation of a complex set of financial guidelines, which will eventually have to be agreed upon by all countries involved.

The ECB has also changed its policies and programs to better protect and stabilize the common currency and to strengthen the financial system. The implementation of its OMT program to support and protect sovereign bond rates of member states has calmed debt markets and reduced damaging speculation by providing a credible commitment to the euro. While the Eurozone may have been slow to use the ECB's power to end the liquidity crisis that occurred after the 2009 Greek debt revelations, they finally did and efforts are now focusing on the credit problems that now depress growth across the currency area.

More, however, can be done. The union lacks a federal system of governance and transfers and a harmonized set of social benefits, and labor mobility could still be improved. Labor markets are still too rigid and barriers still exist in too many countries to protect too many domestic sectors and industries. EU governance structures could be reformed to become more democratic and inclusive, and designed in a way that creates the incentives to promote good European policy. A change to a more federal system is unlikely anytime soon, however, political reforms could be implemented to encourage greater European leadership, with greater accountability to the electorate of Europe as a whole. As noted previously, in regard to all of these areas, complacency, malaise, and policy-fatigue are likely the greatest dangers to accomplishing the more complicated structural reforms still lacking in the economic and political architecture of the Eurozone.

Again, it would be tedious to list in detail the specific improvements the Eurozone might take to rectify the shortcomings that have contributed to the severity of the Euro crisis. These are described daily in policy documents and news magazines, and are added to almost as often. Instead and without summarizing too much of the ground already covered, this chapter focuses on three observations that might be useful for future policy makers and students of the crisis. With these insights in mind, it is hoped the reader may be better able to understand future events in this crisis as they unfold, or the events of the next crisis when it arrives.

Forest Fires

Like the drought ravaged Greek forests that ignited in August 2009, conditions in the Eurozone only needed the necessary trigger. The Euro crisis began rather suddenly later that year when a new Greek government admitted that the country had reported misleading statements regarding the true state of its debt and deficit for some time. Coming on the heels of what had been the most severe worldwide financial crisis since the 1930s, market reaction was harsh and swift to the realization not only that Greece's debt was much less secure that previously thought, but also that sovereign debt in general may not be as safe as had been once assumed. Some, including the European Commission itself have attributed the cause of the Euro crisis to the U.S. financial crisis that occurred the year before, however, the first lesson that might be observed from Europe's experience is that regardless of its trigger, without reforms that were necessary to complete the monetary union and reinforce its stability, conditions were such that in the late 2000s a crisis was bound to happen. Faults in the currency union were well known—so-called euro-skeptics, economists, and other pundits who predicted the failure of the euro even before it was introduced had a long list of reasons why the common currency was doomed and many of these flaws have proven very important. As discussed in the previous pages, attributing the Euro crisis to the U.S. financial crisis is convenient but not necessarily truthful. This would be akin to blaming a raging forest fire that starts in a tinder-dry wood on the lightning.[1] Lightning is difficult to predict and impossible to control, but forest conditions are manageable in the face of such risks.

It seems almost certain that even without that the U.S. financial crisis and absent some reform, the problems of unsustainable debt levels built up by Greece, and the structure of the Eurozone's common currency, its banking system, and political institutions would eventually have led to a Euro crisis. The Eurozone's institutional design, in particular, its lack of political willingness to enforce treaty requirements meant to maintain a stable euro early in the currency union's history led to the breakdown of a set of systems meant to safeguard the economic stability of the union. Market rigidities in member states also ensured economies were less adaptive to economic shocks than what would be desired in an optimal currency area. What became clear in the Euro crisis was that the impact financial market structure could have on the stability of a currency area, something that had been overlooked in much of the euro-skeptic literature earlier. When the world became focused on the problems in Greece in 2009, contagion in sovereign debt markets spread to the European banking sector, which had already been weakened by the earlier world financial crisis. In this way, the problems of one small country representing less than 3% of Eurozone output mushroomed into a crisis that threatened much of the region.

To understand how the crisis has occurred as it has, it is fundamental to understand the context of the Eurozone. The roots of the problems that now beset the region were created long before the crisis began. They can be traced to structures defined in the Maastricht Treaty signed in 1992, but that treaty was only a step along the path toward a more united Europe begun almost 40 years before. The initial currency union was to be an integrated economic union that it was hoped, once underway would lead to a greater political union as borders faded away in importance and Europe became even more tightly integrated. Until that occurred, the monetary union was meant to alleviate barriers to trade, ease the movement of goods and services, ease labor and capital mobility, and allow harmonization of taxes—all inevitable steps necessary to tighter political integration.

In many of these areas the monetary union was a great success. The common currency ended the currency speculation that had for so long been a problem for trade within Europe. It also allowed greater transparency and harmonization of some economic institutions, allowed greater transparency in goods and service pricing, spurred economic growth in many areas, and greatly enhanced the degree of policy collaboration between European countries. Unfortunately, the creation of the common currency did not end speculation—in 2009 it became clear speculation had only moved from currencies to speculation on sovereign debt.

The initial success of the monetary union also had another negative effect. In encouraging growth across the continent it may also have resulted in complacency regarding the need for additional institutional reform, allowing EU leaders to leave undone the challenges of greater political and economic integration. Complacency also allowed leaders to weaken the institutions and policies already created. For example, accomplishing greater fiscal coordination across states could have reduced the problems that led to the crisis by ensuring debt brakes were in place that avoided destabilizing deficits. Unfortunately, instead of strengthening this coordination, the Maastricht Treaty Convergence Criteria that were meant to ensure a sound currency base were weakened and eventually ignored in some countries.

Imbalances in debt and trade that should have signaled the need for reform were also allowed to build. Trade imbalances across the union, coupled with credit booms led to an increase in debt held by southern states. Since a country's income cannot be greater than its total expenditure without debt accumulation (or wealth exhaustion), trade deficits implied that if these countries were to continue spending more than they earned in production, they would have to finance the difference with credit. Although credit could have been allocated to the types of investment that would have increased productivity and competiveness, alleviating structural trade imbalances in southern countries, it instead fueled real estate and consumption bubbles that only worsened these imbalances over time. Public finances were not addressed in countries where these challenges were most pressing, nor were necessary structural reforms that could have improved labor market competitiveness and productivity. This worsened the debt and trade imbalances further.

The implementation of a common currency also exacerbated these effects by causing interest rates to converge across countries, creating easy credit conditions that allowed growth in countries to be fueled by debt instead of productivity gains. The end result was a continuing cycle of worsening trade imbalances between northern and southern countries, with northern credit being used to finance southern expenditures, with the eventual result the catastrophic outcomes still being dealt with today.

The Eurozone's governance, consisting of a club of nations and not a functioning federal system has also increased the political challenges of dealing with the crisis once it began. Policy reaction to the crisis has often been compromised, untimely and inadequate due to the nature of the EU, its lack of centralized and continent-wide policy-making ability and its need to gain the support and approval of all EU members (or at least several of the most important) before adopting any new measures. Markets have often appeared to judge Europe's efforts as too little and too late, leaving them unconvinced that the Eurozone has the leadership and commitment to solve the currency area's problems. The reason for this reaction, however, may not have been in the quality of leadership within the Eurozone so much as the political incentives and constraints the leadership of the Eurozone faced.

Once the crisis began, the types of policies that would have been most effective in dealing with it were often too drastic to be passed through the constraints of the EU and Eurozone political system. For example, agreement to create a much larger fiscal transfer union, the creation of collectivized debt, or a European unity tax to fund new bailouts all would have been politically difficult policies for some national leaders facing voters at home. Domestic narratives within northern countries regarding the causes of the crisis, which often relied on easy, inaccurate, and unfair stereotypes, along with the challenges of domestic politics ensured this. Alternatively, doing nothing risked failure of the Eurozone. Again, the threat of such an outcome and its resulting fallout presented a grave threat to Eurozone leaders who knew they would face the blame for the consequences of such a failure in their respective countries if it occurred. Between a rock and a hard place, leaders had little incentive but to appear to act when is necessary but otherwise to do as little as possible. When faced with a new problem or threat in the Euro crisis saga, Eurozone leaders' most common reaction was first denial, in hopes that the problems might fade away. When that didn't work, a limited response would follow to gain time while hoping for a resolution to occur that didn't require still more action. Too little and too late has often been Eurozone leaders' only political choice.

Given that the evolution of consensus is difficult to predict within the Eurozone, and that national leaders are constrained by internal politics, uncertainty has remained high regarding leaders' ability to find a resolution to the crisis. This implies that domestic political events can then have sudden and significant effects in financial markets.[2] Events within the domestic spheres of important countries have immediately increased uncertainty regarding the markets' expectations of future Eurozone outcomes during the crisis and will continue to do so. One could argue that the Eurozone has come much farther much sooner toward addressing the economic union's shortcomings in the past few years than would have been imaginable in such a short time prior to the crisis. But it has not been a quick enough change. Changes in political outlook move on a far slower timescale than movements in international financial markets.

While European leaders could not come to terms quickly with the crisis, the situation has been worsened by the fact that the EU's central bank was also unwilling and unable to quickly act as a lender of last resort through the crisis's early years. Again, the EU's architecture created the problem as the design of the central bank and its role in the economy limited such powers intentionally. This decision left the bank unable to address market problems with the sort of overwhelming force that historically has been shown to be effective in such conditions. Previous financial crises and much financial theory have shown how immediately a central bank, using capacity as lender of last resort, can stabilize a banking system, allowing policy makers breathing space to make decisions.[3] The effectiveness of the ECB's own eventual liquidity actions, through their LTRO loans in December 2011, and the threat to use OMT actions since August

2012 reinforce this argument. It was only when the ECB actually made or threatened overt use of its powers as a lender of last resort that liquidity began to return to the Eurozone's sovereign debt markets and banking system.

Since the summer of 2012, it appears that Eurozone and ECB actions have begun to convince markets the crisis can be contained. Three actions have bought the Eurozone time to address longer term problems of debt and structural reform. The second bailout for Greece, finalized in March 2012, staved off fears of a disorderly Greek default, at least for a time. In addition to this, the ECB's lending actions noted above appear to have credibly convinced markets that it will use its power as lender of last resort to stabilize the banking sector as necessary should a new crisis occur, significantly reducing speculation in Europe's debt markets (given a country is willing to agree to reforms). The third action was the creation of new institutional structures such as the permanent financial firewall, the fiscal compact and negotiations toward a banking union. These have developed a means of protecting countries in the short term from financial system shocks while creating facilities to ensure better debt brakes will be present in the future. The remaining challenge the Eurozone faces is the need to address how growth can be encouraged on the continent as deep recessions in peripheral countries threaten their ability to maintain stable debt burdens. So far, actions taken have only bought time. The crisis will only truly end when growth and recovery return to the Eurozone.

Growth, or the lack of it, is the most serious challenge to the stability of the crisis currently. In the coming years growth is expected to be very weak across much of the Eurozone, and contractionary conditions are expected to remain severe in GIPSI economies. Bailout terms for Greece include benchmarks that will be very difficult to achieve unless growth returns to its economy. With an unemployment rate near 30% overall, and nearly 60% for young adults, economic conditions and austerity measures continue to undermine the political stability of the country. Similar problems of high unemployment and slow growth also beset Spain and Portugal. All three countries have seen their national governments' policy-making abilities to meet bailout terms imposed by their Troika partners and to institute structural reforms hobbled by eroded public support, which worsens as these economies continue to struggle. Worsening conditions will only reinforce the challenges each of these countries face, and by extension, the currency union and its economies.

What does the future hold for the crisis? It is very difficult to predict, which is why so much uncertainty remains. A disorderly and unexpected Greek default could still wreak havoc in world markets despite recent efforts to reduce the threat. Also, conditions in Europe could change very quickly thus the relative calm sovereign debt markets have enjoyed since late 2012 could quickly erode if market concerns suddenly worsen, or external events increase political and economic uncertainty within and outside the Eurozone. Growth cannot be taken for granted and the risks a lack of growth presents should not be underestimated—it is the key determinant of whether the threats to the Eurozone will recede or persist.

Bumblebees

The euro area is still engulfed in a severe crisis, which is posing a formidable challenge to all European policy-makers
Benoit Cœuré, European Central Bank Executive Board member,
Paris, July 10, 2013[4]

The above statement was recorded almost 4 years after the Greek debt announcements that began the Euro crisis and exemplifies the second lesson of the Euro crisis: conditions can continue to be very bad for a very long time, yet the currency union and the euro continues to persist. Grounded in models that emphasize optimizing and self-interested behavior, many economists would have predicted, if told to consider the conditions that occurred in the Eurozone over the past 4 years, that the currency union would have failed. Many did so during the crisis, with more predicting that minimally, the euro's membership would be reduced, with at least Greece and perhaps Portugal or even Spain having to inevitably leave the euro. While such defections may still occur, every day that the currency union remains intact seems to increase the chance that it will continue to. Economists have continually underestimated the willingness of Germany and its Eurozone partners to pay the price they have to keep Greece in the euro and to maintain the currency union.

Why have economists been so pessimistic of the euro's chances? In part, this comes from past experience—the experience of Europe and the failure of its previous fixed exchange rate regimes. When countries faced fierce speculation in their exchange markets, and combined difficult recessions, they abandoned their commitments to fix exchange rates. Furthermore, models economists use do not include important political considerations and the inertia and political capital Europe has invested in the common currency. While economic forces and the flaws of the Eurozone already described create destabilizing forces that should lead to the currency union flying apart, like the nucleus of an atom packed with similarly charged protons that should repel one another, an invisible and unaccounted for force seems to have kept the Eurozone together.[5] Politics have held the currency union together long after economic interests might have implied it should come undone.

Alternatively, and just as likely, it may be larger economic interests and uncertainty that are keeping the union together. Economists know that there are potential merits for countries to leave the euro, but there are also potentially great costs. In southern countries, the benefits of devaluation from returning to a domestic currency could be overwhelmed in the short term by the increased inflation and immediate lack of credit-market access, not to mention the economic uncertainty such a departure would create. In the north, for example in Germany, the effects of moving to a domestic currency would be the opposite. Economic conditions and uncertainty in the Eurozone have caused the euro's exchange rate to be depressed relative to what the exchange rate of the deutschmark would be if it were readopted. Germany has benefited from greater exports and reduced imports due to the euro's depressed state, which has helped the economy with its export-based orientation to avoid recessions other countries have fallen into since the crisis began. While a collapse in the euro would likely cause an immediate flow of credit into Germany as a safe haven, the effects of these positive financial flows would likely be offset by the trade impacts a suddenly less competitive deutschmark would have on Germany's trade balance and growth.

Given Europe's politics, leaders have also been unwilling to jettison the euro for another reason. Europeans, despite their reservations about the EU, the European integration project, and the crisis, like the euro.

An overwhelming majority of people in the countries at the center of the crisis, when asked whether they would prefer to keep the euro or go back to their domestic currency, reported they would prefer to keep the euro. This was despite the fact that a majority of people in many of these same countries report that they think increased economic integration has been bad for their countries, that they prefer less and not more power being transferred to the EU from their own national governments, and that the general favorability of the EU has fallen below 50% in many countries.[6]

Ten years after its introduction in general circulation, Europeans like the common currency. The reasons are difficult to ascertain with certainty. Anyone who has traveled in Europe can appreciate some of the reasons why. One can still experience the frustration, confusion, and inconvenience of exchanging currency traveling between the small countries of Europe that still maintain national currencies if they, for example, leave Germany and travel to the Czech Republic. The experience of currency exchange, once commonplace all over Europe, and the uncertainty caused by prices marked in an unfamiliar currency no longer occur in the Eurozone, the convenience of a single currency is taken for granted. Europeans also seem to have adopted a pride in the euro as their currency, and despite any nostalgia for their previous monies. Certainly nostalgia and nationalist pride have not been strong enough to bring back to their old currencies.[7] Finally, there may be a political reason. While Europeans may mistrust Brussels they also often mistrust their own governments more, and in some countries it may be the case that the euro creates a constraint on the mischief they believe their own governments might otherwise perpetrate with control over their own national currency.

Overall, despite dire predictions of many market-watchers, economists, and other pundits, the euro has remained far more durable than many imagined it could. The currency has endured despite the very difficult conditions that have occurred during the Euro crisis. The flaws in its design are clear, and the difficulties its existence have created since 2009 are many. Still the euro persists. Mario Monti once likened it to a bumblebee, claiming that like a bumblebee, according to experts the euro should not be able to fly, yet it continues to. In evaluating future crises in the currency union, experts and pundits alike would be well served to remember this observation. The euro has proven very resilient.

Hammers and Nails

The third lesson of the Euro crisis stems from the second. It may not so much be a lesson as an observation. A currency union is fundamentally a political undertaking as much as it is an economic one, especially if it is to be maintained. The designers of the euro knew that, and recognized as they have since the 1950s that political integration would occur more easily only if economic integration occurred first. Coming from an economic perspective to understand the Euro crisis may cause observers to underestimate the euro's resilience for this reason. Economists have a standard set of tools and often fall into the trap of having a hammer, and therefore viewing the world's problems as just a lot nails. While swinging a hammer can feel right and often rewarding, there are many times when using a hammer is not appropriate, or at least if a hammer is needed, afterward several other skills and tools are as well. The problems of the European financial crisis fit into such a context. While they are about, among other things, currency, debt, and credit, and therefore seem to be in the bailiwick of economics and finance, solving the problems involves not just an understanding of these disciplines, but also of the politics present that limit the set of potential solutions.

Economics is well suited to identify many flaws in the design of a currency union. In the end, however, a currency union among nations will entail a political decision with very important and symbolic ramifications, primary among these the surrender of a national currency. It also requires, to work, coordination of fiscal policies and the ceding of national sovereignty to a larger union. These are very difficult political decisions. Furthermore, that larger authority, if it is to be effective and accountable to the societies it governs, would be well served if it were organized as a strong federal body. Clearly, in this regard Europe has taken a different path, choosing a governance structure that has tried to find a middle road between federal authority and individual nation's autonomy. The political constraints this decision has imposed have been apparent since the beginning of the Euro crisis, and these have undermined the speed and scale of crisis policies used to combat it. Resource considerations within the currency union have also determined which national viewpoints have received the greatest weight, and in turn policies have been constrained by the interests of those providing the resources. This inequity and national self-interest has also undermined the perception of democracy in Europe, and the willingness to engage in further efforts to unify the continent. While the early impetus for European unity after World War II may have been unity at any cost, it now seems that the crisis has caused many people to wonder whether Europe is worth the cost. While such a viewpoint has always existed, it seems the Euro crisis has made Europeans far more cautious and skeptical on this point.[8]

Moving forward, there are still many challenges to overcome before the crisis is ended, the greatest now being how leaders will approach economic recovery. Since 2009, the millions of people in Europe and millions more worldwide have been affected by the Euro crisis and the fallout that has ensued since the first revelations regarding Greek debt. While 4 years after those revelations the financial crisis finally seems to have eased, the economic damage done will take years to recover from, especially in the Eurozone's southern states. In these periphery nations, debt levels will remain high and banking systems will remain weak for years to come. High levels of unemployment will not be overcome quickly even when growth returns to these countries, and the persistence of joblessness will cause skills to depreciate, undermining any employment recovery. Worse, persistently high levels of unemployment will contribute to political instability that could eventually prove to be the common currency's greatest challenge.

It still remains to be seen whether Europe's leaders will be able to find solutions that keep the currency union intact, or whether it is even optimal to do so. The question of "what is optimal" is also unclear. Given that the interests of Europe may not currently be in the interests, or even preferred by many of Europe's citizens, it is uncertain whether future outcomes will be determined by the chaos of national objectives or whether these will eventually be suppressed to identify a unifying direction with which to continue efforts at greater European integration. While many steps have been taken in the crisis to correct some of the flaws that originally beset the euro's design, there are still many questions regarding the currency union and whether its members will all remain. To maintain the currency union will require willingness among all parties to press on, and to make necessary sacrifices, both politically and economically. The Euro crisis, regardless of its outcome, will prove to be a formative event in European history and efforts to integrate the continent, fundamentally affecting the course of events that follow it. What that course will be remains unclear. There is still smoke in the air, and where there is smoke ...

Notes

Chapter 1

1. See Euro News, February, 2, 2011. http://www.euronews.com/2011/12/
    02/merkel-warns-of-marathon-to-solve-euro-crisis/
2. The Eurozone has consisted of 17 countries since Estonia joined the Euro in
    January 2011. Greek deficit and debt had been hidden using several tactics
    for years, including using special financial accounting practices to present
    misleading government expenditure statistics. See http://www.nytimes.
    com/2010/02/14/business/global/14debt.html?pagewanted=1&hp
3. These figures come from the European Commission (2010), Report on
    Greek Government Deficit and Debt Statistics. Eventually the deficit would
    be re-estimated to be 15.6% of GDP.
4. The ECOFIN statement declared the following:
    "The Council REGRETS the renewed problems in the Greek fiscal
    statistics. The Council CALLS ON the Greek government to urgently take
    measures to restore the confidence of the European Union in Greek
    statistical information and the related institutional setting. The Council
    INVITES the Commission to produce a report before the end of 2009.
    Moreover, the Council INVITES the Commission to propose the
    appropriate measures to be taken in this situation. In this context, the
    Council WELCOMES the commitment by the Government to address this
    issue swiftly and seriously and CONSIDERS the measures announced
    recently, such as those aiming to make the National Statistical Service fully
    independent, to be steps in the right direction." (p. 6, footnote 2 as reported
    in European Commission (2010)).
5. Portugal, Ireland, Italy, Greece, and Spain, or Greece, Ireland, Portugal,
    Spain, and Italy. Neither acronym is politically correct.
6. Slovenia joined the Eurozone on January 1, 2007. On January 1, 2008,
    Malta, and Cyprus joined, while on January 1, 2009 Slovakia entered the
    currency Union. Estonia officially entered on the first day of 2011. Four of
    these new countries have economies smaller than Luxembourg's (which
    while the smallest of the original 12 countries, Luxembourg is by far the
    wealthiest country in the Eurozone on a GDP per capita basis.). Together
    the five newest countries' nominal GDP is also less than that of the next
    smallest country in the Eurozone (Ireland). Using World Bank nominal
    GDP annual data at the start of the Euro crisis (2009), the five newest

members' economies as a share of total Eurozone GDP were as follows: Malta (0.06%), Estonia (0.15%), Cyprus (0.20%), Slovenia (0.39%), Slovakia (0.70%). For comparison Luxembourg's share of total Eurozone nominal GDP in 2009 was 0.42%, while the next three smallest countries (Ireland, Portugal and Finland) accounted for 1.82%, 1.83% and 1.91%, respectively.

Part II

1. This was made clear in the European Commission's report detailing the bookkeeping problems of 2009. See European Commission (2010).
2. For a review of these viewpoints, see Jonung and Drea (2009). The authors argue that as the euro progressed, authors began to question the theory of optimal currency areas.
3. Latvia will join the currency union in 2014, making 18 countries in the currency union

Chapter 2

4. This quote was reportedly penned by Jean Monnet in a memo according to Baudet (2012).
5. Winston Churchill, *Speech to the Academic Youth in Zurich*, University of Zurich, September 9, 1946. http://europa.eu/about-eu/eu-history/founding-fathers/pdf/winston_churchill_en.pdf
6. Robert Schuman, *Schuman Declaration*, Quai d'Orsay, French Foreign Ministry, May 9, 1950. Retrieved from http://www.robert-schuman.eu/en/declaration-of-9-may-1950
7. Other institutions governing the ECSC included the Court of Justice, which adjudicated disputes and ensured ECSC laws were observed, and the Consultative Community. The Court continues in the modern EU. The Consultative Community, an advisory group to the High Authority representing coal and steel consumers and dealers, workers (unions), and employers, functioned in a similar role to today's Economic and Social Committee of the EU.
8. Technically, the European Council follows the rules of the Council of the European Union, formerly the Council of Ministers of the European Union.
9. The stalling of further economic reforms and the implementation of a single market, undermining the purpose and promise of the European Economic Community was often referred to as "eurosclerosis." Policy and reform

efforts by the European Council, including but not limited to those outlined here in the late 1970s and 1980s were aimed at overcoming this problem.

10. While the Rome Treaties outlined an elected Common Assembly, which later developed into the European Parliament, the process defining how elections would be held was delayed throughout the 1960s and early 1970s due to nationalist concerns.

11. Turkey made an application for membership in 1987; however, its application has been delayed since due to poor relations with Greece which were worsened by the Turkish invasion of Cyprus in 1974 and the resulting partition of the island, which remains to this day.

12. See Delors (1989).

13. In 2012 the Eurozone had a population of 331 million people, while the United States had a population of 312 million. U.S. GDP at current prices in 2012 was $15.1 trillion and Eurozone GDP across countries at current prices converted to U.S. dollars was $12.2 trillion (*Source*: IMF April 2013 World Economic Outlook Database, www.imf.org).

14. The description of a confederation is meant narrowly here, and is focused on the decision-making apparatus of major policy initiatives. The EU should not be generalized as a confederation in all issues. The EU has elements and institutions that reflect everything from intergovernmentalism (where national governments are the primary actors in the process of decision making) to federalism, depending on the policy area.

15. Without digressing into a comparative history of the formation of the U.S. and EU governance structures, it could be said that the American revolution allowed the original 13 colonies of the United States to accept the need to create a federal system, though this took a decade and the failure of the original Articles of Confederation before the Constitution of the United States, outlining such a system, was adopted. In Europe as described the tension between maintaining sovereignty and creating limited supranational governance has resulted in the system described. The tension between these two potentially conflicting levels of governance is supposed to be ameliorated by two governing principles in the Treaty of the European Union: subsidiarity and proportionality. Subsidiarity requires decisions be taken at the most decentralized level of government consistent with effective action, while proportionality requires that EU legislation should impose the minimum standards necessary over sovereign member-states to achieve a particular goal. Overall, the structure of the EU's European Council creates incentives for the most conservative governance possible over the EU—a structure that minimizes the potential conflict between EU interests and the interests of single member states. This conservatism, however, has

been at the core of the Eurozone's inability to address the Euro crisis quickly.

16. This problem of commitment to a fixed exchange rate is referred to as a "time inconsistency" problem. Initially, a country sees it as optimal to adopt a specific exchange rate; however, doing so then limits the monetary policy options has in that country as interest rates must be held at levels that support the target exchange rate. If the country's domestic economy then falls into a recession, for example, it now faces a conflict between maintaining higher interest rates to protect the exchange rate or lowering them to assist domestic recovery, which is inconsistent with the commitment to maintain the fixed exchange rate. Since internal politics usually trump a government's priorities, currency speculators will also recognize that higher interest rate policies needed to maintain exchange rates will eventually be abandoned. They then begin to sell these currencies in anticipation, adding further pressure for an exchange-rate devaluation, which makes the conflict the government faces more intense and usually hastening the abandonment of the country's exchange rate policy. This is what happened in Europe in 1992 and 1993, with George Soros being the most famous of the currency speculators involved.

17. The Council of Ministers is most often referred to as ECOFIN when Finance ministers meet to decide economic and financial issues.

18. The euro's early architects understood this. For example, Giscard d'Estaing, the former President of France, and Helmut Schmidt, the former chancellor of Germany were quoted as saying "One must never forget that monetary union, which the two of us were the first to propose more than a decade ago is ultimately a political project. It aims to give a new impulse to the historic movement toward union of the European states. Monetary union is a federative project that needs to be accompanied and followed by other steps." Elliott (1997).

Chapter 3

1. Quoted from Shore (2006).

2. See http://www.bundesverfassungsgericht.de/entscheidungen/rs19980331_2bvr187797.html.

3. For a detailed history of these criticisms, see Jonung and Drea (2009).

4. For a survey of the early literature regarding estimates of the effect the euro's adoption had on member country trade flows, see Baldwin (2006). More recent research by Santos Silva and Tenreyro (2010) suggests little to no effect.

5. Among the original members only Luxembourg might have been deemed specialized with its reliance on banking and financial services. Newer members, beginning with Greece and its reliance on shipping and tourism, and especially Cyprus which was almost wholly dependent on its banking sector and tourism by 2012, have been less diversified.

6. See *Economist* (2012) and Gáková and Dijkstra (2010).

7. The criteria also require that countries maintain an annual average inflation rate no greater than 1.5% more than the average of the lowest three states in the Eurozone.

8. See Council of the European Union (2005).

9. After the currency union was created in Europe, some countries, specifically Greece, exceeded Maastricht debt and deficit limits by reporting misleading economic statistics, thereby causing a severe understatement of their actual debt and deficit levels. Still others began or continued to miss these targets claiming excesses were due to special economic circumstances such as changes in the business cycle. Often, however, excessive deficits and resulting increases in debt levels were due to domestic political pressures to maintain politically popular spending. Sanctions in all cases were neither levied nor seriously considered once the SGP rules were changed in March 2005. Political expediency forced Maastricht limits to be ignored after the precedent set by Germany and France.

10. The EU does allow some transfers among members for economic development, particularly competitiveness and economic convergence programs. These funds are spent as part of the Regional Support or Cohesion programs commonly referred "structural funds" and accounted for approximately 30% of the EU budget, rising to 36% by 2013. Most of these funds flow to east-European countries and lower income regions of the EU and were not meant to be used as countercyclical expenditures.

11. Moral hazard describes a situation in which an economic agent is shielded (in part or completely) from the consequences of their actions, leaving them less (or no) incentive to change their behavior to avoid such consequences.

12. Luxembourg had to create a central bank, as previously it had been part of a currency union with Belgium.

13. The Council of European Banking Supervisors, to which representation from the ECB is mandatory, was formed to coordinate banking regulation within the EU in 2004. It was superseded by the EBA in 2011. The actual regulation of EU country's banking systems is the responsibility of individual member-nation authorities. This has created difficulty in establishing regulatory frameworks in instances when banks or financial institutions operate in multiple countries.

14. Controversially, the ECB did begin more significant interventions in sovereign debt markets in August 2011, but this occurred a year and a half after the bailout of Greece and almost two years from the start of the crisis, and notably Germany's representative to the Governing Council argued vocally that such support was illegal.

15. Private institutions, however, can use funds to purchase national debt in bond markets, thus an indirect channel has existed to finance government debt in the banking system.

16. The Troubled Asset Relief Program (TARP) provided a form of Federal bailout in the United States in October 2008. With authorization to use as much as $700 billion, funds were provided to recapitalize the banking system.

Chapter 4

1. See Eurobarometer polling regarding support for European-wide institutions including the ECB. From Spring of 2008 through Spring 2012 support for the ECB had dropped by 47% across the Eurozone, support for the EU dropped by 46%, and support dropped for the European Parliament, the European Commission and the Euro by 34%, 32%, and 7%, respectively. See Flash Eurobarometer 335, July 2012, and Roth, Jonung, and Nowak-Lehmann (2012).

2. Draghi (2012).

Chapter 5

1. In simple economics the sum of total expenditure across household consumption of domestic goods (C), investment (I), government expenditures of all types (G) and on the trade balance (exports (X) sold to other countries less imports purchased from other countries (M) or ($X M$) must equal national income (Y). As $Y = C + I + G + X M$ is an identity that states total expenditure cannot be greater than total income, it must always be true. Redefining $Y C G$ as national savings (S), that is, total savings by households and government, this relationship can be expressed as $S = I + (X M)$. When a trade deficit occurs ($X M$) < 0 and expenditures on imports exceed exports sold abroad. Rearranging the previous equation, a trade deficit will imply that investment (I) exceeds new savings available to finance it (S) by the same amount ($S - I = (X M)$). In this case, a trade deficit will require that borrowing to finance domestic investment must occur from other countries in an amount equal to the trade deficit as domestic savings

will not be able to finance this level of investment expenditure. This borrowing is referred to as Net Foreign Investment or NFI = $(X M)$ and refers to the positive flow of credit from other nations to satisfy the shortfall of domestic savings and investment in the presence of a trade deficit. Note also as G government spending rises, total savings S falls since $S = Y C G$, thus more must be borrowed from abroad to finance a given level of investment if public expenditures increase. This is known as the "twin deficits" hypothesis and describes the fact that typically countries with expanding government expenditure deficits will also incur larger trade deficits. This was apparent in Europe, particularly in southern countries shown in Figures 10 and 15.

2. These results are more rigorously verified in papers like Holinski, Kool, and Muynsken (2012).

3. In Germany, the Agenda 2010 reforms championed by Gerhard Schröder's government liberalized labor markets, which have led to significant productivity benefits. The reforms have also been blamed for a lack of wage growth in Germany over the decade. See Brenke (2009) as an example. Dutch and Finnish reforms followed periods of economic malaise in the late 1990s.

4. OECD (2011, p. 320).

5. Data on Greek public-sector employment from Sfakianakis (2012).

6. Greece, Ministry of Finance (2010).

Chapter 6

1. The process of bubbles and deleveraging became widely understood in the 1930s. Irving Fisher (1933) coined the term debt-deflation for the effect that such debt unwinding would have on price levels and the economy. In the 1970s through the 1990s the idea was revisited by more contemporary scholars. These notably included Ben Bernanke (1995), who considered the effects of financial crises in the context of modern economies and financial markets. This would prove fortunate for Bernanke, who would find himself at the head of the U.S. Federal Reserve when the U.S. mortgage and financial crisis hit in 2007 and 2008.

2. While well understood, the potential dynamics of financial crises and their potential implications on credit market conditions in the early 21st century were often ignored by mainstream analysts and policy makers, though a few notable exceptions existed before the U.S. housing bubble burst in 2007. Some of the better known examples of academic researchers who sounded warnings of the potential effects leverage could have on the financial system, the United States, and world economies were Robert Shiller, Nouriel

Roubini, and Raghuram Rajan. Famous analysts included Nassim Nicholas Taleb, whose book *Black Swan* detailed his earlier warnings that markets were unprepared for such shocks.

3. See, for example, Creswell and Bowley (2011) for an overview of the role of credit rating agencies.

4. See IMF (2013a).

5. Such optimism was reflected in the IMF's use of a Stand-By Arrangement (or SBA) in its participation in the first Greek bailout, an arrangement by definition not to last more than 36 months. By 2010 the IMF had already begun to reconsider the time that recovery would take. Reflecting that concern, its participation in later bailouts took the form not of an SBA but an Extended Fund Facility, a medium-term program meant to provide assistance to countries over a longer period.

6. For example, see *The Economist* (2010).

7. Poor governance had been Greece's problem. Since the introduction of the euro, as interest rates fell, growth in Greece had been debt driven, particularly in the public sector. Unsustainable increases in the Greek public sector had swelled the size and pay levels of the Greek civil service, and these increases had been driven by political incentives as successive Greek governments used such actions to gain political favor. Simultaneously, Greek pension programs had become increasingly underfunded as entitlements became more generous and publicly provided social benefits expanded. The state had also assumed increasing liability for debts accrued by public enterprises as their borrowing grew over this time.

8. For a description of events see IMF (2013a).

9. The EFSF was funded to a level of €440 billion by Eurozone countries, and an additional €60 billion was made available by European Financial Stability Mechanism (EFSM), a similar facility created and funded by non-euro EU countries.

10. In a later reappraisal the IMF reported that it ignored its own internal rules in supporting a bailout to a bankrupt country. Furthermore, it admitted estimates of the costs to the Greek economy of the austerity measures the first bailout imposed were underestimated. See IMF (2013a).

11. In Germany there have been several challenges to the bailouts. Terms of the bailouts have been debated fiercely before being passed by the German Parliament. On September 7, 2011, the German constitutional court ruled against a challenge brought by a coalition of economists, business executives, and lawmakers who had argued the terms of the bailouts undermined Parliament's ability to determine government spending and budgetary planning. While arguing the bailouts did not infringe on German Parliamentary powers, judges also ruled that bailout agreements entered by

Germany's government in consultation with parliamentary budget committee.

12. Haircuts on privately held debt had apparently been discussed since at least October 2010, when comments regarding this option were leaked to the press at an EU summit in Deauville.

13. France also opposed this policy; however, internally it appeared the proposal had much more traction in France than in Germany.

14. Stark, while often referred to as the ECB's "chief economist" was actually a member of the Executive Board of the ECB, where he was officially responsible for Economics and Monetary Analysis. Purchases of sovereign debt had actually started in May 2010 but on a very limited scale. The decision in August 2011 expanded the powers to do so. Stark's resignation followed the resignation of Germany's head of the Bundesbank (the German central bank) Axel Weber over the same measures. In addition to being opposed to the use of monetary policy to reduce pressure on international interest rates for troubled countries, both men had argued previously that such efforts violated the ECB's prohibition of buying country's sovereign debt and also believed the ECB's political independence was being undermined in the face of political pressures due to the debt crisis. The ECB argued that the actions were an attempt to stabilize financial markets, a responsibility within its mandate. Unlike quantitative easing actions in the United States, these purchases did not result in an increase in the money supply as the ECB sterilized these purchases with offsetting bond sales.

15. Bagehot (1873).

16. The structural deficit refers to the deficit occurring after accounting for expenditures demanded by the business cycle or the deficit that would occur if the economy was at full employment. For example, increases in unemployment and social benefits costs in a recession would be netted out of a structural deficit computation.

17. See Eurogroup Statement, February 21, 2012. National central banks and states in the in the EU, including the ECB holding Greek bonds were exempt from the write-down. Profits made on these debts were to be allocated to the bailout.

18. Actual funds allocated to the ESM included funds previously allocated to the EFSF, and included funds allocated in previous bailout actions were expected to total €700 billion, with €200 billion kept as a capital reserve.

19. The Spanish government argued determinedly that the credit guarantee of €100 billion should be paid directly to banks, thereby avoiding an increase in Spanish sovereign debt levels. Some Eurozone countries, specifically Germany, resisted this plan arguing that under the current rules of the

Eurozone's ESM fund, the debt had to be assumed by the national government, which could then assign it to a national bank recapitalization program. Such ESM aid would also require austerity conditions, defined and supervised by the Troika. The original agreement reached in early June 2012 initially seemed to specify the debt would be assigned to Spain's total sovereign debt load as defined above but dreaded austerity conditions previous bailouts had required, would be limited since Spain had already implemented an austerity program that met European Commission guidelines.

In a dramatic turn of events, however, Germany found itself isolated on these points at an EU leader's summit later that June. Without France to support Germany's position, Angela Merkel found herself in an all-night debate apparently led by Mario Monti, Italy's prime minister, and Spain's Prime Minister Mariano Rajoy who pressed Merkel to allow a rule change regarding the use of ESM bailout funds. In a major concession she eventually agreed to a rule change, allowing ESM funds in future to be disbursed without being overseen by the Troika and its strict austerity conditions as long as a country met the European Commission's budgetary requirements under the terms of the fiscal compact. These rules would allow a Spanish bailout to avoid the type of austerity conditions included in previous bailouts as Spain had met their negotiated EC requirements. Also, she agreed in the future that the ESM would be allowed to provide direct aid to banks, avoiding the requirement the loans be made to national governments, but only once a common mechanism for European banking supervision, under the auspices of the ECB had been defined. This allowed Spain to potentially defer final agreement on its aid package until later in the year after such a mechanism was to be proposed, thereby allowing the country to avoid the inclusion of the bailout costs in its official government debt.

This was considered a major political victory for Italy's Prime Minister Mario Monti, who spearheaded the negotiation, and a major loss for Germany's Angela Merkel. The political defeat was made more painful by the fact that this negotiation took place on the same evening the favored German soccer team lost in its bid to advance to the Euro Cup championship game, also at the hands of Italy. To make matters worse the Italian player who dominated the game and the German team was nicknamed "Super Mario." This symbolic coincidence was not overlooked by the European press, and newspapers trumpeted both the uncommon German soccer loss and even more rare political loss of Germany's Merkel in Euro crisis policy making.

20.   While the Cypriot government, as part of the Eurozone, had approved the recent Greek bailout agreement, a credit downgrade in fall of 2011 and recent events had caused its sovereign rates also to climb to unsustainable

levels, and the costs necessary to stabilize its banking system made bailout aid necessary.

21. Draghi (2012).

22. During Spanish bailout discussions the potential to enter secondary bond markets had been widely discussed by legal and economic experts and officials.

23. The previous SMP had been limited in the sense that all transactions were "sterilized," purchases of one country's sovereign debt were balanced by equivalent value sales of another's, thereby leaving the money supply in the Eurozone unaffected.

Chapter 7

1. Data taken from Der Spiegel (2012).

2. The Eurozone, which fell into recession in the fourth quarter of 2011, officially resumed positive growth in the second quarter of 2013, reporting an initially estimated 0.3% increase in output over the previous quarter in the euro area as a whole. This technically ended what had been the longest recession in the Eurozone since the common currency had been aopted. The EU defines a recession as two consecutive quarters of negative growth or contraction in economic output.

3. In mid-2013, a revised set of government compiled growth figures was released that indicated Ireland had officially entered recession again in the last quarter of 2012 and the first quarter of 2013. Forecasts still indicated growth by the end of 2013; however, the weakening economy put these forecasts at risk. The lower than expected growth was attributed to low consumer and business demand, and weak banking conditions. By mid-2013 the effects of the real-estate crisis in that country were still being felt with 15.8% of all mortgages found to be over 90 days in arrears, and 26.9% over 90 days overdue for buy-to-let mortgages. Twenty-five percent of small- and medium-sized business loans held by banks were judged to be "impaired" and bank lending had slowed significantly, further slowing business and consumer activity. The credit crunch in Ireland was especially obvious in the statistics for bank loan refusal rates compared to other countries in the EU, where Ireland ranked second highest (IMF 2013b).

Chapter 8

1. See EU (2012).

2. The agreement initially limited such uses of ESM funding to €60 billion, and required that funds in the country requiring aid be exhausted first.

Furthermore, for all banks in all countries, recapitalization would first occur at the expense of bank shareholders and creditors, and then depositors with over €100,000 in deposits. Only after these resources were exhausted would EU taxpayers become liable for the remaining costs of recapitalization through ESM efforts.

3. Currently this limit is €100,000 across the Eurozone.

4. Bertelsmann (2013).

5. This is of importance to the EU as some member states, notably the United Kingdom, have recently made clear they are reconsidering their membership.

6. See, for example, EU President Barroso's proposals for an economic and banking union made ahead of the June 2012 European Council meetings (European Commission 2012).

7. The best known of these was likely the American Recovery and Reinvestment Act of 2009 in the United States that allocated over $700 billion in stimulus funds to stem the recession that followed the 2008 financial crisis there.

8. It is important here not to interpret the relationship presented between austerity and growth as causal. The trend-line only summarizes the average correspondence. A more carefully detailed structural study is necessary to determine if this is causal. For example, a traditional Keynesian framework would argue greater austerity is causal with respect to output contraction, and that the degree of contraction is determined by the fiscal multiplier. A discussion can be found in Blanchard and Leigh (2013) regarding the possible size of multipliers at the time of the data presented.

9. See IMF (2012). The analysis did not just rely on the simple relationship shown in Figure 1, it also relied on an analysis of IMF forecasts and actual outcomes to determine whether the IMF estimates of what is known as the "fiscal multiplier" were consistently underestimated. This is reported in more detail in Blanchard and Leigh (2013).

10. Alternatively, efforts could rely on creating external stimulus for the Eurozone, for example, through plans to create a free-trade agreement with the United States. Such agreements, however, take years to negotiate and therefore are not effective short-term policies.

11. When the crisis began in 2009 there were only 16 countries. Estonia joined the currency union in 2011.

12. Estonia does not have a contribution requirement in the EFSF as it joined the Eurozone after this fund was created. It does have a contribution share in the ESM.

13. See IMF (2013a).

14. Several polling agencies have found diminished support for the process of European integration since the start of the crisis. Eurobarometer, the EU's polling agency has found reduced support for questions regarding the benefits of EU membership. See Eurobarometer's interactive website at http://ec.europa.eu/public_opinion/cf/step1.cfm?keyID=200. Pew Research's Global Attitudes Project has also found support for EU membership and for increased European integration falling since the start of the crisis. See, for example, Pew Research (2013).

15. González (2012).

16. Kindleberger (1973, pp. 291–92).

17. Kindleberger (1973). Barry Eichengreen and J. Bradford Delong reflect on the importance of this theory in the academic literature since Kindleberger's book was published, and the quoted passages (both Kindleberger's and the term "anarchic international system") appear in their foreword to the 2013 edition.

18. During the first 2 years of the crisis, France and Germany in effect shared this duty and implicitly coordinated policy making by defining the agenda for action, but the election of François Hollande, coupled with a significantly weaker economic situation in France leaves Germany as the only potential leader in the Eurozone currently. The socialist Hollande government is an unlikely partner for Merkel's more conservative coalition. Furthermore, it could be argued that France was never really a necessary partner in the first part of the crisis, and that the Franco–Germanic partnership the two countries presented was merely a partnership based on mutual convenience. France was able to maintain the appearance of relevance as a partner while Germany was able to avoid appearing as a unilateral dictator through France's presence. The coordination of two countries, however, could have its advantages politically and diplomatically. There is a long history of cooperation in European integration that focuses on the need and idea of a Franco–German partnership thus the rise of a benevolent hegemonic leadership might be more likely if the two countries could work together again.

19. It is possible that Chancellor Angela Merkel, if elected to a new term might decide to leave as her legacy a more united and integrated Europe, and following elections she could proceed down such a path. Given her high popularity across Europe and in Germany she would likely have the political capital to lead such an effort. Prior to such elections though, which will occur in Fall 2013, all German politics will be focused not on Europe but on domestic considerations. What Merkel's agenda will be after those occur is unclear.

20. In June and early July 2013 the European Council announced plans to create over €30 billion in funding to increase youth training in troubled states but these promises in part were made by reallocating funds already pledged to help development in less wealthy nations of the EU, and were pledged over several years. Little impact was expected to be seen from these promises.

21. Krugman (2013). The actual Mencken quote comes from H. L. Mencken's *A Book of Burlesques*, "Sententiæ" (1920), quoted from the *Columbia Dictionary of Quotations*.

22. This is particularly true in southern states where the ECB's own data shows lending continuing to contract across the Eurozone and particularly the south. Despite improving crisis conditions in Europe between 2012 and 2013 and the ECB lowering its interest rate targets to the lowest levels ever offered, the ECB's banking data showed that in May 2013 lending to corporations excluding banks had declined at an annual rate of 3.1%, continuing a trend that had been ongoing in Europe for some time.

23. Such an error could be something unanticipated. For example, in June 2013 the Greek government, in a surprise move, announced the shutdown of its state-broadcaster in an attempt to meet Troika demands that the government reduce public employment by 5,000 workers before the end of the year, with half of that level being accomplished before the end of summer of 2013. The resulting backlash to this seemingly hurried and ill-advised action nearly brought down the weak coalition government in Greece, undermining its already weak support and the limited public support remaining to maintain bailout commitments.

Chapter 9

1. As an example, general information material including videos describing the Euro crisis and the EU's response casually argue the crisis began in the United States. For example, see http://www.youtube.com/watch?v=0B3zNcFYqj0. While technically true—the financial crisis in the United States and international fallout that followed contributed to the weak banking conditions in the Eurozone, and therefore the weakened sovereign debt position of countries like Ireland and Spain caused by the need to deal with these banking problems, one should not necessarily assume causation due to origination. It is argued here that the crisis began in Europe with Greece and sovereign debt market shock that created then metastasized into what has become the Euro crisis due to the Eurozone's currency union and banking system arrangement.

2. For an excellent and more detailed explanation of this linkage, see Elliott (2011b).

3. See, for example, early descriptions of such a role in Walter Bagehot's *Lombard Street* (1873) where he famously wrote "We must keep a great store of ready money always available, and advance out of it very freely in periods of panic, and in times of incipient alarm. Any notion that money is not to be had, or that it may not be had at any price, only raises alarm to panic and enhances panic to madness." Later examples of similar sentiments include Hyman Minsky's *Stabilizing an Unstable Economy* (1986), Bernanke (1995), or several more recent papers written since the events of the 2008 financial crisis.

4. Extracted from the ECB's website. Retrieved July 18, 2013 from http://www.ecb.int/press/key/date/2013/html/sp130710.en.html

5. In physics, it is the "strong interaction" or "strong force" that holds the nucleus of an atom together when it is composed of two or more similarly charged protons. Prior to its discovery, physicists were uncertain how to explain why the nuclei of atoms composed of positively charged protons and neutrons with a neutral charge were able to stay bound together.

6. See Pew Research (2013).

7. This effect was foreseen by the ECB's first President Wim Duisenberg when he said, "The euro is far more than a medium of exchange... It is part of the identity of a people. It reflects what they have in common now and in the future." ("Welcome to Euroland," *The Guardian*, January 1, 1999, reporting on the official launch of the euro) Retrieved July 21, 2013 from http://www.guardian.co.uk/world/1999/jan/01/eu.politics

8. One could argue that European unity has also been most strongly supported by European elites and that its popularity has always been lower among the general population. This contention seems supported by the number of EU referendums on EU policies that have failed in Europe. For a detailed discussion of the political constraints present in Europe during the early part of the crisis, see Elliott (2011a).

References

Bagehot, W. (1873). *Lombard street*. Greenbook Publications, Sioux Falls, SD.

Baldwin, R. (2006). The euro's trade effects. European Central Bank Working Papers, No. 594, March.

Baldwin, R., & Wyplosz, C. (2004). *The economics of European integration* (3rd ed.). Berkshire, McGraw-Hill, New York.

Baudet, R. (2012). *The significance of borders: Why representative government and the rule of law require nation states*. Brill Publishing, Boston, MA.

Bernanke, B. (1995). The macroeconomics of the Great Depression: A comparative approach. *Journal of Money, Credit, and Banking*, 27(1), 1–28.

Bertelsmann Foundation (2013). Transatlantic Trade and Investment Partnership (TTIP)—who benefits from a free trade deal? Bertelsmann Stiftung, June 2013.

Blanchard, O., & Leigh, D. (2013). Growth forecast errors and fiscal multipliers. *IMF working Paper WP/13/1*.

Brenke, K. (2009). Real wages in Germany: Numerous years of decline. German Institute for Economic Research. Retrieved June 18, 2013 from http://www.diw.de/sixcms/media.php/73/diw_wr_2009-28.pdf

Council of the European Union. (2005). Presidential conclusions: Brussels, 22 and 23 March 2005. Retrieved May 15, 2013 from http://ue.eu.int/ueDocs/cms_Data/docs/pressData/en/ec/84335.pdf

Creswell, J., & Bowley, G. (2011). Ratings firms misread signs of Greek woes. *New York Times*, November 30, 2011. Retrieved June 5, 2013 from http://www.nytimes.com/2011/11/30/business/ratings-firms-misread-signs-of-greek-woes.html?pagewanted=all&_r=0

Delors, J. (1989). Report on economic and monetary union in the economic community. Committee for the Study of Economic and Monetary Union, European Council. Retrieved July 17, 2013 from http://aei.pitt.edu/1007/1/monetary_delors.pdf

Der Spiegel. (2012, June 25). Imagining the unthinkable: The disastrous consequences of a euro crash. Retrieved June 26, 2012 from http://translate.google.com/translate?sl=de&tl=en&js=n&prev=_t&hl=en&ie=UTF-8&layout=2&eotf=1&u=http%3A%2F%2Fwww.spiegel.de%2Finternational%2Feurope%2Ffears-grow-of-consequences-of-potential-euro-collapse-a-840634.html

Draghi, M. (2012, July 26). Speech to the Global Investment Conference, London. Retrieved June 8, 2013 from http://www.ecb.int/press/key/date/2012/html/sp120726.en.html

Economist (2012, January 27). Europe's debt crisis: At a bursting point? Retrieved June 8, 2013 from http://www.economist.com/blogs/charlemagne/2012/01/europes-debt-crisis

The Economist (2010, January 28). A Greek bailout, and soon? Retrieved June 8, 2013 from http://www.economist.com/blogs/charlemagne/2010/01/greek_bailout_within_months

Elliott, D. J. (2011a, August 22). Why can't Europe get it right the first time ... or the second ... or the third? Brookings InstitutionResearch Paper.

Elliott, D. J. (2011b, October 12). Eurozone governments and the financial markets: A troubled marriage. Brookings InstitutionResearch Paper.

Elliott, M. (1997, October 14). Monetary union has always been mainly about politics. *International Herald Tribune*, p. 8.

Eurogroup Statement. (2012, February 21). Retrieved June 8 2013 from http://www.consilium.europa.eu/uedocs/cms_data/docs/pressdata/en/ecofin/128075.pdf

European Commission. (2010, August 1). Report on Greek government deficit and debt statistics. Retrieved January 18, 2013 from http://eur-lex.europa.eu/LexUriServ/LexUriServ.do?uri=SPLIT_COM:2010:0001(01):FIN:EN:PDF

European Commission. (2012, June 27). Europe 2020: President Barroso proposes banking Union. Retrieved June 8, 2013 from http://ec.europa.eu/europe2020/banking-union/

EU. (2012, September 12). A roadmap towards a banking union. Communication from the Commission to the European Parliament.

Fisher, I. (1933). The debt deflation theory of Great Depressions. *Econometrica, 1*, 537–57.

Gáková, Z., & Dijkstra, L. (2008). Labour mobility between the regions of the EU-27 and a comparison with the USA. European Union Regional Policy 02/2008.

Greece, Ministry of Finance. (2010, January). Update of the Hellenic stability and growth programme (14 pp.). Submitted to the European Commission.

González, F., Der Spiegel. (2012, July 2). Solidarity plea: Germans always looking out for own interests. *Der Siegel International Online*.

Holinski, N., Kool, C., & Muyske, J. (2012). Persistent macroeconomic imbalances in the euro area: Causes and consequences. *Federal Reserve Bank of St. Louis Review*, 94(1), 1–20.

IMF. (2012, October). *World economic outlook: Coping with high debt and sluggish growth*. Washington, DC: International Monetary Fund.

IMF. (2013a, June). Greece: Ex post evaluation of exceptional access under the 2010 Stand-By Arrangement. IMF Country Report 13/156.

IMF. (2013b, June). Ireland, tenth review under the extended arrangement. IMF Country Report 13/163.

Jonung, L., & Drea, E. (2009). The euro: It can't happen, it's a bad idea, it won't last. US economists on the EMU, 1989–2002. *Economic Papers*, Economic and Financial Affairs Directorate, European Commission. Retrieved April 18, 2012 from http://ec.europa.eu/economy_finance/publications

Kindelberger, C. P. (1973). *World in depression, 1929–1939* (40th Anniv. Edn. 2013). Berkeley: University of California Press.

Krugman, P. Defining prosperity down. *New York Times column*, Opinion Section, July 8, 2013.

Minsky, H. P. (1986). *Managing an unstable economy*. Yale University Press, New Haven, CT.

OECD. (2011). Economic outlook, May 2011.

Pew Research, Global Attitudes Project. The new sick man of Europe: The European Union. Survey results released May 13, 2013. Retrieved June 8, 2013 from http://www.pewglobal.org/2013/05/13/the-new-sick-man-of-europe-the-european-union/.

Rodrik, D. (2000). How far will international economic integration go? *Journal of Economic Perspectives*, 14(1), 177–86.

Rogoff, K., & Reinhart, C. (2009). *This time is different: A panoramic view of eight centuries of financial crises*. Princeton University Press, Princeton, NJ.

Roth, F., Jonung, L., & and Nowak-Lehmann, F. D. (2012). Public support for the single European currency, the euro, 1990 to 2011. Does the financial crisis matter? *Lund University Working Paper*, Department of Economics. Retrieved June 15, 2013 from http://www.nek.lu.se/publications/workpap/papers/WP12_20.pdf

Santos Silva, J. M. C., & Tenreyro, S. (2010). Currency unions in prospect and retrospect. *Annual Review of Economics*, 2, 51–74.

Shore, P. (2006). Fighting against federalism. In P. Whyman, M. Baimbridge, & B. Burkitt (Eds.), *Implications of the euro: A critical perspective from the left*. 196-201. New York: Rouledge.

Sfakianakis, J. (2012, October 10). The cost of protecting Greece's public sector. *NY Times*, New York.

Unpublished Documents Cited

IMF. Greece: Preliminary debt sustainability analysis, February 15, 2012, M Visser. Retrieved February 23, 2012 from http://av.r.ftdata.co.uk/ and http://ftalphaville.ft.com/blog/2012/02/21/889521/that-greek-debt-sustainability-analysis-in-full/

International Institute of Finance: Implications of a disorderly Greek default. Retrieved from http://www.athensnews.gr/portal/11/53784

Data sources

Flash Eurobarometer 335, July 2012. http://ec.europa.eu/public_opinion/archives/flash_arch_344_330_en.htm

Eurostat. Retrieved from http://epp.eurostat.ec.europa.eu/portal/page/portal/interest_rates/data/main_tables

OECD. Retrieved from http://www.oecd.org/home/0,2987,en_2649_201185_1_1_1_1_1,00.html

GlobalPropertyGuide.com. Retrieved from http://www.globalpropertyguide.com/Europe/

IMF. Retrieved from http://www.imf.org/external/data.htm

IMF World Economic Outlook. Retrieved from http://www.imf.org/external/pubs/ft/weo/2011/01/

IMF, April 2013 World Economic Outlook Database. Retrieved from www.imf.org

Pacific Exchange Rate Service. Retrieved from http://fx.sauder.ubc.ca/data.html

Treaties

Maastricht Treaty. Retrieved from http://www.eurotreaties.com/maastrichtext.html

Treaty on Stability, Coordination and Governance in the Economic and Monetary Union. Retrieved from http://european-council.europa.eu/Eurozone-governance/treaty-on-stability

About the Author

Robert Godby is an Associate Professor at the University of Wyoming, where he has been an active researcher and taught undergraduate through PhD students in the areas of macroeconomic policy, behavioral economics, energy economics, industrial organization, and environmental economics and policy. Godby received his formal economics training in Canada, graduating with his PhD from McMaster University in Hamilton, Ontario. He also chaired the Department of Economics and Finance at the University of Wyoming from 2005 to 2010. In 2010, the National Research Council (NRC) ranked the department as the nation's leader in faculty research output and eighth overall in research productivity out of 120 U.S. PhD programs. The department has also been ranked among the 10 best environmental and resource economics departments in the world (econPhD.net) and one of the top three public research departments in environment economics (Southern Economic Journal).

In 2011–12, Robert spent a sabbatical year in Germany engaging academics, EU, and Bundesbank officials as well as other scholars and policymakers regarding the causes of the Euro crisis, and about the policy options available to potentially resolve them. This book is in part the result of that experience. In addition to publishing scholarly articles, Godby has written research papers for government and makes regular public presentations on the state of the economy and the financial system. He is also often asked to comment on regional and national economic policy by media at the local, regional, and national levels including *The Wall Street Journal, New York Times, USA Today*, television, and radio outlets.

Index

OTHER TITLES IN OUR ECONOMICS COLLECTION

Philip Romero, The University of Oregon and Jeffrey Edwards, North Carolina A&T State University, Editors

- *Managerial Economics: Concepts and Principles* by Donald Stengel
- *Your Macroeconomic Edge: Investing Strategies for the Post-Recession World* by Philip Romero
- *Working with Economic Indicators: Interpretation and Sources* by Donald Stengel
- *Innovative Pricing Strategies to Increase Profits* by Daniel Marburger
- *Regression for Economics* by Shahdad Naghshpour
- *Statistics for Economics* by Shahdad Naghshpour
- *How Strong Is Your Firm's Competitive Advantage?* By Daniel Marburger
- *A Primer on Microeconomics* by Thomas Beveridge
- *Game Theory: Anticipating Reactions for Winning Actions* by Mark L. Burkey
- *A Primer on Macroeconomics* by Thomas Beveridge
- *Economic Decision Making Using Cost Data: A Guide for Managers* by Daniel M. Marburger
- *The Fundamentals of Money and Financial Systems* by Shahdad Naghshpour
- *International Economics: Understanding the Forces of Globalization for Managers* by Paul Torelli
- *The Economics of Crime* by Zagros Madjd-Sadjadi
- *Money and Banking: An Intermediate Market-Based Approach* by William D. Gerdes

Announcing the Business Expert Press Digital Library

Concise E-books Business Students
Need for Classroom and Research

This book can also be purchased in an e-book collection by your library as
- a one-time purchase,
- that is owned forever,
- allows for simultaneous readers,
- has no restrictions on printing, and
- can be downloaded as PDFs from within the library community.

Our digital library collections are a great solution to beat the rising cost of textbooks. e-books can be loaded into their course management systems or onto student's e-book readers.

The **Business Expert Press** digital libraries are very affordable, with no obligation to buy in future years. For more information, please visit **www.businessexpertpress.com/librarians**. To set up a trial in the United States, please contact **Adam Chesler** at *adam.chesler@ businessexpertpress.com* for all other regions, contact **Nicole Lee** at *nicole.lee@igroupnet.com*.

CPSIA information can be obtained at www.ICGtesting.com
Printed in the USA
BVOW07s1433071213

338101BV00003B/10/P